STORE

Economy and Environment
in the Caribbean

1954

Economy and Environment in the Caribbean

Barbados and the Windwards in the late 1800s

Bonham C. Richardson

with a Foreword
by David Lowenthal

The Press University of the West Indies

Barbados • Jamaica • Trinidad and Tobago

University Press of Florida

Gainesville • Tallahassee • Tampa • Boca Raton
Pensacola • Orlando • Miami • Jacksonville

F 2011

Published by The Press University of the West Indies
ISBN 976-640-038-5 (paper)

Published simultaneously in North America by
The University Press of Florida
ISBN 0-8130-1539-1 (cloth)

Set in Adobe Garamond with Barmeno Extra Bold display
Book design and composition by Dariel Mayer

01 00 99 98 97   5 4 3 2 1

Cataloguing-in-Publication Data

Richardson, Bonham C.
    Economic depression, environmental
disaster and change : Barbados and the
Windwards in the late 1800s /
    Bonham C. Richardson.
    p. cm.

    Includes bibliographical references.
    ISBN 976-640-038-5

    1. Man - Influence of environ-
ment - West Indies, British. 2.
Environmental economic - West
Indies, British.
3. Human ecology - West Indies,
British 19th century. I. Title.
GF51.R43 1997   304.2

01 00 99 98 97   5 4 3 2 1

Library of Congress
Cataloging-in-Publication Data

Richardson, Bonham C., 1939-
    Economy and environment in the
Caribbean: Barbados and the Windwards in
the late 1800s / Bonham C. Richardson.
    p. cm.

    Includes bibliographical references and
index.
    ISBN 0-8130-1539-1 (cloth)
    1. Economic development—Environ-
mental aspects—Barbados—History—19th
century. 2. Economic development—
Environmental aspects—Windward
Islands—History—19th century. 3. Human
ecology—Barbados—History—19th
century. 4. Human ecology—Windward
Islands—History—19th century. I. Title.
HC155.7.Z9E57   1997
333.7'0972981—dc21   97-28120

*To the Memory
of my Mother and my Father*

Contents

Illustrations

Photographs

Figures and Maps

Tables

Foreword

America was long viewed primarily as a place to be acted on by Europeans, Bonham Richardson reminds us at the start of his book. The Caribbean, earliest colonized and longest controlled by European powers, was the quintessential transatlantic appendage. Almost all West Indians were imported or bred, just as their locales were exploited, to service European interests.

What happens to such people and places when their owners have no more use for them? That agonizing conundrum suffuses the chronicle told here. Among the most bereft of Britain's outworn, virtually cast-off colonies in the late nineteenth century were those of the southeastern Caribbean. The parlous plight of Barbados and the Windwards, the causes thought responsible, and the measures urged to alleviate them are trenchantly exposed in these pages.

In common with all the Caribbean, Barbados and the Windwards had been exploited since the seventeenth and eighteenth centuries to raise tropical crops for European consumers. Of these, by far the most profitable and extensively grown was sugar cane. Sugar and other export commodities were produced largely by slaves brought from Africa; by the eighteenth century slaves vastly outnumbered free West Indians. A handful of Europeans ran the plantations and governed the colonies, but absenteeism was rife; few landowners or colonial officials stayed in the Caribbean of their own choice. But sugar was so lucrative that some islands, notably Barbados, grew little else; even food for slave labourers had to be imported.

Two mid nineteenth century events transformed the British Caribbean. Emancipation in the 1800s freed the slaves but left them under planter subjugation. In many islands former slaves cultivated higher ground off the estates, but most had to supplement produce from provision grounds with plantation wage-labour. And restrictive suffrages denied the large majority any elective role in local government. 'A race has been freed', commented a colonial official in 1848, 'but a society has not been formed'.

The second change was a sharp decline of imperial interest in the West Indies, signalled first by the withdrawal of tariff protection for West Indian sugar. Several circumstances combined to cripple the planters and to impoverish their former slaves. The promotion of European beet sugar; the exhaustion and erosion of long abused Antillean soils; the indebtedness of the planters and the obsolescence of their technology; not least, a general shift of attention from the Caribbean toward more profitable markets in India and elsewhere. Numerous Caribbean sugar enterprises went bankrupt or survived only in reduced form. Estates previously in sugar were planted to less labour intensive tree crops (cacao, coffee, nutmeg) or abandoned to peasant cultivators. Many of the unemployed were forced to emigrate, notably to mine gold in Guiana or to work on the Panama Canal. Islanders left behind were sorely destitute.

Conditions in Barbados and the southernmost Lesser Antilles were especially grievous – Barbados owing to total reliance on sugar and massive overpopulation, the Windward Islands owing to the wellnigh total collapse of their plantations. Such was their distress that hundreds if not thousands of Barbadians in the late nineteenth century took up lands vacated in the Windwards.

Indeed, Britain's Colonial Office hoped in the 1870 to alleviate Barbadian unemployment and shore up Windward enterprise by unifying the islands under one regime. But the so-called Federation Riots of 1876 put paid to this marriage of misery. Unlike in climate, in land forms, and in agriculture, the two paupers were also socially incompatible. Barbados, an anglophone white plantocracy, was proudly self-governing and substantially literate; the Windwards, French patois-speaking save for St Vincent, were virtually devoid of local whites, run by the Colonial Office, and largely illiterate. Impoverishment and mutual grievances were all these realms had in common.

Their fin-de-siècle plight is not unfamiliar to Caribbean historians. But it is newly animated here with intimate and vivid details from first-hand accounts. Drawing on local newspapers, court cases, and visitors' comments, Richardson makes extensive use of testimony given at the 1897 Royal Commission set up to gauge the extent of distress, to clarify its causes, and to find ways of providing people with a securer livelihood and a modicum of self-respect. Thanks to these abundant sources, conditions only sketchily inferred from statistical data and summary reports come fully to life. West Indians of the 1890s gain an immediacy, an individuality, a reality no less palpable than that modern chroniclers limn for their great-grandchildren today.

We hear the frustration of men and women scratching a meagre living from mountain lands they cannot call their own. We hear the anger of Barbadians helpless against slave-like servitude. We read of men left so bereft of local hope they venture as far afield as Amazonia or central Africa, few ever to return. At the same time, we hear the laments of planters who live in fear of peasants armed with cutlasses, yet cling to perquisites tainted by slavery. We hear British officials and advisers who admit the old plantation regimen is doomed, agree on the need for a landowning peasantry – yet cannot dream of letting control pass from whites, however hidebound, to blacks, however hard up. Such bias was bolstered by pseudoscientific racism that held blacks incapable of managing tropical milieux adjudged inaccessibly unviable, dangerously overexploited, and yet somehow also so fruitful as to encourage reversion to slothful savagery.

A century on, some circumstances seem remarkably unchanged. The same degradation of steep soils by logging and charcoal burning: the same insecurity against hurricanes and volcanic eruptions; the same fragmented complex of tenures commingling private with family lands and Crown re-serves, tenants and share-croppers; the same frenzied search for alternative staple exports to insure against market collapse or drought or plant disease.

Social responses to environmental and economic stress also seem much the same: local laws flouted, because seen to feather the nests of those in power; outside experts and entrepreneurs welcomed as saviours yet simulta-neously rejected as scoundrels. Insular identity is pervasive: folk memories bind each island community in a network of narrative tradition continuous since slavery. Yet boundaries are regularly breached: smuggling between Petit St Vincent and Petit Martinique is as much a way of life today as in Richardson's account of conditions a century ago.

Opposing such continuities are changes unimaginable yesteryear, either to Royal Commissioners or to residents. Tourism has displaced sugar from economic primacy even in Barbados; banana cultivation is the peasant mainstay of the Windwards: hunger and epidemic disease are all but van-quished: post-war emigration to America and to Britain has augmented many if not most islanders' economic options and expands insular cultural horizons.

Most momentous are the social and political metamorphoses. Yet an-other Royal Commission in the 1930s paved the way first for universal adult suffrage, then for self-government. Within a few postwar decades planter hegemony in every island yielded to control by coloured elites and at length by black majorities. And the last remnants of imperial British pres-ence gave way to demands for freedom that made each colony, however small and impoverished, an autonomous sovereign state. Foreign interests continue to dominate many realms, notably tourism, the islands' economic life blood. But neocolonialism notwithstanding, the descendants of the folk depicted in this book have come a long way. Whereas colour and class barred their forebears from any effective role, their great-grandchildren today are, and know themselves as, masters of their own house.

The 1897 Commissioners proved prescient in one major respect: foreseeing planter demise in the Windwards, they acted to enlarge peasant smallholdings. In St Vincent, the most regressive plantocracy, land reform was most needed and bore the earliest fruits. Grenada's energetic and progressive peasant proprietors were held up as a model the other Windwards should follow. It is ironic that a century later Grenada again became a model of new peasant reforms – reforms seen as so fearsomely marxisant that metropolitan powers and Grenada's own neighbours stepped in to quash them.

Let me conclude on a happier irony. Who could have dreamed that little patois-speaking St Lucia, a century back the least integrated and worst schooled of the Windwards, would emerge as the seed-bed of two Nobel laureates, whose insights in global economics and Creole literature today enlighten the whole world? From exporting logwood, St Lucians have graduated to disseminating Logos – a more sustainable resource than any envisioned by Colonial Office or colonials of the era this book so fully re-evokes.

David Lowenthal
January 1997

Preface

The 1992 Earth Summit in Rio de Janeiro marked, according to some, the defining moment for new ways of thinking about our finite planet, inspiring green movements everywhere, affecting policy and diplomacy, even ushering in a new world order. Similarly, the frequency with which we hear or read the terms 'ecology', 'sustainable' and 'global' from academics, government officials and policy makers alike would suggest a genuine preoccupation with things environmental.

Yet if substance is to outdistance rhetoric and a true environmentalism set in motion it seems sensible to truly "think globally and act locally" as the bumper stickers suggest. That means focus on and attention to real places and real problems because environmental knowledge, although subject to the laws of science and nature, really comes to life in particular localities, among rocks, trees, hillsides of different places and – more and more – physical features built or modified by human action. And it is difficult to think of a region of the world – or, really, the region's series of different places – for which these remarks are more true than they are for the Caribbean.

The Caribbean's physical geographical commonalities – beyond the sand and surf images that form the basis for its valuable tourist industry – nurture its human populations but also pose the threats of recurring hazards. The region's identity as a series of islands and coastlands makes it susceptible to sea level oscillations in an era of possible global warming. Further, the Caribbean's seismic instability, hurricane autumns and eroded landscapes are features of long standing. Within these general features, however, are located scores of varying island environments along with their human societies that have adapted to each of these unique and different environments over the past half millennium.

The idea that a wide variety of Caribbean environments and histories are bound up with one another – a point that Caribbean writers and poets always seem to emphasize – comprises in large part the subject matter of this book. And I hope very much that this study of the Eastern Caribbean's geographical experiences of one century ago will interest not only historically oriented academics but also today's future oriented planners and policy makers as well. I make no policy recommendations here nor do I offer suggestions beyond emphasizing by implication how important it is to understand the particularities of each individual place. Yet this profoundly commonsensical point – the danger of the sweeping regional generalization – is probably more important at the end of the twentieth century than it was at the end of the nineteenth. And it was certainly a problem then as I try to show in the chapters that follow.

If I have indeed been successful in writing a book of both academic and practical interest for the Caribbean region, or even if I have not, I have a great many direct and indirect debts to acknowledge here. The great bulk of the primary material in this study comes from information I located and researched in London-area archives during academic year 1986–87. The research would have been impossible without the generous support from grants from both the Committee for Research and Exploration of the National Geographic Society in Washington, DC, as well as a grant from the Geography and Regional Science branch of the United States National Science Foundation. I am also grateful to the research-study leave programme at Virginia Polytechnic Institute and State University which provided a year with half salary so that I could pursue this work.

These funds from various sources allowed my wife and two daughters and me to live in the London area for a year. The librarians and staff at the various archives that I mention preceding the bibliography were exceptionally helpful. Perhaps more important was the opportunity to interact with fellow Caribbeanists while I was in London and to talk with them informally and frequently about what I was finding in the archives. Hilary Beckles from UWI Cave Hill had an appointment at the Institute of Commonwealth Studies paralleling my stay in London, and we had numerous opportunities for conversations over lunch. Caribbeanist colleagues Peter Fraser and Clem Seecharran provided stimulating company on an almost daily basis as they were also pursuing their own research projects at the Public Record Office. As always, David and Mary Alice Lowenthal were both encouraging and generous.

The decade–long lag between the research period and the published book requires explanation. First, I wrote another book during the period; it was published in 1992. Second, I have published a series of academic articles, beginning in 1989, from this same research material. These articles do not duplicate the information I provide in this book. Rather, they explore byways of some of the issues I discuss here. I would like to thank various editors and journal referees for poring over this written material and helping to improve it and thereby indirectly helping me write material for this book. Also, thanks to the Johns Hopkins Atlantic history seminar for inviting me to present to them in 1992 an early draft of what is now the chapter about climate.

Thanks to my colleague and friend Vanessa Scott for all of the word processing. I have also always been able to call on my other departmental colleagues at Virginia Tech for help and encouragement; Jim Campbell and Larry Grossman especially have been sources of wisdom, good humour and help with maps and diagrams. Linda Cameron of The Press UWI was punctual and encouraging while the manuscript was under consideration, and she put it into the hands of two knowledgeable referees whose suggestions, both general and very specific, improved the study. John Boyer expertly re-drafted the maps at the last minute.

My wife and daughters have suffered through the period I have been writing this book, listening – usually with patience – to my anecdotes about century–old sugar cane blights in Barbados or smuggling in the Grenadines at the turn of the century. I hope that they will enjoy reading the final product. I wish my parents could have read it as well, but they both passed away while I was working on it. The book is appropriately dedicated to their memory, although it is a trivial memento to a lifetime of love, understanding, and generosity that I received from both of them.

Chapter One
Introduction

On the morning of Thursday, 18 February 1897, the three members of the visiting British Royal Commission interviewed witnesses in the Council Chamber of the Public Buildings in Bridgetown, the capital of the British West Indian colony of Barbados. The commission had been convened in London two months earlier to investigate the nature, extent and implications for the immediate future of the severe economic depression that had afflicted the British West Indies for more than a decade.

The commissioners, beginning their second full day on Barbados, already had heard testimony concerning the plight of that island's workforce during the depression: Barbados, a low-lying, coralline island, was monopolized by sugar cane plantations. Portions of each Barbadian estate were devoted to subsistence gardens allocated to the black descendants of plantation slaves, but their vegetables usually had to be supplemented with food imports. The prevailing low sugar prices had lowered wages, reducing black workers' ability to buy imported food. The results included malnutrition, high infant mortality and a malaise accented with bitterness among members of the black Barbadian workforce. Drought prevalence on low-lying Barbados—such as the drought of 1894–95 that had desiccated black workers' subsistence grounds—compounded the local misery already created by economic depression.

Not all British West Indian islands were similar to Barbados. On this morning the commissioners sought comparative evidence about life and livelihood in the volcanic Windwards, one hundred miles to the west, islands that had highland interiors not cultivated in sugar cane. Portions of the Windwards, moreover, were occupied by small-scale subsistence and cash crop cultivators, a much different pattern than in Barbados. The commissioners questioned the Reverend J. Payne, a Wesleyan minister familiar with the entire region. Were conditions better for the black labourers on mountainous St Vincent than on Barbados? "Yes," responded Payne, "in St Vincent the people get breadfruit and a great many other things for nothing. With a few acres of mountain land the labourer of St Vincent can do a good deal for himself."[1]

This book describes these geographical contrasts and explores the comparative human-environment interactions as they differed among people in Barbados and the three British Windwards—St Lucia, St Vincent and Grenada—during the economic depression of the late nineteenth century. The dates of the depression, so far as this study is concerned, are 1884 to 1902. In the former year, the London price of sugar plunged in response to a (mainly German) dumping of European beet sugar on the open British market. The latter date is that of the Brussels Convention where Western European nations agreed to rescind the so-called bounty system that had helped create the low sugar prices, although the overall price of sugar on the London market would not rise to pre 1884 levels again until after the onset of World War I.

This study focuses on the ecological characteristics of the eastern Caribbean during the depression. Accordingly, the book's substantive chapters deal with "the Climate", "the Waters", "the Lowlands" and "the Highlands", although the emphasis here is on the human activities that took place within each of these zones or environmental categories. The meanings and importance of these seemingly passive environmental categories were changing at the end of the nineteenth century because of unprecedented economic and social changes in the British Caribbean, changes linked directly to the depression. Except in a few places, such as Barbados, absolute planter control in the region was in decline and a smallholder class emerging. The same hills and valleys that had sustained planters' tropical export crops for many decades now were being inherited by the region's working peoples. So the landscapes of the several small British Caribbean islands, heretofore regarded (by members of the plantocracy) as backdrops necessary for the production of tropical staples, had, by the late 1800s, somewhat suddenly become the objects of earnest, self-conscious, official colonial plans and schemes designed for smallholders.

The appealing geographical characteristics of the British Caribbean—optimum intercontinental location, subtropical climate, fertile soils and accessible insular topographies—had together comprised an ideal physical setting for the original core of the New World plantation system.[2] But the spectacular economic success of the English and later British West Indian plantation system beginning in the seventeenth century had depended ultimately on its complex and changing market connections with London. Compared with the political, economic and social linkages between Europe and the Caribbean that directed and reinforced the flows of agricultural surpluses to metropolitan destinations, furthermore, the physical environmental characteristics of the British Caribbean islands in the heyday of the colonial plantation era were often taken for granted.

A corollary of such an argument is that the local geographies of the islands had themselves been formed and transformed to accommodate the plantation system. So that Jack P. Greene's recent assertion that, during the first three centuries of European colonization, "America . . . came to be known primarily as a place to be acted upon by Europeans", is, as far as the Caribbean is concerned, an understatement.[3] By the early nineteenth century, the principal characteristics of insular geographies of the Caribbean—infrastructure, settlement patterns, demographic characteristics, crop complexes—had been etched into local landscapes because of the overriding influences of metropolitan control. And the well-known sentiments of planters (absentee and otherwise) and transient colonial officials, whose personal wealth and career trajectories had eventual meaning in a British—not a Caribbean—setting, did little to enhance their concern about or understanding of local Caribbean environments. Planters could hardly ignore physical geographical realities; yet their concerns about local water supplies or soil fertility, for example, usually were limited to an understanding driven by their desire to produce sugar cane for external markets, the activity that was, after all, the business of the islands. Overall environmental concerns might best be left to the random visits by scientists from London or the naturalist who tended the occasional botanic garden, tucked away in a corner of a local capital town.

But a geographical complacency initiated and reinforced by an overriding concern with economic connections with Britain could be rudely interrupted. If a damaging hurricane or pest invasion reduced crop yields, the orderly flow of goods and profits were reduced, thereby calling for local corrective attention. Such attention was of course necessary in order to reestablish linkages with the mother country, thereby restoring equilibrium to the region's externally focused plantation system.

It hardly needs emphasis that the material benefits of the plantation system's economic success accrued only to a small fraction of the people residing in the British Caribbean. Similarly, the luxury of an elitist geographical complacency was not shared by the region's Afro-Caribbean slaves and their emancipated descendants. Indeed, the region's slaves might be said to have suffered all of the Caribbean environment's negative consequences and almost none of its benefits. Although they toiled daily under a broiling tropical sun, their captive status limited them severely from tilling the region's soils for their own benefit. And those periodic disruptions in the flow of materials that comprised the externally focused plantation system often curtailed slaves' food imports.[4] Locked into a perverse geographical system over which they had absolutely no control, Caribbean slaves experienced occasional famine, malnourishment and early death on the same island environments that produced the agricultural wealth which flowed "into the European metropolises in great rivers, nourishing infant industry, making possible the foundation of great families, and supporting the growth and spread of culture and civilization".[5]

Slave emancipation in the British Caribbean in the 1830s had a varied geographical impact throughout the region; this variation was based less on the general, London-decreed guidelines dealing with people than it was on the difference in insular landscapes and the ways these lands were and were not made available to freedmen.[6] Sidney Mintz's term "reconstituted peasantries" has thus not only illuminated the Caribbean's unique colonial history, but it also has identified an interdisciplinary research agenda dealing with the many ways in which ex-slaves of the region and their descendants have come to grips with a variety of environments and planter imposed rules concerning those environments.

As ex-slaves and their children then began to gain greater control over some of the region's local lands as freeholders, squatters, or in a variety of sharecropping arrangements, the human geography of the British Caribbean expanded into marginal, previously unoccupied environments. A 'highland adaptation' unfolded on mountainous islands, where former slaves established village settlements above fertile lowlands that still were preempted by sugar cane plantations; in other areas, former estate labourers occupied swampy lowland zones adjacent to ongoing plantations.[7] These geographical changes, although imperfectly known and under-researched, were of momentous regional significance. By mid nineteenth century, Caribbean lands, heretofore a near monopoly jealously guarded by the plantocracy, were beginning to sustain a sizeable, freed human populace.

Interrelated with these changes were increasingly favourable official attitudes toward smallholder proprietorship, attitudes emanating in Britain itself. Thomas Holt's recent research traces the importance of the writing and thinking of John Stuart Mill in the latter decades of the nineteenth century that began to champion the practicality of a peasant proprietorship, not necessarily for Britain, but for certain other parts of the British empire.[8] Holt shows that Mill drew examples from Ireland and India to assert that the encouragement of a smallholder populace was a fair, prudent and forward looking strategy for matching people and land. Mill's views inspired bitter opposition in Britain and were considered near unthinkable among members of the British Caribbean plantocracy. Despite this opposition, Mill's ideas were sufficiently attractive to some of the younger members of the Colonial Office that commentary about the feasibility, even the desirability, of "peasant proprietary schemes" for some of the British Caribbean islands began to appear in official correspondence as early as the 1870s.

So when the externally influenced economic depression descended upon the British Caribbean in 1884, there were at least theoretical metropolitan alternatives, combined with incipient applied knowledge in the form of free villages, to cane sugar production on large-scale estates. More immediately, a reduction in the flow of capital from London, combined with the associated collapse of a number of longstanding merchant/financier establishments in the British Caribbean islands, had had the combined effect of weakening the planters' control over local lands. The reduced financial and market control from London had therefore heightened the importance of looking inward toward local resources. When the members of the 1897 royal commission visited St Lucia, two weeks after they had left Barbados, they heard St Lucia's treasurer D.G. Garraway explain that the island's labourers could no longer count on obtaining wage labour on sugar cane estates. Instead, according to Garraway, these same labourers needed "to pay greater attention to their holdings, and to raise more permanent crops upon them for the support of their families".[9] Garraway's observations were, in many ways, applicable to the entire region and to planters and workers alike, all of whom had been thrown back on local resources and local environments because of the effects of the economic depression.

For the late nineteenth century in the British Caribbean, ecological and economic themes therefore intersect and overlap. The entire region, consisting of a series of discrete insular societies whose geographies had been created by their economic linkages with London, was suffering greatly because of a general economic depression ultimately based on the weakening of those same linkages. And just as the development of local settlement patterns, plantation forms and postemancipation smallholder adaptations all had been influenced by the particular terrain, climate and configuration of each of the islands, the varying ways in which Caribbean peoples in different islands adapted to economic depression were similarly conditioned by these same geographical characteristics.

At a broader level, the Caribbean region at the end of the 1800s was undergoing profound change in response to global shifts in political and economic power. The opening paragraphs of the following chapter describe Britain's overall colonial strategies in light of her international rivalries and new territorial opportunities at the time. Geopolitically, these influences had reduced the importance of the Caribbean in London's eyes. Economically, the British Caribbean's outdated colonial infrastructures that had evolved in response to earlier technologies were no longer attractive as investment opportunities. More promising were new tropical areas being developed with new technologies. The most obvious contrast to the depression-yoked sugar islands of the British Caribbean was in the Caribbean region itself. The momentous late nineteenth century surge in sugar production in the Greater Antilles, particularly in Cuba, was interrelated with the growing economic might of the United States. The British Caribbean islands, anxious to formalize their longstanding trading ties with the United States, established modified trade reciprocity with that country during the depression but were then rebuffed in 1894 by US commercial arrangements that greatly favoured Cuba, Puerto Rico and the Dominican Republic.[10]

The wider Caribbean at the end of the nineteenth century was thereby a region between empires, a generalization exemplified no better than in its small British colonies. Caught in the middle between a rising regionwide United States hegemony and longstanding British economic control, these small islands were gripped by both yet embraced by neither. And the local adaptations and changes made by individuals and groups, planters and labourers alike, in response to these overall conditions have been imprinted upon these same islands well into the twentieth century.

The Royal Commission of 1897

Despite the Caribbean's decline within Britain's colonial empire, the West India Royal Commission of 1897 was nevertheless convened to assess the region's economic malaise. It was the first full-scale, investigative, regionwide commission since 1842.[11] And the immediate events precipitating the formation of the commission, beyond the obvious effects of the depression, probably were a series of workers' riots in the islands themselves. In this way, the working peoples of the region were not simply passive recipients of external demands but had a direct hand in framing their own destinies, a point discussed further at the conclusion of the following chapter.

The resulting presence of the delegation of commissioners from London in the British Caribbean was itself a pivotal historical event. When they reached St Vincent early in February 1897, the commissioners received, among other memoranda, a handwritten statement signed by twenty-one men and women from Barrouallie on the island's leeward coast, likening the commissioners' arrival to the coming "of Moses of yore into Egypt, delivering the children of Israel from Pharoah's bondage".[12] Although the members of the commission were not always greeted with such exuberance, it is important that their hearings throughout the region, combined with the volumes of documentary evidence and analysis they generated from local testimony, represented at once a mirror and mould of the region during the 1890s.

The three commissioners, their secretary, and their agricultural consultant were neither unfamiliar with the Caribbean nor with the events that had led to the depression there. Indeed, it has been suggested that they probably were already predisposed to recommending the substitution of a 'peasant proprietary' for the region's antiquated sugar plantations in most of the islands, a strategy that, by 1897, was being discussed regularly in colonial correspondence.[13] The commission's well published agricultural consultant, Daniel Morris, the assistant director of Kew Gardens and a former agricultural officer in Jamaica, had written about British Caribbean agriculture for *Nature* a decade earlier. While acknowledging sugar cane's longevity and importance in the British islands and the plantation capital invested there, his main predictive observation was that "it is estimated that more than one-half of the actual surface of the West Indian Islands is suitable for other cultivations than sugar-cane".[14]

So it is not surprising that, after their months of research and testimony in both London and the British Caribbean colonies, the commission's principal and unanimous recommendation and remedy for the economically depressed islands was "The settlement of the labouring population on small plots of land as peasant proprietors." The commissioners were however careful not to appear to abandon altogether the local plantocracy; the commission also recommended unanimously the modernization of Barbados' sugar cane industry by establishing central mills there with the aid of a loan from the Imperial Exchequer.[15] Similarly, the Colonial Office was cautious not to appear to favour unduly the emergence of a smallholder class that would overturn the local social order. After reviewing the commission's findings, Colonial Secretary Joseph Chamberlain informed the various British West

Indian officials to encourage the establishment of smallholders on the islands but not if such encouragement meant either widespread squatting or the abandonment by workers of ongoing sugar cane estates.[16]

Despite these ambivalences, the 1897 commission's findings and recommendations, derived from the commissioners' observations of the islands in the depression decades, marked a major geographical watershed for the British West Indies as a whole. The findings justified the emergence of a widespread presence of smallholders on several islands that had heretofore been nearly monopolized by plantations. The concluding chapter of this book describes some of the first hesitant steps at establishing some of these smallholdings following the commission's recommendations, yet the unfolding of changing land use patterns in the islands later in the twentieth century is beyond the scope of the present study. But the overall impact of the 1897 commission's findings—and, by extension, the influence of the economic depression of the late nineteenth century—on the peoples of the Commonwealth Caribbean throughout the twentieth century is difficult to overemphasize. Writing in 1947, a half century after the commission, C. Y. Shephard, the Carnegie Professor of Economics at the Imperial College of Tropical Agriculture in Trinidad, asserted: "The report of the 1897 Commission may be regarded as the Magna Charta of the West Indian peasant."[17]

Caribbean Geography

The suggestion that early British West Indian planters took local environments for granted might be considered a geographical corollary of the Caribbean's uniqueness in colonial history. The Caribbean's aboriginal peoples, whose small insular habitats provided few buffers against a relentless European quest for economic accessibility, provided little lasting resistance, and they were decimated within decades by European cruelty and introduced diseases. Europeans thereby inherited an 'uninhabited' environment that they subsequently transformed by introducing capital, cultigens, planting techniques and an exotic labour force. In discussing "a distinctive commonality of leading features" distinguishing the Caribbean from other world regions, the late Gordon K. Lewis pointed out that "The first of these features, and that from which everything else flows, is . . . that the European colonial powers created Caribbean colonies *de novo* . . . once . . . the original Taino-Arawak-Carib Indian stocks had been reduced."[18]

Insularity—especially when combined with a disappearing aboriginal populace—doubtless enhanced an assumed environmental familiarity and a confidence reinforced by total control. On Columbus' second voyage from Spain late in 1493, his party's landfall was Dominica, from where they sailed generally northwest to Hispaniola, dutifully mapping and naming the islands along the way and thereby adding each place, both cartographically and semantically, to a growing constellation of colonies within Europe's economic orbit.[19] As Michael T. Ryan has suggested, such activities "implied a certain ownership, if not legal then at least intellectual and psychological".[20] Decades later, after the demise of the original human inhabitants and their replacement with imported African slaves, the perception of total environmental domination must have been reinforced for the European colonists of the various Caribbean colonies by simply being able to sail around each island, a journey that, for the smaller colonies, could be completed between the dawn and dusk of a single day.

The subsequent European colonization of much larger, continent-sized areas of the world reinforced, later in colonial history, an outlook that took the character of Caribbean environments for granted. The Caribbean lacked vast interiors populated by sizeable and enigmatic aboriginal civilizations who were able to buffer and mediate European encroachment and demands by seeking refuge in local subsistence systems based on local environments. The mountainous centres of British Caribbean islands, in contrast, though not risk free and sometimes inaccessible, were hardly the settings for safaris or explorers' expeditions. And even though the volcanic interiors of some of the places were dangerously steep, a few of the smaller islands were—for all practical purposes—completely tamed by a very early date: "When [Hans] Sloane climbed Nevis peak in 1687, searching for botanical specimens, he passed through cleared fields almost all the way up until he came to a patch of woods at the top."[21]

Environmental challenges in the British Caribbean were not unknown. The tropics, after all, were and are environmentally different from mid latitudes. And a steady stream of correspondence between planters of the region and British scientists at Kew Gardens at the end of the nineteenth century, complete with enclosed plant and insect specimens, were ample evidence that, even after many decades of colonial control of the Caribbean, there was still much to understand. Yet the understanding, pioneering, and exploration of the Caribbean environment was of a commercial, internal quality—a directed, exploitative activity that reduced local ecosystems in order to enhance the externally oriented flow of tropical staples to impersonal

European markets. According to anthropologist Robert Dirks, Caribbean colonial success in terms of monetary reward

was to be made by the pioneering planter, the man first on the scene, the opportunist, more miner than either farmer or gardener, who could reduce a primeval biomass and its wealth of nutrients to sugar. For this reason there always existed a cutting edge, an expanding frontier of cultivation, which, for all its artificially conceived constructiveness, actually thrived on massive ecological destruction, a degradation of complex natural and cultural assemblages that left in its wake a more or less rundown monoculture of standardized fields and regimented communities.[22]

Dirks is one of the comparatively few academics who has incorporated a blatantly ecological perspective into a historical study of the English-speaking Caribbean. The reason, furthermore, seems clear. The historical incongruity between the Caribbean's externally introduced peoples and the lands they occupy represents a far different situation than, for example, in the Pacific, where peoples and the lands they occupy are intimately related and where ecological studies of these relationships abound. Nor have the particular qualities of the historical relationships between people and land in the Caribbean been amenable to the broad-scale historical studies of competing ecological traditions such as in colonial New England, on which scholars have thrown new light for the ways in which European settlers came to dominate the land.[23] Until recently, academics dealing with the Caribbean, particularly those of an historical bent, seem to have taken the Caribbean environment very much for granted, much as the early British planters did.

There have, of course, been exceptions. The famous geographer Carl Sauer—writing decades before it became academically fashionable to equate Christopher Columbus with ecological rape—described the demise of the aboriginal peoples of the Greater Antilles at the hands of the invading Spaniards in stark, ecological terms, showing how the productive Arawak agricultural adaptations were swept away with the people themselves.[24] And Otis P. Starkey years earlier wrote an under-appreciated environmental study of Barbados, including a useful discussion of how Barbados's climate—mainly the recurrence of drought—was interrelated with the island's historical trends in sugar cane production.[25]

More recent work by academic geographers has begun to reduce the ecological void in Commonwealth Caribbean studies. Riva Berleant-Schiller and Lydia Pulsipher have carefully crafted a typology, based on field research and archival sources, that identifies similarities in small-scale subsis-

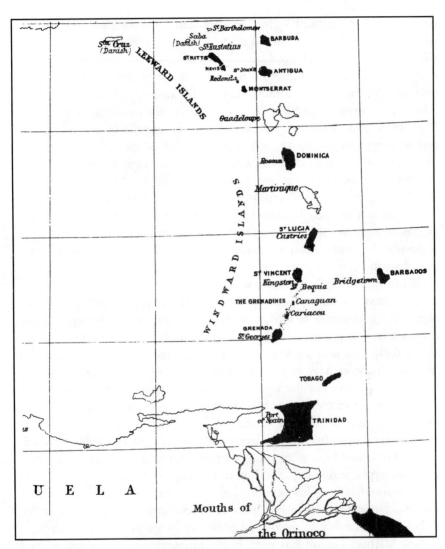

Figure 1.1. A portion of the map that augmented the *Report of the West India Royal Commission* (1897)

tence agriculture in the English-speaking Caribbean with an eye to establishing local gardening as part of a "New World creolization process" with African, European and pre-Columbian antecedents.[26] David Watts has compiled a far more voluminous historical survey of the entire Caribbean environment since pre-Columbian times with an emphasis on eastern Caribbean sugar production from the seventeenth to the nineteenth centuries.[27] Most important as far as the local study of the region's geography is concerned, there have emerged in recent years local geographical journals edited by Caribbean based personnel as well as primary and secondary school texts dealing with Caribbean environments.[28] The latter trend finally has rendered anachronistic the oft-repeated commentary about traditional schooling in the British West Indies which provided students with detailed geographical narratives about, for example, coal mining in the British Midlands or Kentish hop cultivation without any information whatever about breadfruit, bauxite, or sugar cane.

In an interdisciplinary sense, it is perhaps inevitable that recent historically oriented scholarship dealing with the Caribbean also has begun to recognize the importance of environmental characteristics of the region more than before. The growing emphasis on the Caribbean's social history invariably attempts to seek answers as to how enslaved and otherwise coerced labouring peoples have coped with the region's power holders. These attempts cannot avoid exploring the ways in which these oppressed peoples have attempted to compete for local resources, a competition that mirrors the longstanding asymmetry of the Caribbean's social order. Accordingly, these explorations often involve grassroots descriptions and analyses of village or household level adaptations that are intimately associated with hillsides, soil types, seasonality, flooding or evaporation rates.

The interrelationships between Caribbean resistance and local environmental adaptations now have a number of scholarly examples upon which to build. In his study of the overall resistance by slaves in the British West Indies, Michael Craton has used maps, physiographic descriptions, and photographs of the impenetrable mountainous sanctuaries that were so important in sustaining the Maroon societies of pre-emancipation Jamaica.[29] Walter Rodney, in a brief but now oft-cited passage describing the misery of what living through slavery must have involved in coastal Guyana, refers to the travails of shovelling "tons of heavy, waterlogged clay . . . while enduring conditions of perpetual mud and water".[30] Barry Gaspar, in seeking ways to understand differing styles of resistance in New World slave societies, has appealed strongly to these societies' varying physical backdrops or settings as explanatory variables.[31] And Sidney Mintz has pointed out that the act of establishing the region's "reconstituted peasantries"—often on lands that were too inaccessible, economically marginal or both—was in itself an enduring example of resistance against the plantation regime.[32]

In a more abstract way, the recognition of the importance to Caribbean peoples of land, as both resource and symbol, has provided a recent and now increasingly common thread in the fabric of academic work dealing with the region. As early as 1961, the geographer David Lowenthal, inspired by the literature created by West Indian writers as well as his own prolonged residence in the region, identified land as a valued and idealized entity among Caribbean peoples.[33] This theme has now inspired others, notably the anthropologist Jean Besson and the geographer Janet Henshall Momsen, to contribute to a growing literature on the subject.[34] In perhaps the most important historical-environmental statement to date about the Caribbean, the geographer/historian B. W. Higman has addressed specifically the "ecological determinism" in Caribbean history, perhaps introducing a new idiom that will be fruitful in historical studies of the region.[35]

The present study attempts to reinforce and extend the incorporation of environmental considerations into historically oriented scholarship dealing with the British Caribbean region. The Eastern Caribbean of the late 1800s is ideal for such an effort because the region's lands had begun to be interpreted as the lifeblood of a newly invented peasantry rather than the basis for ongoing plantation production, and one is struck by the many ways in which British Caribbean officials were beginning to appeal to local geographical characteristics for clearer understandings of the societies they governed. The 1897 commissioners received a memorandum, for example, when they reached St Lucia, urging caution in considering the suggestion of a land tax. Such a tax in the colony would be "unpopular and objectionable" perhaps goading "the ignorant to resistance" which could perhaps be "quelled only by bloodshed".[36] The observations are of course consistent with the realization of the importance of land among working peoples of the region. But colonial officials of the eastern Caribbean in the 1890s took the importance of land a good deal further than that. Among an apparent majority of administrators in the region the notion that land was a "drug" for the labouring class helped them to "explain" the lackadaisical character of the Windward islanders as opposed to the hard-driving (landless) Barbadians, issues considered further in chapter five.[37]

Yet attitudes held by Caribbean officials were not the same, and, perhaps more often than not, were exactly the opposite, from those felt and acted upon by the region's working peoples. And although a full-blown cultural-ecological study of these peoples' activities in the 1880s and 1890s is near impossible because they left few detailed records, their voices are nevertheless heard in the official written records to a surprising degree. The occasional passionate laments to Queen Victoria for more land or freedom, signed by groups of villagers, are sprinkled through the conventional archival records. And small-scale farmers sometimes recorded their perspectives in local newspapers or passed them on to officials who included these remarks in reports that subsequently appeared in the colonial correspondence. These working peoples were, after all, the future backbone of the 'peasant proprietary' group destined to inherit much of the region if the sugar industry failed. Occasionally one finds lengthy, verbatim testimony describing the ways in which these peoples coped with elements of the local environment. One example is the description of how one small crew of Barbadian fishermen survived the gale of 12 October 1894 that blew them all the way to St Lucia, a passage that concludes the discussion in chapter four about the region's waters.

A highland-lowland distinction is emphasized throughout this study, and it provides the contrasting subject matter in chapters five and six. When the first African slaves came to the Caribbean, to Hispaniola probably in the first decade of the sixteenth century, several escaped into the island's mountainous interior almost immediately.[38] Since then, Caribbean highlands have been associated with a relative absence of planter control, in contrast, of course, with the region's lowlands. Many of the other polarities of the region—in terms of scale, technology and accessibility—are well recognized as highland-lowland differences.

Reverend Payne's testimony before the 1897 commissioners in Barbados also recognized this contrast when he described the relatively advantageous position of Vincentian highlanders versus Barbados' lowland labourers. Others echoed Payne's advice to the commissioners when they emphasized, for example, the amenities of the mountainous and forested interior of Jamaica in contrast to flat, deforested Barbados.[39] And the conventional medical wisdom of the time that the highlands of the region were healthier than the lowlands was reinforced by the correspondence and records left by medical officers and other officials that dealt with both particular places and also inter-island differences.

Yet the relationship between residential location and health—illustrated indirectly by the tables of death rates and infant mortality (see Appendix)—cannot demonstrate empirically that the highlands were always healthier than the lowlands. Furthermore, as discussed below, one must be wary as always of official testimony. Despite Reverend Payne's assertions before the commission about Vincentians' access to fruitful highland interiors, for example, the black labourers of St Vincent in general were frightfully poor and ill-nourished, a point that most observers of the time reinforced, especially when they compared the overall conditions in St Vincent with those in Grenada and St Lucia.

A comparative inter-island theme also is facilitated here by using the principal physical features of the eastern Caribbean as chapter headings. And by focusing on four neighbouring but internally quite different islands, the highland-lowland contrast leads to back-and-forth assessments of likenesses and differences among islands and islanders. These comparisons, in turn, help lead to clearer understandings of how West Indians characterized and stereotyped themselves and one another, much as they did late in the nineteenth century and much as they do today, one century later. This middle-range approach comparing four islands, as opposed to a single focus on either one territory, on the one hand, or the entire region, on the other, is thereby different from the majority of book-length studies of the Caribbean.

A general point about the highland-lowland contrast is obvious yet necessary. Excepting the strict altitudinal differences, the division is of course artificial and somewhat arbitrary. That is because human settlements and especially human activities on Caribbean islands ascend from the low country into the highlands and descend from the mountains to the seacoasts. Although colonial officials of St Lucia, for example, were generally ignorant of the patois-speaking peoples of the island's mountainous interior of the 1890s, everyday they saw village market women bringing fresh fruit and vegetables from the highlands to Castries. And the attempts in St Vincent actually to survey a boundary to delineate highlands from lowlands in the 1890s was a subject of great planter-labourer contention as discussed in chapter five.

Overlap also is inevitable between chapter three ("The Climate") and chapter four ("The Waters"), and, for that matter, between these two chapters and the others. Using the example of the hydrologic cycle illustrates the point. Precipitation is a climatic event in which water vapour evaporated from the surface of the earth cools and condenses. It then becomes surface water after reaching the ground. Then the resultant water affects highlands or lowlands or both through runoff, seepage, aiding photosynthesis, or in any number of other ways. Again, a certain artificiality is necessary in identifying environmental categories as chapter topics, and this organizational necessity is not intended to reduce the obvious importance of the interrelatedness of environmental elements.

The suggestion that traditional British West Indian planters and others were insufficiently attentive to environmental realities and inherited an attitude that took Caribbean geographical conditions for granted is reinforced by noting the indifference toward possible hurricane dangers in Barbados in the 1890s. These complacencies are discussed in chapter three. Similar misper-ceptions failed to recognize the possible earthquake and volcanic eruption hazards in the Eastern Caribbean and instead influenced an indifference toward possible catastrophe among both French and British officials in the region. In St Vincent, the Soufrière volcano was considered more a source of pleasure and beauty than of potential danger. In the 1890s, it was common for bands of hardy holiday makers to gather at the edge of the crater's summit to watch the changing colours of the volcano's water, and "No one cherished the slightest suspicions of evil, lurking under the serene water of the crater" despite occasional volcanic jolts and tremors on the island.[40]

But environmental complacency vanished after the geophysical catastrophes that visited the eastern Caribbean at the turn of the century. The great hurricane of September 1898 ravaged Barbados and St Vincent, then veered north and dealt a blow to St Lucia. The conclusion of chapter three describes its trajectory, destruction and immediate consequences. Then less than four years later, Soufrière's eruption on St Vincent—which occurred almost simultaneously with the more famous explosion of Mt Pelée in Martinique—created similar havoc and despair (but fewer deaths) on the former island. The final part of chapter six considers Soufrière's eruption and its aftermath.

These twin disasters magnified and publicized the economic misery that already had afflicted the region for nearly two decades, thereby exposing more clearly "the underlying structures of social and political life" in the region as have other Caribbean disasters.[41] These catastrophes also helped to condition the region for the eventual unfolding of the smallholder schemes, discussed in chapter seven, that had been recommended increasingly in the British colonial correspondence of the late nineteenth century and reinforced by the recommendations of the 1897 royal commission. These land use changes cannot be interpreted as having been 'caused' by environmental catastrophes in a deterministic sense, but the disasters helped in no small way in pushing some islands along toward smallholder developments.[42]

After these two catastrophes struck the eastern Caribbean, local officials, especially in St Vincent but also in nearby islands, seemed to vie with
one another for superlatives with which to describe the suffering in the region. Never before, they insisted, had British subjects faced such difficulties.
For two decades the people of the region had suffered the consequences of
externally produced economic depression. Now they faced the dire circumstances of coping with ecological disaster. At the beginning of the twentieth
century in the eastern Caribbean, the intersection of economic depression
and the environmental characteristics of the region was by no means an ar-
cane, theoretical construct. And the ways in which the peoples of Barbados
and the Windwards coped with the economic depression in the 1880s and
1890s using the environmental resources at their disposal provides the subject material of this book.

Chapter Two
The Eastern Caribbean in Depression, 1880–1900

In the forty years between 1875 and 1915, a remarkable burst of world co-lonialism created global patterns that in large part are still evident at the end of the twentieth century. During that four-decade period "about one-quar-ter of the globe's land surface was distributed or redistributed as colonies among a half-dozen states".[1] It was a partitioning of economically weak ar-eas and their peoples by the strong, helping to create and reinforce the gulf between the developed and underdeveloped world regions that we recognize today. Although this staking out of territory at the end of the nineteenth century has been interpreted as a spatial expression of limitlessness engen-dered by the successes of industrial capitalism, this final era of colonization in practice and on the ground had obvious limits. The colonial powers' lo-gistical problems associated with coordinating and redirecting non-Western labour systems, patrolling sea lanes, and defending colonial boundaries, combined with growing demands at home from labouring classes who de-manded better lives, meant that the recolouring of the world map was to be a shared—though still competitive—experience.

At least that is the way officials in the United Kingdom seem to have interpreted the unfolding of geopolitical events at the time. The British, ob-viously, were old hands at colonialism, having established the so-called Pax Britannica of the early nineteenth century after the Napoleonic Wars and extending their lightly challenged influence throughout the world. But by the early twentieth century, under the threat of growing German naval power, Britain is said to have reached accommodations with erstwhile rivals in a number of strategic world areas. They accepted Japanese preeminence in the northwestern Pacific, established harmonious relations with the French in the Mediterranean, North Africa and Southeast Asia, and resolved previous differences with the Russians in the Far East. These agreements thus allowed the British to pursue aggressively territorial opportunities in tropical Africa while attempting to cope with German military and eco-nomic rivalry in Europe.[2]

The British similarly came to terms with the United States in the Caribbean—Europe's original overseas colonial region—by acquiescing to American supremacy there through the resolution of the Venezuela-British Guiana boundary dispute during the 1890s in accord with American wishes and also by withdrawing the British naval squadron from Jamaica in 1906. American geopolitical preeminence over European rivals in the Caribbean was further solidified in 1898 through its military removal of Spain from the region and the successful completion of the Panama Canal in the next two decades, although the United States continued to face a German threat in the region until the termination of World War I.[3]

Yet the Americans had by no means ousted the British from the Caribbean. United States control was strongest in the Greater Antilles and along the eastern rim of Central America. The British in 1900 continued to maintain a significant territorial presence in the region in the form of a fragmented, 2,000-mile arc of colonies extending from the timber camps of British Honduras in the far west to the sugar cane plantations along the mudflats of British Guiana in the east. In between were the aging sugar colonies of Jamaica and the Lesser Antilles. Most were tiny islands, densely populated by the descendants of black slaves and a sprinkling of more recently introduced indentured labourers from India. The main economic activity of the working peoples of these colonies was sporadic and seasonal work on relic sugar cane estates interspersed with labour on their own tiny garden plots. Both the estate-produced sugar and surplus subsistence crops ended up at the small port cities for export or for sale at Saturday morning markets. The port towns were also the seats of local colonial governments where a handful of British administrators enviously followed the course of empire from afar by reading in their weekly newspapers of events in Ceylon or South Africa.

Conquering new territories doubtless seemed far more glamorous to them than dealing with their own mounting local problems. The British Caribbean at the turn of the century was in the second decade of a severe economic depression, creating a malaise resulting from both cumulative global economic changes and regional conditions. Everyone realized, moreover, that the British Caribbean colonies had become economic backwaters and that the immediate depression conditions were in many ways symptomatic of the region's economic decline. The activities of the anti-slavery forces of the late eighteenth century in Britain and Western Europe, in concert with the rise of industrial capitalism, had together led to the abolition of the British Caribbean slave trade in 1807 followed by slave emancipation in the 1830s.[4] Then in 1846 the British Parliament had removed preferential pricing for colonial sugar imported to the mother country. British Caribbean sugar cane planters, now forced to deal with free labourers and without market advantages in London, had struggled back to realize profits in most years. Yet anyone with an eye to the future and access to comparative cane sugar production data knew that the British Caribbean islands really were anachronisms of an earlier empire.

The islands' small size had been advantageous in the earliest decades of colonization. During the seventeenth and eighteenth centuries small grinding mills, powered by animals and then by wind or water, processed the cane cultivated on 300-acre estates, and small-scale insularity assured ready access to local port facilities. But the steam engine had revolutionized cane sugar production in the nineteenth century. Large tracts of virgin lands, not the worn-out soils of the Lesser Antilles, now were necessary to support the overhead cost of erecting modern, steam-driven grinding mills and to ensure the subsequent production of sufficient quantities of sugar cane once the mills were in place. These new techniques had revolutionized cane sugar production throughout the tropics by the late nineteenth century. One had to look no farther than Cuba to see examples of the dramatic results of the pairing of modern technology with new lands. In 1815 Cuban sugar exports had been only half those of Jamaica; by 1894 Cuba produced fifty times the sugar cane grown in Jamaica and four times the total of all the territories of the British Caribbean combined![5] Further, the qualitative differences in American-financed Cuban cane sugar production and marketing and those same activities in the British islands had, by the late nineteenth century, become so marked that it was almost as if one were comparing two completely different industries. In Cuba most sugar was ground in large, steam-driven factories; in the British Caribbean much of it still produced by windmills. Once produced, the Cuban sugar was stacked, stored and shipped in warehouse bags, not in the old-fashioned wooden barrels still used in the British islands. And Cuban sugar was subject to market intelligence and price information relayed by sophisticated telecommunication networks, not marketed through the haggling among consignees and marketing agents as was the case in much of the British Caribbean, despite the British islands' recent telecommunication linkages with the mother country.[6]

Nor was all British Caribbean sugar production so antiquated. As the nineteenth century had progressed, modern techniques had been adopted in the larger southern territories of Trinidad and British Guiana. The first colonial vacuum pan—which had the unique feature of boiling sugar juice at low temperatures and thus avoiding the scorching of the semi-refined sugar—was installed at Vreed-en-Hoop in British Guiana in 1832, an innovation leading to the production of the famous, high quality 'Demerara crystals' of sugar.[7] Forty years later the construction of the central grinding factory St Madeleine—at the time, the second largest sugar factory in the world—in southern Trinidad reoriented agricultural patterns and helped to inspire small-scale cane farming there.[8] St Lucia also had established a central factory by the 1870s, following similar developments in Guadeloupe and Martinique late in the 1840s. The southerly shift of the centre of gravity of the British Caribbean sugar industry after emancipation also was accompanied by intraregional demographic changes as the nineteenth century progressed; thousands of black freedmen from the small, worn-out 'old islands' to the north—mainly the Leewards (St Kitts, Nevis, Montserrat and Antigua) and from Barbados as well—migrated south permanently and temporarily to work for higher wages and to avoid the lower wages that were part of the relative decline in the sugar plantations on their home islands.[9]

But no amount of internal reorientation within the region could alter the direction of the global economy and its impact on the small British Caribbean colonies. By the late nineteenth century, British industry produced massive surpluses of manufactured goods, and an open market, *laissez faire* economic policy was advantageous so that British industrialists could ship their goods worldwide in exchange for unrefined minerals and agricultural staples. The seventeenth and eighteenth century policies of monopoly capitalism and jealously protected metropolitan markets, policies under which the Caribbean sugar colonies had originated, evolved and thrived, had long since been abandoned by London. Unfortunately for most of the Commonwealth Caribbean, the infrastructures and peoples that those earlier policies had called for were still in place. To make matters worse by the end of the nineteenth century, the Great Depression of 1873–1896 in Europe, marked by "universal catastrophe" in European agriculture, was making itself felt worldwide.[10]

It was indeed European agriculture that created most directly the depression conditions in the British Caribbean in the late 1800s. Since early in the century, European beet sugar had made ever increasing penetrations into the global sugar market. Begun as a series of German laboratory experiments showing that common forms of European beets yielded sugar, the commercial production of beet sugar had started to gain importance in Western Europe after the 1820s. The sugar beet represented an alternative European cash crop to grain which increasingly was imported from elsewhere, and it also required deep plowing and heavy applications of fertilizers, thereby helping to raise the outputs from other crops within local agricultural rotations. Sugar cane planters in the French Caribbean complained as early as the 1830s that favouritism accorded continental French beet sugar producers was a violation of the *pacte colonial*; French continental beet producers responded, perhaps prophetically, that the ruin of the French beet sugar industry would affect as many people in a single French *arrondisement* at home as there were whites in all the French colonies combined.[11]

From mid nineteenth century, world beet sugar production, mainly from Europe but also increasingly from the United States, gained dramatically on global cane sugar and finally caught it in the early 1880s.[12] The success of beet sugar, however, lay only partially in European cultivation techniques and agricultural science as it was understood at the time. Much more important in the eyes of their Caribbean sugar cane competitors was that continental European governments had introduced a complex system of payment incentives to their local beet sugar refiners which were refunds of internal excise taxes for exported beet sugar; the refunds were based on conventional sugar extraction standards, so refiners were encouraged to improve their techniques to receive higher refunds ('bounties') for the greatest amount of sugar that possibly could be produced from a given weight of sugar beet.[13] These financial incentives—which were of course protective government strategies aimed, ironically, at London's open market—encouraged ever greater beet production throughout Western Europe. In 1884 the dumping of a massive amount of German beet sugar on the open London market lowered the price of sugar there from 19 to 13 shillings per 100 pounds. Thus began the so-called bounty depression that ravaged the Commonwealth Caribbean for two decades and more because sugar prices did not reach 1883 levels again until World War I.[14]

Besides having the advantages of large-scale production leading to lower prices, European producers of sugar and sugar-based products developed other techniques intended to capture the British market. They used charcoal in their refining process to adsorb impurities and produce white sugar crystals, as opposed to the less attractive grayish crystals usually coming from the Caribbean sugar colonies. British refiners also used yellow dyes to colour beet sugar and therefore replicate the characteristic colour of the

Demerara crystals, which were a popular British grocery store item. German liquor manufacturers even developed a type of rum using a cane sugar elixir adulterated with juices derived from sugar beets. And transportation costs, of course, gave European sugar producers a sizeable advantage over Caribbean cane growers. Some of the German beet producers, for example, stored their finished product in Hamburg for less cost than they could in London and then shipped their product directly to British buyers.[15]

British Caribbean sugar cane producers during the bounty depression were not being outcompeted for a share of a static market. Rather, their production was being curtailed at the very time that British consumption of sugar was soaring; since the mid nineteenth century consumption of sugar in the United Kingdom had increased steadily to nearly 90 pounds annually per person by the 1890s.[16] And it was not, strictly speaking, a competition between identical products. Besides the subtle differences in the colours of sugar crystals, cane sugar had a higher sucrose content than did beet sugar. It was said, for example, that the residents of eastern England, near the ports where European beet sugar was brought in, had grown accustomed to a 'beety' taste in their sugar.

But the importance of the British sugar market of the late nineteenth century was not because of the direct consumption of granulated sugar. Sugar's cheap price had helped make it an important additive for biscuits, sweets, marmalade and jam consumed by the members of the British working class, food items formerly considered luxuries. By the late 1890s sugar was, next to corn, the most important food item imported into Britain. Sugar also was a key ingredient in the confectionery, cocoa and biscuit industries that not only served the growing demand for better diets among working-class Britons but also employed thousands. These food items also were important British exports. Cheap imported sugar, moreover, was helping to stimulate the spread of fruit orchards, especially in southern and eastern England.[17]

These were some of the formidable obstacles, not to mention the massive free-trade lobby led by British industrialists, faced by British Caribbean sugar cane planters who pleaded unanimously to the home government for countervailing tariffs against bounty-inspired beet sugar from Europe. Yet local industries in the mother country had not profited uniformly from the influx of massive amounts of European beet sugar, and some had been hurt badly so that they too called for tariff protection. The cane sugar refiners of England and Scotland had declined in both number and overall refining capacity, and they warned of the "progressive extinction" of the British sugar refining industry owing to the "unfair, unjust competition by means of bounties" and warned of eventual price increases once European refiners controlled the entire market.[18] Nevile Lubbock, chairman of the West India Committee in Britain, similarly warned that a decline in the British sugar refining industry would mean losses in shipping as well as to those supplying machinery, engineering expertise, disposable sugar bags and similar goods and services.[19] Nor was the concern about European sugar bounties confined to the highest levels of Britain's industrial society. A conference of members of the London trades' council at the Westminster Palace Hotel in March 1888 involved trade union representatives from throughout the city who feared widespread job losses owing to the unfair competition from cheap European sugar prices.[20]

The ambivalence among British industrial and commercial interests over European sugar bounties was absent in the Caribbean sugar colonies. Planters, officials and most administrators there appealed long and loud for relief from bounty-lowered prices. Planter groups were the most vociferous. Reading the reports and memoranda from these sugar cane colonies at the time suggests that the two decades starting in the early 1880s consisted simply of one planter meeting after another, each resulting in another condemnation of London's free trade policy; more details of the disastrous conditions in the islands; and one more appeal for action against European sugar bounties. To be sure, financial conditions were grim in the islands; during the fifteen-year period starting in 1884, some of the oldest merchant houses in the British Caribbean that traditionally had provided credit to local planters—and thereby represented the financial underpinning of the region's sugar cane industry—had failed. They included George Little & Co., Cotton Morton & Co., and A. W. Perot & Co. in British Guiana; A. M. Gillespie & Co. of Tobago and Grenada; DuBoulay, Mackay & Co. in St Lucia; Swindell and Matthews in St Kitts; F. and G. Garraway in Antigua and Dominica; Thos. Daniel & Co. of Barbados; Gregor, Turnbull & Co. and Wm. Burnley & Co. in Trinidad; and Hawthorn and Watson in Jamaica.[21]

But a litany of failed British Caribbean commercial houses was only a caricature of the grassroots devastation that the bounty sugar depression brought to the region's working peoples. The descendants of black slaves in the region never had prospered in the half century following emancipation, but in most places they had established village based societies that were partly independent from ongoing estates, and a growing number of black and brown peoples of the British Caribbean had become artisans and shopkeepers, and had profited from a modicum of education. Then in the 1880s depression-lowered wages quickly absorbed household savings, reduced the quantity and variety of food imported to augment village subsistence crops, and sent labourers in droves to distant estates and other islands to seek work. Scarcely a week passed at the British Colonial Office in London in the last two decades of the nineteenth century without officials there receiving a report from the Caribbean colonies outlining in poignant detail estates closing or reducing their labour needs, the impoverishment of working peoples, or widespread undernourishment accented by disease, all of these conditions exacerbated by the depression. The effects of the depression were perhaps most obvious to visitors and the newly arrived. Robert Baxter Llewelyn, a colonial officer with twenty years' experience at posts that included Jamaica, Tobago, and the Turks Islands, arrived in St Vincent late in 1887 to become the island's administrator. He declined to append an extensive narrative to the end of that year's annual report to London because he had not been at Kingstown for the entire calendar year. But he had witnessed an islandwide malaise so pervasive that he hoped 1887 would "be found hereafter to have been the worst year the Island has ever experienced".[22]

Despite its preoccupation with the newer, richer and larger areas of the empire, the British Colonial Office was unable to ignore this regionwide calamity among its oldest overseas territories. Since emancipation in the 1830s the Colonial Office had adjudicated the rivalries between British Caribbean planters—who attempted to coerce the newly freed labourers into providing cheap, reliable and docile labour—and the black freedmen themselves who pressed just as hard in the opposite direction to attempt to consolidate their meager gains. Often, decisions in London had tended to protect the latter from the former. But a rising 'coloured' class in the region after mid century inevitably demanded more political power, and they coveted seats in the elected colonial assemblies. Declining sugar prices and associated labour crises also clouded the atmosphere. Then the Morant Bay Rebellion in Jamaica in 1865 was followed by a rescinding of the old Jamaica constitution and the imposing of Crown Colony government there. The Crown Colony system meant near autocracy by an appointed governor and vastly reduced power by local legislators. In the following decade the Crown Colony system was extended to nearly all the British Caribbean colonies with the notable exception of Barbados. And these changes have been interpreted as responses to a widespread fear of possible black political control in the region and an associated "means of protecting the interests of European planterdom".[23]

From the perspective of the British Colonial Office, the longstanding Caribbean antagonisms based on the interrelationships among economics, class and colour reduced the possibility of easy political solutions to the local effects of the bounty sugar depression of the 1880s and 1890s. The Crown's Caribbean possessions could hardly be governed by indirect rule through local chiefs as in some of the recently partitioned colonies of Africa. Nor were British Caribbean possessions similar to the 'settler colonies' of Canada, Australia or New Zealand where a high degree of local autonomy relieved the Colonial Office from dealing directly with many local problems. Furthermore, each Caribbean colony—despite the regional depression—was different in size, economy and social character. So when a new constitutional change was inaugurated in Jamaica in 1884 which entered "the largely uncharted field between pure crown colony government and representative government" it did not necessarily mean the extension of similar arrangements for all of Britain's Caribbean colonies.[24]

Whatever new forms or configurations the British Caribbean colonies were likely to assume would, in any case, be influenced greatly by the men of the British Colonial Office. These men read widely, entertained a variety of new ideas, and, though not necessarily thoroughly committed to the rise of a landed black peasantry, were nevertheless deeply suspicious of the region's planter class.[25] On the one hand, the Colonial Office officials knew, for example, the development logic forwarded by writers like Benjamin Kidd, who articulated a compelling urgency for white control of the tropics, an untapped biotic domain that had lain dormant because of the indolent, unenergetic peoples who always had lived there.[26] On the other hand, they were deeply influenced by John Stuart Mill and his followers who had stressed, among other points, cultural variation within the empire. If the Crown's influence was to be extended and consolidated, according to Mill, the idea of absolute property rights might have to be modified in favour of governed (rather than governing) peoples, in effect conceding small land plots to colonial cultivators.[27]

Colonial Office personnel were not restricted by what they read or heard from writers and journalists, nor were their thoughts necessarily directed into a single, orthodox viewpoint. By the late nineteenth century there existed a small army of military officers, teachers, accountants and administrators who had served the empire in a number of different capacities and in many different places. And it had become common to share governing philosophies and experiences from one colony to another, formal exchanges of ideas and opinions that were encouraged and mediated through London. By the 1890s these exchanges were influenced by the partition of Africa which had introduced a nakedly exploitative dimension to the thrust of British colonialism whereby British entrepreneurs sought control of large numbers of (to them) undifferentiated black African labourers. It was perhaps inevitable that these activities came to be justified through an idiom equating Africans with 'savage' and 'primitive'. These terms and attitudes inevitably spilled over into the pronouncements about the character of black West Indians, though a number of Colonial Office officials consciously resisted these comparisons.[28]

Yet they were used time and again in the late nineteenth century as British colonial officers considered the possibilities of some kind of self-rule for their Caribbean colonies. According to James H. Stark, author of a guidebook to the region, the geographical results of blacks taking over Barbados probably would lead to a settlement pattern of "African hut[s] of wattles and thatch" whose inhabitants "would be found cooking their bananas and yams on the ruins of warehouses". Writing in the 1890s, Stark even went so far as to draw a perverse comparison between black Africans and Caribbean blacks, describing the latter as "the lowest race on earth . . . coarsely formed in limb and feature" who "would have been slaves in their own country if they had not been brought to ours".[29]

A most influential observer (whose ideas Stark may very well have borrowed) of the British Caribbean during the depression decades was James Anthony Froude, eventually the Regius Professor of Modern History at Oxford University. Froude toured the islands in 1886—87 with an eye to assessing the possibility of some kind of parliamentary self-rule for the Caribbean colonies, islands that had become "a burden upon our resources" and that "were no longer of value to us". Froude's research consisted of an incredibly naive series of travel vignettes published as a book that sought to elucidate the nature of West Indian blacks' mental capacities and character from observations made from aboard ship, on carriage rides or from the verandahs of governors' mansions. Even in the context of the late nineteenth century, his observations appear lamentably racist. West Indian blacks, according to Froude, had never really "shaken off the old traditions" and if the

British islands ever were to fall under their control "the state of Hayti stands as a ghastly example of the condition into which they will then inevitably fall".[30]

Froude was not without contemporary detractors. The most famous was John Jacob Thomas, a self-taught Trinidadian teacher and linguist whose book *Froudacity*, published in London in 1889, exposed Froude's lack of insight and endless oversimplifications; it also sharply criticized the nature of colonial rule: "The Colonial Office has for a long time been responsible for the presence in superior posts of highly salaried gentry . . . who have delighted in showing themselves off as the unquestionable masters of those who supply them with the pay that gives them the livelihood and position they so ungratefully requite."[31]

British officials at the time probably took more seriously the anti-Froude writings of C.S. Salmon, a Colonial Office official who had held posts in West Africa and Seychelles besides the Caribbean. Salmon's 1888 monograph, *The Caribbean Confederation*, proposed a political union of the British Caribbean colonies seventy years before that same solution marked the islands' eventual freedom from colonial rule. His proposal was also a scathing, line-for-line indictment of both the substance and recommendations in Froude's book.[32] Yet despite these contemporary critiques, Froude's observations often were cited approvingly by Colonial Office officials during the late 1880s and the 1890s. Froude's most notable supporter (and occasional dinner partner) was Joseph Chamberlain who became Secretary of State for the Colonies in 1895. In the following year, Chamberlain observed, reminiscent of Froude's notions, that "liberal constitutions" such as Jamaica's were "not really suited to a black population".[33]

The many influences on British government officials notwithstanding, the depression conditions in the islands had to be dealt with in one way or another. Finally, in November 1896 the Colonial Office announced the formation of a Royal Commission "to inquire into the effect of the foreign Sugar Bounties upon the British Colonial industry, more particularly in regard to the West Indies". The announcement cited the failures of sugar estates and allied business in the region, the distress among the local black and indentured Indian populations, and it noted the intention to seek perspective about what would become of these peoples if there were "extensive abandonment of sugar estates".[34] It was the first regionwide commission to assess conditions in the British Caribbean colonies in more than half a century. The commissioners held hearings in London early in January 1897, spent the next four months travelling throughout the British Caribbean, stopped briefly in New York before returning home, and then held concluding hearings again in London. Altogether, the West India Royal Commission of 1897 held forty-five formal sittings, interviewed hundreds of witnesses from all social levels, and amassed an extraordinary amount of data and information. Most important, the commission's recommendations in favour of the establishment of black smallholders on the land eventually led to momentous changes in some islands of the region.

The commission's chairman was Henry Wylie Norman who, at age seventy, had been a military official in India and later the governor of Jamaica and also Queensland. His fellow commissioners were David Barbour, author of a number of economics treatises, and also Edward Grey, who had served the Crown in several official capacities. The secretary of the commission, Sydney Olivier, had entered the employ of the Colonial Office in 1882, had acted as secretary of the Fabian socialist society from 1886 to 1890, and would later serve as the governor of Jamaica. Daniel Morris, the assistant director of Kew Gardens and former agriculture officer in Jamaica, accompanied the commission to provide botanical and agricultural expertise. The five men interviewed witnesses in London for the first week of 1897, sailed from Southampton on 13 January, and, after two weeks at sea, arrived at Georgetown, British Guiana on 27 January 1897.

Barbados and the Windwards

The commissioners were men with first-hand experience in the West Indies, so they understood when, during the preliminary hearings in London, their witnesses emphasized the wide geographical diversity of the region. Yet it was an observation that they themselves would make time and again during their four months in the islands early in 1897. For one thing, the sizes and resources of the various places were so very different. British Guiana with interior goldmines and an incipient rice industry, Trinidad with asphalt and cacao, and Jamaica with bananas and forest products, all were somewhat better off than the smaller islands depending solely on sugar cane, but these larger places also had larger populations to support. Furthermore, some of the tiny places, such as Nevis with mainly subsistence crops and Anguilla with seafaring, hardly depended on sugar cane at all. Then there were the great differences in environments from one place to the next, such as the aridity of flat Antigua compared with nearby but mountainous and rainy Dominica.

This variety was perhaps no better exemplified than in the southern islands of the eastern Caribbean. The three Windward islands of St Lucia, St Vincent and Grenada had highland volcanic cores because they lay along the intersection of two of the earth's crustal plates and, like most of the other islands of the Lesser Antilles, had been formed from extrusions of molten material from deep in the earth's interior.[35] Barbados, 100 miles to the east, was geologically unrelated to the other three; it was a low-lying island whose soils consisted of weathered coral. The four islands were, however, sufficiently close to one another that they, together with Tobago, had been administered jointly by a single British governor-in-chief from 1833 to 1885. In the latter year Barbados had begun to be administered by a single governor and the other four by a governor whose office was in Grenada. Then in 1889 Tobago became administratively detached from the three Windwards and united with Trinidad to form a single, two-island colony.

Barbados and the three Windwards had been incorporated into the British empire in different ways. Barbados had been settled by the English in 1627 and had never been under any other colonial jurisdiction, a rarity among Caribbean colonies. St Vincent had been ceded to Britain from France in 1763; then the British army had battled the island's aboriginal Caribs intermittently until 1797, when the British deported some of the remaining Caribs to eastern Central America and isolated the remainder on a reserve at the northern end of St Vincent. Grenada and St Lucia each had changed hands between the French and British several times in the eighteenth century and, like St Vincent, had come under formal British jurisdiction in 1763; British troops had fought and pacified French-influenced rebels in both Grenada and St Lucia one century earlier, in the 1790s.

Despite the divergence in land use and much else during the following century, the four islands—Barbados, St Lucia, St Vincent and Grenada—were all numerically dominated by the descendants of black slaves. The largest of the four, St Lucia (233 square miles) had 42,220 people counted in the 1891 census; St Vincent (150 square miles) had 41,054; Grenada (133 square miles) had 53,209; and densely settled Barbados (166 square miles) had 182,306 (Table 2.1). The tiny Grenadines were located between St Vincent and Grenada; in 1891, 3,071 people inhabited the St Vincent Grenadines, and 6,031 inhabited Carriacou, the latter island administered as part of Grenada. A brisk, informal traffic in sailing sloops and schooners

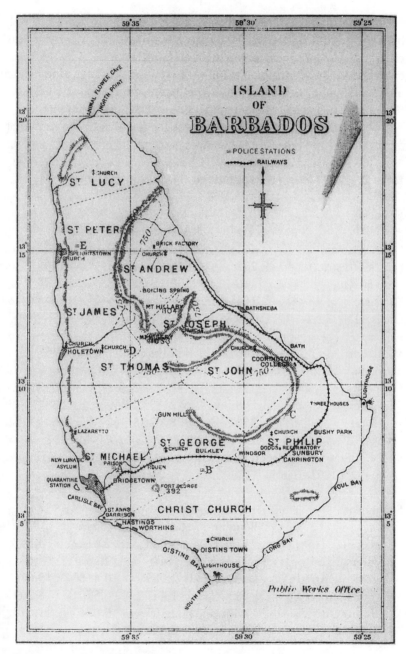

Figure 2.1. Barbados, 1909

among the islands had existed since slavery days and steamer travel had been introduced in the 1830s. By the late nineteenth century steamships provided scheduled yet intermittent passenger connections between the eastern Caribbean and the outside world, and also brought the foodstuffs, building supplies and nearly all of the manufactured goods used by island residents in exchange for locally produced tropical staple products.

The first stop from Southampton for the fortnightly Royal Mail Steam

Table 2.1 1891 Human Populations

St Lucia

	White	Mixed	Black	Asiatics	Total
Castries (town)	444	2,242	3,980	22	6,688
Castries (district)	202	915	4,543	843	6,503
Anse-la-Raye	16	690	1,403	136	2,245
Soufriere	154	1,771	3,954	162	6,041
Choiseul	19	1,771	3,077	45	4,312
Laborie	23	989	2,188	155	3,355
Vieux Fort	46	482	2,547	453	
Micoud	9	574	1,757	56	2,396
Dennery	29	472	2,368	566	3,435
Gros-Islet	8	672	2,949	88	3,717
Total	**950**	**9,978**	**28,766**	**2,526**	**42,220**

Source: Alex. Clavier, "Report on the Census of St Lucia 1891, *St. Lucia Gazette* (January 29, 1892), Table V

St Vincent

	White	Colored	Black	Total
Kingstown	512	1,423	2,612	4,547
The Grenadine	152	488	2,431	3,071
Kingstown District	1,109	2,089	10,418	13,616
Leeward District	185	1,447	6,570	8,202
Windward District	487	2,107	9,024	11,618
Total	**2,445**	**7,554**	**31,055**	**41,054**

Source: C.O. 264/17, "Census taken on 5th April 1891, No. III," *St Vincent Official Gazette, 1891*

Table 2.1 , Continued
Barbados

	White	Mixed	Black	Total
Bridgetown	3,336	9,227	8,433	20,996
St Michael	3,646	9,609	21,932	35,187
ChristChurch	1,483	3,081	16,928	21,492
St Philip	1,301	4,025	13,337	18,663
St George	694	3,087	12,273	16,054
St John	1,170	1,850	7,936	10,956
St Peter	825	2,663	7,312	10,800
St James	486	2,351	7,667	10,504
St Thomas	394	1,831	7,873	10,098
St Lucy	509	2,332	6,921	9,762
St Joseph	995	2,153	5,900	9,048
St Andrew	774	1,767	6,205	8,746
Total	**15,613**	**43,976**	**122,717**	**182,306**

Source: Report on Census of Barbados (1881-91) (Bridgetown 1891), p 17.

Grenada

Town of St George	4,919
Parish of St George	8,816
St John	6,204
St Mark	2,902
St Patrick	7,482
St Andrew	12,512
St David	4,343
Carriacou	6,031
Total	**53,209**

Source: Grenada Report and General Abstracts of the Census of 1891 (St George 1891), p 17, table 4.

Packet Company bound for the Caribbean was Bridgetown, Barbados, a port served by several other steamer lines providing passage to North America, South America, and other Caribbean ports. Visitors to Barbados boarded lighters at the deep-water anchorage in Carlisle Bay; then they were rowed by black lightermen along the estuary of the Constitution River to Bridge-town's landing place where the customs, harbour master, and health officials maintained offices. Not far away was the imposing complex of public buildings, gray edifices of masonry and stone, where the legislative halls, post office, treasury and public library were located. Compared with Bridgetown, the other main port towns, including Kingstown in St Vincent and St George's in Grenada, were picturesque but obviously less important. And Castries in St Lucia in the 1870s had been unromantically described as "a little town, small, dirty, dilapidated, and unwholesome", although the British Admiralty's decision to construct major port facilities there—a project begun in November 1885—eventually transformed Castries into a major coaling centre.[36]

The urban amenities of telephones, streetlights and piped water had all been introduced into each of the capital towns by the early 1890s. Also, the Colonial Bank, whose head office was in London, had offices in each of the four capital towns; these banks maintained accounts of the working funds for local colonial governments, merchants' accounts, and thousands of tiny deposits of small-scale tradesmen and labourers. Silver British coins were the islands' official currency, although coins from elsewhere were commonly exchanged in the weekly markets that convened each Saturday morning in the small cities. Rural cultivators brought vegetables to these markets on foot, and more rarely by horse-drawn carriage—the means of transport for the local social elites—via the road networks on each of the four islands.

The roads were of varying quality, best on Barbados where the near-flat terrain facilitated intra-island movements, and the Barbadian highways' crushed coral surfaces were still passable during rainy periods. Conversely, the roads of the three mountainous islands often were seasonally impassable. From Kingstown in St Vincent, carriage travel via the coastal road was possible along the Windward coast only to Georgetown, and travel farther north usually via sailing sloops; on the leeward side of the island, the road was decent only to Chauteaubelair, and coastal travel by canoe common from there to the northern end of the island. On St Lucia, the few interior roads were augmented with bridle paths. Grenada embarked on a road improvement programme during the 1890s, including the construction of sev-

Table 2.2. Percentage of Sugar Products in Total Exports, 1896

Jamaica	18
British Guiana	70.5
Trinidad	57
Tobago	35
Barbados	97
Grenada	nil
St Lucia	74
St Vincent	42
Antigua	94.5
St. Kitts-Nevis	96.5
Dominica	15
Montserrat	62

Source: Royal Commission (1897) Report, p 3.

eral bridges and tunnels. Barbados was the only island of the four with a railway, a small-gauge line having been laid east from Bridgetown in 1881, eventually to run along the Atlantic coast past Bathsheba to Belleplaine, in St Andrew parish, in 1883. In the early 1870s the four islands were linked to the outside world by a cable of the West India and the Panama Telegraph Company. Thereafter, local residents in each of the four islands could read with increasing frequency news bulletins from elsewhere in their weekly newspapers.[37]

The 1897 commission, charged with determining the varying severity of results within the region in case the Caribbean sugar cane industry failed altogether, considered the percentage of sugar cane products in an island's total exports a rough statistical rule of thumb as a means of ranking each place's susceptibility to possible collapse. Using this index, Barbados (97%)—with St Kitts (96.5%) and Antigua (94.5%) close behind—was considered the most vulnerable in the region (Table 2.2).

Barbados' large and very dense human population also made it an object of the commissioners' particular concern. The island's settlement pattern was indeed related directly to the plantation production of sugar cane. The typical black resident of the island resided in his or her own house on a rented plot within a plantation 'tenantry' or settlement area. The labourer rented a tiny garden plot and worked on the estate owner's lands under conditions stipulated by a series of 'located labourer' statutes inherited from the days immediately following slave emancipation. These overall conditions were directly related to the plantocracy's domination of Barbados' flat terrain, domination that had left little land for the emergence of village areas as on other islands.[38]

The dense settlement and resultant surplus of estate labour gave black Barbadians little local latitude to cope with planter demands, and it also meant that planters had little incentive to modernize their cane grinding and boiling factories. The traditional small Barbadian estate, subsidized by redundant and underpaid workers, had yielded steady profits until the depression, income misinterpreted by members of the local plantocracy as payoffs for their canny agricultural and managerial expertise. In July 1884, Barbadian Acting Governor Browne observed that problems in Barbados' sugar industry came not only from the depression but also from the backward production methods of the local producers themselves who eschewed the efficiencies and higher quality sugar that economies of scale could produce.[39]

The near monopolization of Barbadian land for the cultivation of sugar cane also limited local subsistence agriculture. So black Barbadian estate workers depended heavily upon imported, cash-purchased food that they bought with plantation wages. The reduction of wages during the bounty depression therefore led to food shortages, malnutrition and high incidences of diseases. Time and again during the depression decades, parish medical officials commented on the emaciated, ulcered and generally ill-nourished black working populace of the island. Disease flourished under these conditions. Typhoid, dysentery and a variety of bowel disorders were common in the crowded, rural tenantries where lack of sanitation was the rule.

Public officials maintained few records of death and disease in Barbados, and, unlike even in the Windwards, kept no track of infant mortality or stillbirths until the mid 1890s. In mid August 1891, Acting Governor Broome submitted a strongly worded statement before the island's Executive Committee wondering if there was any other "civilized community in the world where deaths are not officially registered" and other vital statistics not collected and published. Broome's anger was because of the selective indifference on the part of white Barbadian officials who were all too eager to ensnare black workers for petty crimes, yet oblivious to more fundamental health problems:

If a sugar cane is stolen, or if a thief puts his hand through a window at night and robs an old woman of a saucepan, I receive an elaborate report on the matter from the police; but, if one or two cases of undoubted yellow fever occur and end fatally, I hear nothing about it.[40]

Lowered depression field wages put all members of black Barbadian families into the fields, even children who earned as little as 3 cents per day by weeding or tending small animal stock. Wage necessities thereby kept many working-class children from school. Primary education was available in all the parishes through the Anglican churches for a penny per week per student, but even this fee—combined with a lack of proper clothing for small children—kept many of them away from school. When the members of the 1897 commission visited Barbados in mid February, they learned that one of the effects of the sugar bounty depression was that "the effort to keep the children at school is not so great as it was years ago".[41]

A means of coping with the seasonal and meager wages was emigration to nearby islands. Since emancipation, Barbadian men had been travelling to Trinidad and British Guiana for higher wages. Their travel in the early days had been aboard sailing schooners, but in the latter decades of the century, many had become seasonal 'deckers' on steamships usually destined for the cane harvest in British Guiana. As with health records, reliable data for human migration from Barbados were notoriously vague and unreliable. One estimate given the visiting royal commission was that 1,000 black workers left the island permanently each year. Whatever the number, the Barbadians heading for nearby islands were sufficiently numerous to establish noticeable Barbadian enclaves of policemen, teachers and artisans in these other places by the late nineteenth century.

Barbados' relatively high number of resident whites meant that, unlike in the other islands, it had long been the Colonial Office's practice to employ local men in high appointed positions rather than importing them. White Barbadians were concentrated in the southwestern part of the island in the greater Bridgetown area. But white Barbadians were influential throughout the rural parishes too; they often served as resident plantation managers who, along with white assistant managers and bookkeepers, coordinated the daily running of estates with the plantations' agents who were Bridgetown attorneys. A few hundred poor whites, Barbados 'redlegs', lived in the island's windward parishes, and, by the turn of the century, a growing number of them were migrating to Canada.

Half of Barbados' 'mixed blood' peoples resided in the Bridgetown area

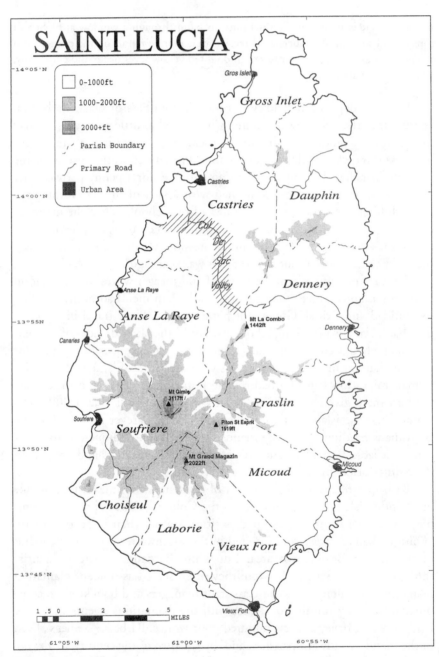

Figure 2.2. St Lucia

where they were artisans or clerks. The bounty depression also had brought rural blacks into the city to seek relief from the pitiful conditions on the rural estates. Lower-class black housing by 1890 was scattered throughout the Bridgetown area, wooden houses packed closely together and interspersed with fetid cesspits. One notable result from rural to urban movements was labour redundancy in the urban area with black Barbadian men even performing some of the hauling and carting jobs accomplished by animals in nearby islands. Black Barbadian market women, long acquainted with the Bridgetown area as a destination for the produce they carried from the farthest points of the island, began to settle there or in the city's periurban areas by the late 1800s.[42]

The export data for St Lucia, noting a heavy dependency on the local sugar industry in 1896 and thereby indirectly suggesting similarity with Barbados in this and other ways, provide an example of how misleading statistics sometimes can be. Within the context of the Commonwealth Caribbean at the time, it would have been difficult to have found two more different islands. The physical dissimilarities—St Lucia's soaring volcanic mountains compared with the rolling limestone plain of Barbados—were paralleled by vast social differences. Sugar production in St Lucia also was very different from that in Barbados and oddly unrelated to the daily activities of the majority of the island's people. And, as far as the importance of St Lucia's sugar industry was concerned, colonial officials could not have been more gloomy. In July 1895, Governor Charles Bruce of the Windwards compared St Lucia very unfavourably with Grenada, mainly because of the dismal condition of St Lucia's collective sugar cane cultivation which he characterized as a "moribund industry" and a "sinking ship".[43]

Unlike Barbados' sugar plantation culture that was two and a half centuries old, St Lucia's had been resuscitated only in the past few decades. Authorities in St Lucia—said to be influenced by the relative successes of large central grinding mills recently erected in the French Antilles—had helped to sponsor the construction of a central factory in St Lucia's Cul-de-Sac Valley in the early 1870s. The factory opened in 1876, and it was followed by the building of three other central mills in St Lucia by 1890. Yet fundamental problems had dogged these projects from the start. The centrals had expected local estate owners of small and medium-sized holdings to provide cane for the factories, yet a sufficient quality and quantity of sugar cane never had been forthcoming. The factories, especially the Cul-de-Sac operation, also had been mismanaged and plagued by key personnel changes during grinding seasons. In August 1887, the factory at Dennery, on the wind-

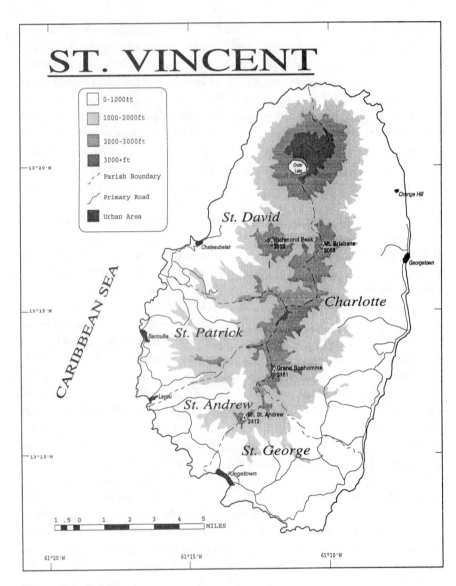

Figure 2.3. St Vincent

ward coast, failed financially, and its operation was financed with government funds until it could be sold. In January 1895, the Cul-de-Sac factory "was wound up" leading to a loss in government funds of £30,000. The mortgages on two of the other St Lucia factories—amounting to over £50,000—also were in deep trouble.[44]

The disappointing economic results of the recent recapitalization of St Lucia's sugar industry—depression conditions notwithstanding—were directly related to the island's social configuration. There were only a small number of white administrators on the island "with English ideas" compared with an educated class of white landowners with "French ideas, sympathies, and leanings". The typical French planter's daily contact with a few brown and white small landholders meant that the loyalty of this small landholding group to Britain could only "be safely depended upon . . . at present".[45] British capital and management for the factories had led to disgruntlement on the part of the francophone landowners who had been taxed to support factory construction, had little voice in the factories' management, and thereby constituted a "strong wrecker party" who were suspected of wanting to take the factories over for cheap prices after they failed.[46]

Roughly similar divisions existed within the black labour force. The 1891 census of St Lucia enumerated over 2,600 Barbadians and nearly 1,000 Vincentians residing there, most of whom were concentrated in the Castries area. They were policemen, small shopkeepers, employees in the public works and services, and generally favoured over the black St Lucians for factory construction jobs and work on the harbour improvement project. It was therefore little wonder that within the black, patois-speaking St Lucian majority, the "peasants, artisans, and respectable young men dislike[d] the Government".[47] Language differences between St Lucia's administrators and the black populace they governed were expressed geographically by a series of English-speaking enclaves—the coastal towns of Castries and Soufrière and the main sugar factories—in a mountainous island of forest hamlets and agricultural villages where the language was exclusively a French-based patois. These language differences excluded most black St Lucians from work overseen by British bosses who, when they did employ them, condemned them as "unintelligent" and "unreliable". Primary education was mainly the responsibility of a French-speaking Catholic clergy paid by government stipends. The incongruity between the black St Lucians and the formal economy of the island on which they resided was thus completely different from the situation in Barbados.

Black St Lucians, however, emigrated routinely for wages as did their Barbadian counterparts. But their destinations usually varied from those preferred by most Barbadian migrants. Thousands of St Lucians, along with Barbadians, Jamaicans and others, headed for Panama during the French effort to construct a canal across the isthmus in the 1880s. An estimated 4,000 to 5,000 St Lucians were then stranded in Colón in 1889 when the French terminated the project. The St Lucia government grudgingly paid the return passage for more than 1,000 of those stranded, and officials in Castries offered cynical views of some of these 'destitute' travellers said to have brought back loads of baggage and considerable sums of money.[48] During the next decade, many (migration data were never specific) men from St Lucia travelled to French Guiana to earn as much as £3/week as porters, carrying supplies through the forests to support the gold mining there.[49]

St Lucia's demographic complexity in the late nineteenth century also was reinforced by the presence of indentured labourers from India (Table 2.1). Claiming a locally "unreliable" labour force, St Lucian planters had imported small numbers of Indians in 1859. In the next forty years 4,427 Indians came to the island and 2,075 were repatriated to India. After their indenture terms expired, St Lucian Indians often drifted down to Trinidad and Guyana where there were larger Indian populations. St Lucia's Protector of Immigrants reported only 721 indentured Indians in St Lucia in 1895. Even as the sugar depression and factory-finance complications reduced sharply the few estate jobs available, planters were said to prefer hiring indentured Indians to St Lucian blacks, as labour performed by the former was "more reliable, being compulsory".[50]

Although topographically similar to St Lucia, St Vincent was economically akin to Barbados because of a close correspondence between dependency on local employment and the monopolization of land by sugar cane planters.[51] Accordingly, St Vincent also was similar to Barbados as far as the desperation of its working peoples was concerned. 'Misery' and 'starvation' were among the common terms used to describe conditions in St Vincent during the years of the bounty sugar depression, even more so than in most other islands of the region. Although the vast majority of Vincentians descended from black slaves, there were a few hundred Portuguese, indentured Indians, and Caribs, the latter group inhabiting a reserve on the northern end of the island.

St Vincent's settlement pattern in the depression decades paralleled the coast, estates and workers' villages linked by a winding coastal road except

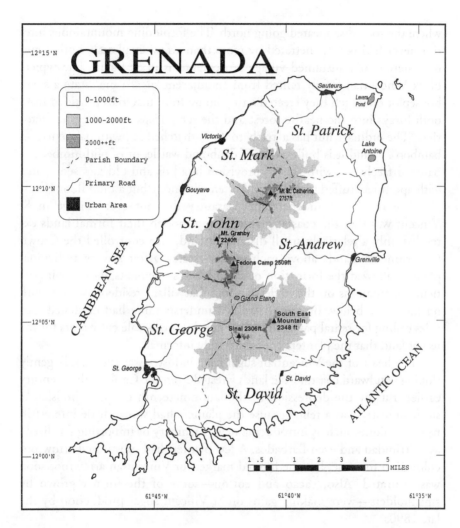

Figure 2.4. Grenada

where the road disappeared going north. The forbidding mountainous interior never had been penetrated by more than a few small-scale settlers and had thereby not sustained village settlements as in St Lucia. The typical black Vincentian family rented from an adjacent sugar cane estate a small houseplot on which they erected a tiny house from materials provided from both forays into the nearby forest and the scrapheaps around estate factories: "The ordinary hut has a 'trash' roof . . . thatched . . . with palmetto and bamboo . . . and it is built either of daub and wattle, or of odd lumber . . . patched freely . . . with bits of provision box lids and old kerosene pans, with apertures stuffed with rag, and often with none but a mud floor."[52]

One reason an independent peasantry did not ever emerge in St Vincent was that the coastal plantations, although their formal lands extended only a relatively small distance inland, also controlled the Crown (government) Lands above each of the estates. After slavery individual planters allowed the formation of small black settlements above their particular plantations on the understanding that village residents would work on the estate below. By the 1880s, this understanding had hardened into rules calling for rental payments to planters by small-scale cultivators for the use of land that the planters controlled only informally.[53]

The heart of the Vincentian sugar cane industry was the island's gently sloping windward coast, fertile lands wrested from the Caribs only a century earlier. But by the depression of the late nineteenth century the island's sugar industry was a relic because the planters had shown little interest in new techniques such as introducing new machinery or importing fertilizers, as in Trinidad and even Barbados. A few planters had substituted arrowroot cultivation for cane, but the limited market for Vincentian arrowroot soon was saturated. Also, cacao and cotton—some of the former grown by smallholders—were making gains on St Vincent sugar production by the late 1890s.

By 1897 the problem of St Vincent, according to the island's administrator, was that "her cultivable lands are in the hands of a few persons, who cling to them with a tenacity worthy of a better cause, and who thus . . . have the power to decide what products shall be exclusively cultivated". The 44,049 cultivated acres on St Vincent were divided unevenly among 516 landholders, with the 270 persons who owned 5 acres or less accounting for only 505 acres. At the other extreme, the ten largest landholders on the island each controlled several estates and together owned 29,141 of St Vincent's cultivated acreage. Alexander Porter—said by some to control personally the entire island's sugar cane industry—owned 22 estates totalling 11,936 acres, more than one-quarter of St Vincent's cultivated acreage in 1897.[54]

More fundamental than specifying what products were to be grown, the St Vincent planters could of course decide whether or not their lands were to be planted at all, and several cultivated only limited cane acreage when the price of sugar dipped very low in the 1890s. Reports were plentiful of black workers—who lived in the shadows of estates whose lands were idle or planted only partially—starved for wages and selling off their small livestock to the few people who had disposable income. The lack of money circulating on the island already had become noticeable by mid 1885, an overall condition that affected merchants and shopkeepers suffering from "short importations of dry goods, lumber and breadstuffs".[55] The near monopolization of cultivated lands and by custom of government lands, also by the few large planters was so pervasive and pitiless that discussions of land reform seemed inevitable. By the mid 1880s, St Vincent government officials, several of whom disdained the hidebound character of the island's plantocracy, advocated opening interior Crown Lands to landless labourers.[56] In the next two decades these first calls for land reform would extend to the planters' lands as well.

As in the nearby islands, black Vincentians emigrated to supplement their locally based livelihoods, a customary activity now vitally necessary to individuals and families as the depression dried up local wages. Venezuela, Costa Rica, Panama and even Chile were destinations of migrating St Vincent men. Data for these movements were typically unreliable and fragmentary; one Wesleyan minister testified to members of the visiting royal commission that "during the last six or seven years 625 able-bodied male members" of his congregation alone had left the island.[57]

Although the two islands were close to one another and superficially similar, St Vincent was far different from Grenada at the end of the nineteenth century, a contrast that few colonial administrators missed underlining. In virtually all of the general reports about the region, Grenada was identified as the sole island relatively unaffected by the sugar depression. When the members of the Royal Commission of 1897 came to Grenada early in February, they were reminded that the production of sugar had virtually ceased, although they spoke with witnesses who could recall as far back as the 1860s when sugar cane was the dominant crop in Grenada's coastal areas and also into the interior. After that, cane production dimin-

1. Market Square, St George's, Grenada, *ca.* 1900
By permission of the Syndics of Cambridge University Library.

ished quickly so that by 1884, the sugar bounty depression's first year, the value of sugar exported from Grenada was only one-tenth that of the value of exported cocoa.[58]

Grenada's interior topography was not as forbidding as St Vincent's so that on the former island "with the exception of the mountain tops, cultivable land may be said to be accessible almost everywhere".[59] Grenada and tiny Carriacou together reported 30,239 acres cultivated in the 1891 census, this total divided into 3,024 different parcels of which 2,508 were of fewer than 5 acres each. An even 1,700 of the small land holdings were classified as "cocoa holdings", although census compilers noted that many were interspersed with nutmeg plants and food crops.[60] The differences between Grenada's prosperous smallholders and the impoverished plantation labourers of the nearby sugar islands was often remarked upon; most, not all, colonial authorities associated self-sufficient peasant virtues with Grenada's small-scale producers. Wesleyan Minister W. Saywell of Grenada, testifying before the members of the visiting 1897 commission, offered that the small landholder "will seek to excel, by realising that he has something more to do than merely perform a task . . . He is more likely to take a greater part in . . . government . . . The education and training of such a man must be superior to that of the mere labourer."[61]

The seasonal flush of money from cocoa sales within the Grenadian villages also had important social implications; in the early 1890s the incidence of marriage always was high during the second quarter of the year because of the money circulation from cocoa sales.[62] But producing small quantities of a cash crop by many hundreds of producers involved marketing complexities not easily regulated. Individual producers sold their crops to licensed dealers who acted as brokers for exporters. In the late 1880s the small cost of a licence encouraged crop pilferage in the countryside.[63] Yet raising the cost of such a licence a few years later did little to eliminate thievery.[64] Government control of cocoa sales also inhibited street vending market women who produced from the beans a beverage that they sold throughout the island, activities curbed by increased cocoa licence fees.[65] But cocoa bean thievery was the worst problem overall, an issue small-scale cultivators raised time and again. The Grenadian government considered legal restrictions to stop the cocoa stealing, including the re-enactment of vagrancy laws used decades earlier by postemancipation planters to immobilize newly freed labourers.[66]

Despite the relative prosperity that the typical Grenadian smallholder had over sugar cane labourers elsewhere, he was not immune to boom-and-bust commodity prices. Some small producers, owing to low cocoa prices, were selling off their lands in the late 1890s. Overall living conditions, furthermore, were not always better in Grenadian villages than in the disease-ridden Barbadian tenantries. Many rural Grenadian houses were crowded and fresh air shut out at night, and notably unsanitary conditions prevailed in some of the hillside villages.[67]

Most Grenadians in the late 1800s spoke a French patois as in St Lucia. The most commonly reported religion was Catholicism, and individual families included both Catholics and Anglicans. Overall, authorities considered Grenada, along with St Vincent, an 'English' island, not a place where the local populace was estranged from the local government as in St Lucia. These considerations were more than random observations because multi-island political federations were contemplated from time to time.[68] Slightly over 1,000 East Indians lived in Grenada in 1891, some of whom had migrated from St Vincent after their indenture contracts expired, and a few of the Grenadian Indians even were shopkeepers and smallholders.[69] Seasonal labour migration was common among black Grenadians though not as pronounced as in nearby islands, doubtless a consequence of the local populace having a greater stake in their own lands than in Barbados, St Lucia or St Vincent.

Brown-skinned peoples of 'respectable' (*ie* light coloured) backgrounds played more important roles in Grenada than in the other three islands; one reason was the tiny number of whites there. In 1891, since "the number of white people in Grenada is so small (probably not more than 250 or 300) . . . it was not considered worthwhile to introduce a coloured column into the census".[70] Accordingly, that year's census provided no distinction whatever as to colour or race in Grenada. Yet brown Grenadians dominated the rural areas. A system of parish-level boards, with membership both appointed and elected by ratepayers, began on the island in 1886, with powers formerly held by the central government. "These boards were invariably dominated by the wealthy, Coloured upper and middle classes."[71]

In between Grenada and St Vincent lay the tiny Grenadines where small, village-based human populations divided their livelihood pursuits among subsistence gardening, limited cash crop agriculture and seafaring activities. Members of the visiting royal commission learned that there had been a few sugar cane estates "some years ago" on Bequia, the largest of the St Vincent Grenadines, although the low sugar prices had long since eliminated cane production there. Residents of some of the other St Vincent Grenadines, notably Canouan, Mayreau and Union Island, occasionally produced small amounts of cotton. But most of the men on those islands left seasonally to work elsewhere.

Male migration and local agriculture were intimately bound up with one another on Carriacou, the largest of the Grenada Grenadines. On Carriacou, estate owners leased small land plots to renters or sharecroppers whose families harvested the corn, peas and cotton from late in the calendar year until March or so. Then cattle and sheep browsed on the crop stubble from March until June while Carriacouan men travelled to Trinidad or even Venezuela for wage labour. The men usually returned during the summer rains for the planting season and spent about two months at home to ensure that the crops were established. Then they usually left again for another two or three months before returning to Carriacou for harvest.[72] The inter-island mobility of men from Carriacou and the other Grenadines was accomplished via a flotilla of fishing sloops and sailing schooners. Although British colonial officials recognized a formal administrative boundary in the Grenadines between Union (St Vincent) and Carriacou (Grenada), the reality of a continual water-borne movement of goods and peoples throughout the tiny islands in the southern Caribbean led inevitably to a thriving contraband trade.

The resident human populations of Barbados and the Windwards in the late nineteenth century were augmented by a small yet highly visible contingent of British and West Indian soldiers. White officers and soldiers represented units from the United Kingdom that rotated with military detachments stationed in the larger and more strategic places in the region. They served alongside units of the British West Indian regiment composed of white officers, black noncommissioned officers and black troops recruited from throughout the islands. Barbados had had a longstanding garrison of several hundred white troops who directed black members of a "corps of military labourers". In December 1888, a detachment of soldiers was transferred to St Lucia to help protect the harbour renovations there. By the end of the century, in 1899, there were 713 soldiers (495 white, 218 black) in Barbados and 537 (242 white, 295 black) stationed in St Lucia.[73] The social impact of the military presence on civilian populations was often fraught with tension and conflict. Especially in Castries, St Lucia, whose social complexity and resulting antagonisms guaranteed a certain amount of animosity, soldiers of the West India Regiment were involved in an endless

series of scuffles and disturbances after dark. On a late August evening in
1891, for example, a general fracas, including fighting and rock throwing,
involved several black soldiers, local St Lucian women, and a few of the police constables who originally had been imported to St Lucia from Barbados.[74]

Colonial Political Control

St Lucia was not the only British Caribbean island where authorities selected immigrant Barbadians to act as local police constables, thereby capi-
talizing on inter-island rivalries to bolster colonial regimes. Barbadians also
dominated police ranks in Grenada and, according to J.J. Thomas, "Barbadian rowdies . . . formed the major part of the constabulary of Trinidad . . .
[men whose] bitter hatred of the older residents had been not only plainly
expressed, but often brutally exemplified." The policemen throughout the
region seem to have been a relatively unsavoury lot, many of whom were
themselves former soldiers from the West India Regiment who often "had
barely escaped the law in their own islands". The chief police officers, moreover, were usually retired British military officers so that the term police
'force' had literal meaning. Police constables and officers brought offenders
to trial before local magistrates who usually were white but sometimes of
mixed blood. Local magistrates had jurisdiction over geographically defined
"chief stipendiary magistracies". In theory, the magistrates adjudicated local
issues in a spirit of legal objectivity, shielding West Indian colonial subjects
from oppression in the best traditions of British law. In practice, according
to Thomas and other observers, police magistrates not only were
unprotective of the islands' poor but were more often "direct scourges" who
aggravated local inequities, occasionally provoking complaints even from
other officials.[75]

Police control of the islands' inhabitants was, of course, part of the
overall political structures of Barbados and the Windwards in the late
1800s. From his office in St George's, Grenada, the governor of the Crown
Colony of the Windward Islands answered directly to the British Colonial
Secretary in London. In turn, the governor had direct authority over each
administrator in St Vincent and St Lucia as well as Grenada. The administrators, who were paid, full-time colonial officials, chaired meetings of the
Executive Councils in each island, a body of appointed government officials

composed of the attorney general, treasurer, chief surgeon and, in the case of St Lucia, the commanding officer of the British soldiers on the island. Besides the Executive Council, each of the Windwards also had an appointed Legislative Council of nine or ten men. Usually, members of the Executive Council were also members of the Legislative Council whose remaining members usually were local planters and businessmen.

These governmental arrangements, very obviously, left the vast majority of the Windwards' residents with no voice whatever in local matters. And these inequities, in light of rising expectations of the islands' black and brown residents, were periodically articulated in petitions sent directly to Queen Victoria from her Caribbean subjects, lists of signatures that were intercepted and filed by colonial officers in London. In July 1887, for instance, several inhabitants of St Lucia wrote directly to the queen to explain that

. . . the black man in these Islands does not enjoy the political liberty, that his white brother enjoys in the Mother Country; in this Island with a population of 40,000 inhabitants, not seven hundred are white; still they make laws to which we the 39,300 submit, they levy taxes, that we the 39,300 pay, and . . . we have submitted patiently to this political slavery.[76]

London officials and the appointed government officers in the islands were not altogether unsympathetic to this and similar viewpoints, but in dealing on a daily basis with islands whose economies were monopolized by tiny, white elites, it was rare to extend local decision making beyond those elites. The situation in St Vincent in the mid 1880s suggests that immutable colour and status barriers restricted unalterably the list of potential 'legislators' even under the most extreme circumstances. In November 1885, Alexander Porter, the island's leading planter, declined to serve on St Vincent's Legislative Council partly because of his dislike for the local administrator, Lieutenant Governor Gore, an official whose lack of popularity was widespread among Vincentian whites. Within a year, two other leading planters resigned from the St Vincent council, creating a governance crisis because all of the island's possible candidates either supported the dissidents or were too old. At this point, the Governor of the Windwards, Walter Sendall, considered the appointment of two leading members of St Vincent's "coloured population" to the council. On reflection, and on learning that one of the latter was a mere blacksmith, Sendall withdrew his suggestion and decided that, under the circumstances, "it would be perfectly right to suspend . . . [the Legislative Council] . . . altogether, and to legislate directly by the Crown".[77] Sendall later remarked about the issue that

. . . I have not yet been able to ascertain that any member of the negro race in this Colony has attained such a character and position as would render it expedient to place him in a small council of nominated members. In an enlarged council having an elective element, room might be found for one or two of this class.[78]

Small islands provided, however, precisely the sorts of settings where the hypocrisy and essential impracticality of colour lines were apparent to any and all local observers. London officials apparently considered their small, late nineteenth century Caribbean postings insufficiently important to be filled by the best and brightest of the Crown's colonial administrative officers. But these small-island positions, unlike in, say, India or even Jamaica, were not buffered from the public at large by layers of bureaucracy, and the incompetence of local white officials was therefore mercilessly, and routinely, exposed. The 1897 commissioners already had learned of this problem in the earliest phase of its information gathering in London. When H. W. Estridge, a permanent resident of Wiltshire but also the proprietor of an estate in St Kitts, asserted that he was certain "that the Colonial Office send[s] out the worst men to govern the islands that they possibly can" he was asked if he considered his opinion confidential. "Oh no," replied Estridge, "You can read it all here. Here are my two official letters to Mr Chamberlain when I came back from the West Indies."[79]

Incompetence by local white officials was bad enough, but it was often accompanied by slovenliness, drunkenness and petty swindling of public funds and even postage stamps so as to become, at times, intolerable. As one example, St George's, Grenada, was without water for nearly three days early in 1885, as Mr Risk, the head of the Public Works Department, was unavailable to lend technical help because he was incapacitated through drunkenness during the entire period.[80] Eight years later in Grenada, W.G. Donovan, a newspaper editor, denounced the jealously guarded decision-making powers on the island that were confined to a very few men, officials who, according to Donovan, were regarded by a large majority of the Grenadian populace as "the public enemy".[81]

As notoriously incompetent as many British officials of the late nineteenth century Windwards seemed to have been, it would be facile and inappropriate to suggest that they were uniformly corrupt and maladroit. Especially among the appointed governors, men with longstanding military and administrative careers in the British Caribbean and elsewhere, there often was a protective interest in the overall welfare of the islands they served. Sir Cornelius Alfred Moloney, for instance, was governor of the Windwards from 1897 to 1900. Moloney had served as a field officer in the Ashanti Wars in the early 1870s and had had various colonial administrative posts in West Africa until 1890. Through his experience in West Africa, Moloney had become an authority on the establishment of coffee production and tropical horticulture in general, and he had published several papers on these topics. Moloney's concerns about and public pronouncements against, for example, rampant deforestation of Grenada's interior while he was governor of the Windwards were therefore based on his long-term involvement and expertise in tropical colonization.[82]

Although outside the local sociopolitical hierarchies, the curators of the islands' botanic gardens seem also to have exhibited similar ecological good sense. New gardens were established in Grenada in 1886 and St Lucia in 1887, and the famous St Vincent garden (of breadfruit fame) was resuscitated in 1890. Daniel Morris, the 1897 commission's agriculture advisor, had influenced the establishment of these gardens in the Windwards and elsewhere in the region. It is difficult to determine the actual extent of the curators' influence in each of the islands they served, although their reports bristled with data from extension surveys and professed concern for the islands' small-scale cultivators. Special mention is appropriate for Henry Powell, the St Vincent curator from 1890 until his transfer to East Africa in 1904. Powell's name appears time and again in reports of the era, whether it be telephoning barometric observations to the police, planning highway routes or accompanying visiting scientists to the rim of the Soufrière crater on St Vincent, activities suggesting an active and energetic public servant who may have been typical of other curators of his day.[83]

The tradition of filling high-level administrative posts with local whites rather than imported colonial officers was only one of the ways in which Barbados was politically exceptional from its closest neighbours. The Barbadian plantocracy had avoided political federation with the Windwards (and Crown Colony status) in the 1870s, although the relative autonomy of the planter-dominated Barbadian assembly had been slightly curtailed by the formation of the island's governor-appointed Executive Committee in 1881. The committee's most important responsibility was the initiation of all colonywide financial acts, authority formerly invested in any member of the Barbadian legislature. The Executive Committee also had assumed overall authority for the island's public works and institutions.

Yet Barbados had retained intact its overall parliamentary system from earlier days. The members of the Executive Committee were selected from among the nine members of the appointed Legislative Council and the twenty-four elected members of the island's House of Assembly. The House of Assembly members (two from each of Barbados' eleven parishes and two from Bridgetown) were elected by fewer than 2,000 qualified—through education, income or land holdings—electors on the island. And qualifications for the positions themselves in the House of Assembly were restricted by income or landholding to the most prosperous men on the island. Although the Barbadian assembly actually was based on little more than a codified set of constraints designed to sustain an unyielding planter domination of the island's lands and its dependent black labour force, much was made of Barbados' constitutional exceptionalism, love of freedom and relative autonomy from the Crown. A typically self-righteous affirmation of the island's special status came from a Mr Cottle on the floor of the Barbados House of Assembly in April 1893 during a discussion of planned harbour renovations for Bridgetown. Cottle objected to the way the British Colonial Secretary had commented about the scheme "in the most arbitrary and dictatorial manner". Cottle observed that "His Lordship had evidently forgotten that we were not yet a Crown Colony", a statement greeted approvingly from the assembly's other members.[84]

The 1881 formation of the Barbados Executive Committee actually represented a constitutional compromise between stronger executive control advocated by London and 'representative' government favoured by the Barbadian plantocracy; the compromise itself was created by a mulatto lawyer of Barbados, Conrad Reeves, who served as the island's chief justice from 1882 to 1901. Reeves also was responsible for a slight lowering of the voting franchise during the 1880s. Reeves' surprising prominence, given his skin colour, was however more indicative of Barbadian exceptionalism than it was of a benign local attitude toward blacks. The vast majority of local blacks were enmeshed in a web of the assembly's statutes that had been little changed since emancipation and had them tied to particular sugar cane plantations and therefore to the whims of estate owners and managers.[85]

Not only did white colonial administrators exert overriding political control in the Commonwealth Caribbean in the late nineteenth century, but they also derived their incomes from the tax revenues they extracted from the islands' local economies. Taxes of course supported a variety of local activities, including road building, church support and schools, but it is doubtless safe to suggest that the average West Indian begrudged these governments any kind of taxation because he felt they helped pay the administrators who he regarded as "merely a set of rulers, making a living out of his country and . . . the taxes they make him pay, because they cannot make it at home".[86] Colonial taxation strategies varied from one island to the next and changed through time. And during the Caribbean's bounty sugar depression, volumes of anxious correspondence to London focused on taxation shortfalls and the reduced ability of island economies to support the government office holders in power there.

The principal element of public revenue for each of the four islands in the late 1800s came from import duties on foodstuffs. These taxes usually amounted to well over half of the annual revenue for both Barbados and St Vincent and sometimes more than half for St Lucia. The next largest category was 'excise and licences' that were, in effect, taxes on local lands or economic activities, usually exports. On Barbados a parish vestry taxation system augmented islandwide colonial finances. The Barbadian vestries could be traced back to the island's settlement in 1627 by the English and the associated necessity to finance the building and maintenance of Anglican churches with taxes raised from each parish. In the late 1800s Barbadian vestry taxes—principally from assessments on planters' lands—supported churches, road maintenance and parish poorhouses, although the operations of the latter made them destinations of last resort for all but the very poorest Barbadians.[87] There also was limited, tax-supported poor relief in St Vincent and some public medical care on each island but no overall poor laws in the Windwards as there were in Barbados.[88]

Taxation policies in each of the Windwards were geared to the economies of each place, policies used by colonial authorities to achieve various desired ends. An 1885 excise tax on sugar exports from St Vincent to compensate for declining public revenues was opposed, to no one's surprise, by the island's leading planter, Alexander Porter.[89] Porter's influential foot-dragging in paying taxes, combined with his intransigence in other land related issues on St Vincent, such as not providing rights-of-way for footpaths and water pipes, made him the target of subsequent tax schemes; proponents of a government tax proposal in 1899 suggested confidentially that a dramatically increased land tax on St Vincent "could . . . be made into a useful instrument for evicting Mr Porter".[90] In Grenada, where local resources were more evenly distributed, a house tax was a main source of tax licence revenue; in many cases, however, the annual tax of 6 shillings caused the poorer residents of the interior of the island to abandon their dwellings and to move in with relatives! In St Lucia a 6 shilling 'road tax' was actually a head tax levied on each adult male. The origin of the road tax was said to come from the days of French colonization when each man was required to perform labour on road maintenance. Whatever its origin, the tax was exceptionally difficult for English-speaking police magistrates to collect in St Lucia's interior in the 1890s because their objects of taxation went by more than one name, lived in more than one place, and often were absent from the island, having gone to Panama or French Guiana.

Varying tax schemes notwithstanding, the sugar bounty depression reduced local government incomes severely. And the strategy of increasing tax rates on depressed property or incomes yielded little extra revenue, alienated those persons taxed, and drove some local economic activities underground. There was simply not much money locally available. In remarking on the low excise tax returns from the islands' rum distillers in July 1896, Governor Charles Bruce of the Windwards explained that "the real cause of the falling off of duty from excise in St Vincent is the restricted circulation of money among the rum-consuming class".[91] The cumulative effect of these conditions in the Windwards had created by the end of 1896 a public debt in the three islands combined of over £340,000, and the governor suggested that the imperial government take on the responsibility of paying for public salaries, the mail and the upkeep of the islands' botanic stations.[92] Barbados' relative independence did not allow this financial latitude, and revenue shortfalls there had to be met from local sources. So when the island's drought-stricken sugar cane crops of 1895 and 1896 came in "considerably below the average of recent years . . . increased taxation became necessary". In June 1896 the Barbados legislature increased the duty on all imports by 20 percent.[93] That meant squeezing more tax revenue, through higher food prices, from the Barbadian labour force that already was underpaid because of lowered wages derived from less work owing to a drought-reduced cane acreage. From all indications, conditions in Barbados by the late 1890s had come close to the breaking point.

Depression and Riots

Seven months before Barbadian import duties were raised, the island's House of Assembly in November 1895 again implored the British Colonial Secretary to impose countervailing tariffs on European beet sugar. Such a move, they maintained, would help relieve local conditions in Barbados where it was "impossible that this large population can be supported" with reduced sugar prices.[94] Economic depression and its low wages, in other words, had reduced Barbados' wage-sustained carrying capacity. Early in 1896 the Barbadian government even made enquiries as to whether Grenada, St Vincent or Dominica would be interested in relieving Barbados of some of its "surplus population" by helping to support, on their own islands, "branch reformatories" for some of Barbados' younger prison inmates. The offer was not accepted.[95]

One reason Barbadian authorities were unable to dump unwanted people onto nearby islands was, obviously, that the depression's reductions in wages had affected these other places as well. When they came to Kingstown in mid February, the visiting members of the 1897 commission found St Vincent's sugar cane industry nearly bankrupt. The few Vincentian labourers left who still depended on estate wages always had to wait until the end of the month for payment, even if they had worked only a few days during the period. And the reduced amount of money in St Vincent had also led to tax revenue shortfalls; between 1870 and 1884, Alexander Porter's cash outlay for wages on his sugar cane estates had averaged £60,000 annually—in 1896 the figure was down to £12,000 to support a population "reduced only by the emigration of most of the wage earners".[96] Even in Grenada, the island seemingly impervious to the effects of the sugar bounty depression, a decrease in cacao prices late in the 1890s had been "ruinous to peasant proprietors, resulting either in the loss of their properties or . . . [resulting] in a condition of present want".[97]

The limited amount of money in the depression years created a downward economic spiral in the eastern Caribbean that engulfed everyone, not just wage workers and their families. In better years, local merchants routinely lent money to planters in order to finance the next year's crop. But less money on the islands meant less profit for the store owners and therefore less to lend sugar cane estate managers. When the lowered sugar prices hit St Lucia in the mid 1880s, for example, the effects on local merchants was "disastrous . . . and the result was that the work on the estates was brought to a sudden standstill".[98]

Longstanding debt and credit relationships, moreover, actually inhibited many British Caribbean planters in the depression years from seeking the highest possible prices for their sugar. From the earliest days of the West Indian sugar industry, some English financiers ('consignees') had acted as agents both for the sale of sugar in England and also the supply of equipment and capital to Caribbean planters. These arrangements resulted in the so-called consignee's lien, by which the British creditors often had first call on money resulting from the sale of estate crops or even the estate itself. By the 1880s the global transformation of the world sugar cane industry—characterized by steamer transport, telegraphs and growing markets—had provided, in theory, the possibility for any planter to seek the highest possible prices for his output at any market and likewise to seek the lowest price possible for his equipment. Yet the ongoing consignee's lien arrangement for some British Caribbean planters funnelled their product into the low-priced British market, thereby reducing their potential income.[99]

Despite these long-established credit arrangements, the depressed prices on the London market had made New York increasingly attractive so that by the end of the nineteenth century, the majority of sugar from Barbados and the Windwards was being exported to the United States. In 1882, 60 percent of Barbadian sugar had gone to the United Kingdom; fourteen years later 93 percent was going to the United States. The latter market imposed difficulties of its own: there was a 40 percent *ad valorem* duty placed on West Indian sugar by the American authorities; and Americans in Barbados representing the United States sugar market drove hard bargains, often bidding on the basis of current telegraphed market prices from both London and New York.[100] Non-Barbados sugar from the region also was tilting toward the American market; by 1896, three-quarters of St Lucia's exported sugar was going to New York. Perhaps more important was the continuing dependence of the region, especially Barbados, on the United States for its food supply. And although imported rice from British India was an important food staple, particularly in St Lucia, and dried fish imported from Canada a critical commodity for St Vincent, the wheat flour and lumber from the United States were crucial imports for the Windwards, having been transshipped through Barbados.[101]

The growing dependence on the United States market by no means created instant prosperity in the region, but it did reorient the planters' concerns about which external events would have the greatest influence on their own incomes. For decades, very obviously, events in London had been monitored carefully in the islands. In the early years of the bounty depression, activities of German farm lobbies or beet-refining procedures in France had become important considerations of West Indian planters, and intense local commentary about these and similar developments are sprinkled through the archival records from the British Caribbean of that time. By the mid 1890s, not surprisingly, the character of the United States sugar market came under closer scrutiny by West Indian planters than ever before. So when armed revolution against Spain broke out in Cuba during the 1895 cane harvest, it had economic repercussions felt throughout the region. In his annual report for 1895, Barbadian Governor Hay referred (probably not unhappily) to the "unhappy war of Cuba" resulting in a dramatic shortfall in the Cuban sugar tonnage directed toward the US market. Hay suggested that the Cuban war, combined with a reported deficiency in Western Europe's beet crop, had not gone unnoticed by the Barbadian planters who, under the altered circumstances, had "energetically set to work to repair their losses".[102]

It is, however, more likely that the Cuban Revolution was regarded with more trepidation than as a case of expanded market opportunity by British West Indian planters and officials. At the end of the nineteenth century, the memory of Haiti was only a century old, and "Hayti" had been invoked time and again by Professor Froude in the report of his travels through the region in the 1880s. Froude had referred to Haiti as the prototype of hopeless political anarchy, but his references doubtless carried much more vivid subliminal meaning to planters and other whites who had little difficulty imagining what might happen if their own labour gangs turned against them. British Caribbean whites, furthermore, really did not need to refer to Hispaniola or Cuba for examples of riot and rebellion. The Morant Bay rebellion in Jamaica in 1865 had involved the killing of a number of white landholders, and the federation riots in Barbados in 1876—which many local residents of the island remembered first-hand—had seen eight deaths and 400 rioters jailed.[103] The carnival or "Camboulay" riots in Trinidad in early 1881 were put down by police, soldiers and special constables. Three years later in Trinidad, in October 1884—after the bounty depression had begun—the police and British soldiers had shot and killed an estimated sixteen Indian participants in the Shia Muslim celebration of Muharram, a celebration the police had attempted to control but which, in their view, had turned into a riot.[104]

By early 1896 the rebel army in Cuba was estimated at 60,000 and the entire island engulfed in a savage conflict.[105] Telecommunication reports of the war were monitored at the Colonial Office in London and also published in the newspapers of the British Caribbean where they were read by an increasingly literate populace. If Cuba, two hundred times larger than one of the tiny British islands in the eastern Caribbean, was ablaze in a matter of months after conflict erupted, how long would it take in Barbados or one of the Windwards? It is a near certainty that members of local

plantocracies asked themselves similar questions as the depression conditions of the 1880s and 1890s produced an accelerating volume of grumbling and threats from members of local working classes.

Colonial West Indian authorities always had been mindful of the latent
capacity on the part of their black subjects for disturbances and riots.[106]
Whereas the numerous and touching reports of high infant mortality rates
or outbreaks of typhoid from the eastern Caribbean were noted and filed in
London, threats of possible violence in the Caribbean colonies always elic-
ited greater attention; at least this greater attention is suggested by the numerous marginal notes about "exciteable blacks" or suggested preventive,
anti-riot strategies that were added to the reports of threats or violence that
came to London. The possibility of violence also showed that governors and
Colonial Office officials were mindful of historical precedent that extended
back for decades. The Colonial Office in 1890, for example, had proposed a
land tax for St Lucia to compensate for sagging government revenues; Governor Hely-Hutchinson of the Windwards convinced them that their proposal involved a "bad tax"; he alluded to "the experience of 1849" in St
Lucia when a riot had begun in Castries but had spread quickly to the
countryside where the rural landholders—previously considered happy and
politically inert—had demonstrated, leaving eight dead and many jailed.[107]

The first real civil disturbance in Barbados and the Windwards during
the bounty depression years came from the least likely place. In the evening
hours of 5 November 1885, a disturbance in the centre of St George's,
Grenada, involved several hundred men and women who assailed the police
with rocks, sticks and bottles. No one was killed, although several rioters
were imprisoned for up to three months and a number of them escaped
without being identified. The riot apparently occurred because of the
abrupt government curtailment of Grenada's annual Guy Fawkes celebrations. For years, Grenadians had marked the anniversary of the Gunpowder
Plot by flinging burning, pitch-soaked projectiles about the market square.
Several of the downtown merchants of St George's, understandably dis-
tressed by the annual recurrence of these celebrations, had approached successfully the newly appointed governor, and convinced him—because of fire
hazards to St George's wooden buildings—to curtail this dangerous custom.
A notice then was posted in St George's on 28 October prohibiting the fireworks display. Obvious disgruntlement followed, and 'rowdies' ignited tar
barrels around the town during the next several nights. Then before the riots on 5 November occurred, several of the rioters distributed handbills—
confiscated afterwards by the police—that expressed resentment against the

curtailment of customary rights, indicated an intention to "lash and go" against the police, and demonstrated an obvious capacity to organize.

The pre-riot handbills were written in English and would thereby have been incomprehensible to the majority of patois speakers in the Grenadian countryside. That probably means the rioters were English-speakers from St George's and not, significantly, members of a desperately poor rural stratum of eastern Caribbean society. In fact, newspaper reports about the riots revealed that "certain respectable young men of the town were aiding and abetting" the rioters. Further, the Guy Fawkes protesters apparently all were combatting the "disorderly and uncivil scamps . . .[among] . . . the constabulary of the island" who were transient Barbadians. The rioters directed their damage toward the merchants who had influenced the curtailment of the Guy Fawkes fireworks. In sum, it seems probable that the riots in St George's in 1885 represented a frustrated outburst by an incipient urban middle class chafing under a decrepit and ineffectual colonial hierarchy run by an appointed white elite and their merchant allies, whose rules were carried out by black police ruffians. The Grenada riots were thus not a potentially infectious rebellion among an impoverished sugar proletariat, and these disturbances were therefore accorded only passing notice by Colonial Office authorities.[108]

The disturbances in Kingstown, St Vincent, in November 1891 represented a cause for greater concern. Rumours of political confederation (merging the Legislative Councils) among St Lucia, St Vincent and Grenada had preceded the visit of the Governor of the Windwards, W. F. Hely-Hutchinson, from his residence in Grenada to Kingstown on Friday 20 November. Threats of civil disturbances in St Vincent over these rumours inspired the governor to telegraph Barbados before his departure to request military reinforcements. Accordingly, the HMS *Buzzard* arrived at the Kingstown roadstead from Barbados on the evening of 19 November, the day before the governor arrived. Captain Browne and a detachment of bluejackets walked into town and were greeted with a shower of stones from an assembled crowd; the British marines then quieted the crowd without firing any shots.

Hely-Hutchinson arrived the following morning and was met at the Kingstown dock by a crowd composed mainly of women and children waving handkerchiefs and shouting "No confederation". He met personally with several black leaders of the potential rioters and discovered that they understood that confederation would mean the imposition of a head tax in St Vincent and a ban against emigration; Hely-Hutchinson thereby concluded that potential riot on the island had absolutely nothing to do with possible political confederation but was tied directly to rumours that 'agitators' had spread among the island's black populace. While the governor received the crowd's leaders, the population of Kingstown was being augmented by an estimated 2,000 men who had come from the St Vincent countryside, all carrying sticks, several smashing windows along the way, and some marching ominously to the beat of a drum. A rumoured public gathering in the main square was defused by the bluejackets who, upon hearing the rumour, offloaded a machine gun from the *Buzzard* and dispersed the growing crowd. The feared public riot was thus avoided. On Saturday the potential disturbance was reduced to little more than "gangs of loose women excited by liquor" parading the streets and shouting.[109]

For some days afterwards the Colonial Office monitored events in St Vincent because the word spread among the people that the *Buzzard* could not remain in the harbour indefinitely and that, as soon as it left, the rioters would cut St Vincent's telegraph wires. Although this did not happen, the near-riots in Kingstown were an obvious result of how depression and despair had created an explosive social atmosphere, whose ignition was prevented only by an extraordinary show of force. St Vincent, furthermore, continued to be regarded a potential trouble spot during the 1890s as depression conditions worsened. When they came to St Vincent in February 1897, the visiting commissioners were apprised by Dr W.F. Newsam of a "strong and growing spirit of discontent and disaffection throughout the island, in many quarters openly expressed. The labourer, ordinarily fatalistic, is assuming a sullen, discontented, insolent attitude, which may culminate in open revolt and lawlessness for which we are little prepared." [110]

Although every British Caribbean colony was unique, similar group attitudes as those on St Vincent animated the labourers in other places. Resentment and discontent simmered below the surface, and the police and estate overseers in all the islands took note of strikes, threats, grumbling, vandalism and arson. Riots or major disturbances seemed inevitable in such an atmosphere and were more indicative of a general malaise than of the specific incidents provoking them. In April 1893, for example, the police in Dominica killed four men and wounded four women in the La Plaine district on the island's windward coast. The immediate cause was police action taken to curb the illicit traffic in rum between Dominica and Martinique. The more significant underlying cause was that the La Plaine district, isolated from more prosperous areas of the island, was "poverty-stricken and neglected".[111]

A truly significant outburst occurred in St Kitts in February 1896. Fewer were killed than twelve years earlier in Trinidad, but the St Kitts riots could not be dismissed as an enigmatic Asian religious procession that had simply gotten out of hand. Quite the opposite, St Kitts was—next to Barbados—the British Caribbean island most heavily dependent on sugar cane. Virtually every rural black Kittitian family had survived in the depression years on ever-decreasing estate wages. And the blacks in urban Basseterre joined the 1896 riots that began in the countryside and spread quickly to the capital town. Sympathetic disturbances in Nevis across the channel from St Kitts showed that the infectious character of civil disturbance could jump from one island to another. Here was the riot that carried with it clear implications for a regionwide outburst that the British Colonial Office dreaded.

When the 1896 harvest season opened in mid January on St Kitts, strikes and demonstrations erupted on two estates near Basseterre. On the night of 27 January, cane fires were ignited on both estates, and in the next three weeks over 400 acres of cane set ablaze elsewhere in the island. The widespread incendiarism was accompanied by marches and protests throughout St Kitts. The local administrator summoned the HMS *Cordelia* from Antigua. On 17 February, the *Cordelia* dropped anchor off Basseterre, but the ship's presence seemed more to inflame than to quiet the onlookers. Meanwhile, crowds of black sugar plantation workers from the countryside had entered Basseterre where they were joined by striking boatmen and waterfront workers. The resultant throng smashed windows and looted shops. The *Cordelia* then offloaded eighty-six British bluejackets. They and local police finally quelled the violence at about 3 a.m. Two rioters were shot dead and five others suffered gunshot wounds. Some protestors were reported to have used firearms. Warned of impending trouble and cane fires on Nevis, a detachment of bluejackets went there to prevent what had happened overnight on the larger island. Conditions in both places then returned to normal.[112]

Events in St Kitts must have frightened every white planter and merchant family throughout the British Caribbean. The Basseterre rioters had targeted 'Portuguese shops' for smashing and looting, in part because the countryside disturbances had begun at an estate owned by a particularly hardhearted Portuguese planter. Would similar riots in other islands seek out individuals and families for acts of retribution involving property destruction or even death? The primal fears of incendiarism and black rebellion—planters' fears that were as old as the Caribbean plantation itself—

had been reawakened. And it is more than likely that every planter in the region now assessed his own property and fieldworkers with both a heightened sense of dread and also keen attention to the kinds of overt incidents that might precipitate an even worse conflagration.

The Colonial Office similarly surveyed the region but with a wider focus, attempting to discern diagnostic features among the various islands that might lead to similar riots. London had realized since the confederation riots of the late 1870s that Barbados, with its densely settled and pent-up labour force, presented particular cause for concern. A Colonial Office spokesman in 1886 had hypothesized a possible outcome of "many estates going out of cultivation" there: "When that happens in Barbados, the too large working population, which in the best of times does not get continuous employment even at a very low wage, is reduced to starvation—incendiary fires become numerous, and there is a rising which the troops can with difficulty put down."[113]

In the aftermath of the St Kitts riots, these possibilities on Barbados seemed to increase. Worse yet, as far as white Barbadians were concerned, London was planning to move the local British garrison to St Lucia to protect the recently completed harbour facilities there, leaving Barbados unprotected from its own black labour force. The Colonial Office thus heard from Barbadian officials and received directly letters from anxious Barbadian planter families specifying threats that local blacks were planning to take everything the whites had, only after cutting their throats![114] Barbadian officials considered plans to combat an islandwide 'rising', including the formation of a mounted cavalry troop of planters and estate managers who would coordinate their actions with the police in order to prevent "such a deplorable condition of affairs as recently prevailed in a neighbouring Island".[115]

Then in October 1896, only seven months after the St Kitts riots, a major disturbance among the indentured Indians at plantation Non Pareil in British Guiana alarmed Colonial Office officials even further. The particular incident sparking violence was an attempted transfer of suspected arsonists to a neighbouring estate. When a crowd of Indians gathered in protest the police opened fire, killing five and wounding fifty-nine others. Despite British Guiana's uncrowded landscape and even among that colony's seemingly docile Indian workers, labour conditions had also been at the root of the Guianese riots. So the propensity for riot and bloodshed had transcended ethnic boundaries and now included the indentured Indians for whom the Colonial Office bore direct responsibility.[116]

The 1896 St Kitts and British Guiana riots apparently had made it clear to London that something had to be done. Although the expected rising in Barbados never materialized, neither did its threat readily disappear, and a series of major riots would occur elsewhere in the next several years in the Commonwealth Caribbean—in Dominica and also in Montserrat in 1898, Jamaica in 1902, and again in British Guiana as well as Trinidad in 1903.[117]

The London Colonial Office officials at the turn of the century obviously had the newer, richer parts of the empire on their minds. Already commitments elsewhere had stretched Britain's military capacities so that she was considering shifting her few armed forces from the West Indies altogether. But Britain also feared the distraction and the logistical and military outlays that regionwide West Indian riots might require. Certainly modern armies and weapons augmented by telecommunication innovations prevented the possibility of islandwide rebellions and black takeovers such as had occurred a century earlier in Haiti. But the British Colonial Office, its attention now focused after the St Kitts and British Guiana riots of 1896, simply could not afford to have the violence prone labour forces of the depression ridden West Indies tying up British troops and naval squadrons for months at a time.

The solution was in the formation, in December 1896, of the 1897 Royal Commission to the West Indies.[118] And the eventual unfolding of land use changes in the wake of the commission's findings was in part because its members already were predisposed to favour a landed peasantry in the islands.[119] The stated need of the commission—to enquire into the economic and social distress that sugar bounties had caused in the British Caribbean—had of course been painfully obvious since 1884. Details of this distress were available in any one of the thousands of reports, now bound in the hundreds of volumes, that had come to London from the islands since the depression had started. But the routine reports of planters' reduced profits, emaciated children or even failed mercantile houses that had been sent to London for twelve years never commanded the imperial attention that the capacity and potential for riot did. The commissioners, on the first day of 1897 in London, heard from H.H. Dobree, Chairman of the Colonial Bank, the essence of why the commission had been formed. Asked to predict what would happen if the West Indian sugar industry were to fail, Dobree responded:

Well, it is almost too dreadful to contemplate . . . the labourers would be starved, and I think these men would be very dangerous citizens if they were starving. Al-

ready we have seen that; there have been some riots in St Kitts and in Demerara
. . . that is what we at the bank are most apprehensive of in the event of the sugar
industry suddenly failing and being obliged to be abandoned, of riots and all sorts
of terrible things.[120]

It is likely that one of the last things the British Colonial Office wanted
to orchestrate in the final decade of the nineteenth century were the activities of a commission dealing with the British West Indies. The islands were,
after all, anachronistic remnants of an earlier colonial era. And it was much
easier to receive grim reports from these colonies' officials and write appropriately condescending concerns in the margins about hopeless conditions
in the Caribbean than it was to take immediate action. The working
peoples of the Caribbean living under these conditions were however not so
passive. And their collective resistance to these conditions—taking the
forms of riots, disturbances and threats—was far more than a romanticized
response to colonial indifference. It had the effect of gaining London's attention and convincing the British Colonial Office to dispatch direct representatives of Queen Victoria to see what Caribbean conditions were really
like on the ground.

Chapter Three
The Climate

January shipboard passengers from England heading south, including the 1897 commissioners, had little difficulty recognizing that they were encountering an entirely new climatic realm when the first southerly gusts of warm ocean air encouraged them to shed their heavy coats for their deck promenades. A few days later, the high sun angle of the tropics, and its associated high temperatures and brightness, were even more obvious signs. When they eventually reached Barbados, the visitors often were dazzled by the brilliance of the sun's reflection off beaches, the crushed coral roads and the whitewashed buildings. Lafcadio Hearn described the tropical brightness when he visited the Lesser Antilles in the summer of 1887:

. . . the azure is revealed unflecked, dazzling, wondrous . . . It is a sight worth the whole journey,—the splendor of this noon sky at Barbadoes;—the horizon glow is almost blinding, the sea-line sharp as a razor-edge; and motionless upon the sapphire water nearly a hundred ships lie,—masts, spars, booms, cordage, cutting against the amazing magnificence of blue . . . first you note the long white winding thread-line of beach—coral and bright sand . . . [1]

Not every port in the eastern Caribbean reflected Bridgetown's white radiance, and visitors to the smaller port towns of the Windwards were afforded immediate and striking visual contrasts there from their first sights of Barbados. St George's, Grenada, for example, tumbled down to its sheltered harbour from green wooded hills that surrounded its ship anchorage on three sides, and visitors' ships to St George's glided to rest as passengers observed a relatively inactive harbour with "luxuriant tropical forest trees overhanging the violet-coloured water".[2]

Nor did mid latitude visitors to tropical port towns experience an abundance of twilight that at home always had eased them from the extremes of day and night. Tropical sunsets and sunrises could be spectacular, but they were always abrupt because tropical daylight gave way quickly to darkness and vice versa. The brilliance of the tropical daylight, furthermore, was always equalled by twelve hours of what seemed like the darkest nights on earth. Inky blackness prevailed at night in the scattered forest villages in the

Windwards and, according to colonial officials, helped to explain the villagers' beliefs in the supernatural. And in 1889 in Castries, St Lucia, the few small street lamps in the centre of town served only "to render the darkness more visible" and to reduce the detection of petty crimes there.[3]

Barbados and the Windwards—all lying between 12 and 14 degrees of latitude into the northern hemisphere—were directly within the path of the tropical easterly winds. These winds originated on the equatorward edge of the enormous subtropical high pressure cell of the North Atlantic that dominated directly places as far flung as Bermuda and the Azores. After traversing thousands of miles of subtropical and tropical ocean surfaces, these easterly trade winds arrived at the arc of the Eastern Caribbean heavily laden with water vapour. The absolute humidity of the atmosphere of the eastern Caribbean always was higher in the northern hemisphere's summer, helping to explain the decidedly hazy character of the summer air in the islands as opposed to its relative clarity in the low-sun season.

Speaking very generally, the easterly winds arriving in Barbados and the Windwards were (and are) strongest in the low-sun season and averaged 12 miles per hour during the course of a normal year.[4] Variations among daily wind directions and velocities which, taken altogether, composed annual averages, were very important to sugar cane planters. The lack of predictability of daily wind directions led many of the operators of sugar cane mills on Barbados to install moveable turrets at the tops of their windmills. A crew of several black men could rotate the turrets from below by carrying the elongated wooden extension that reached the ground, thereby positioning the mill's canvas sails at right angles to that day's—or that hour's—prevailing winds. Furthermore, the winds aloft did not always come from the east, a meteorological fact that at times had direct implications for inhabitants of the southern Caribbean. In early May 1902, and again in late October 1902, volcanic ash from the eruptions of the Soufrière volcano on St Vincent fell on Barbados. The raining of "coarse gritty dust" on Barbados was most dramatic during Soufrière's major eruption in May. At about 2 p.m. on 7 May Barbadians heard Soufrière (100 miles west) explode, and soon they saw black clouds to the west; by 5 p.m. Barbados "was shrouded in darkness", and volcanic dust then fell throughout Barbados during a very hot night so that the entire island was covered with gray dust by the next morning: ". . . It is conjectured that there were upper currents of air blowing Eastward, that the dust was hurled from the Volcano into these upper currents and so borne Eastward against the direction of the wind then prevailing."[5]

Although the islands' moist atmospheres were, in effect, produced by evaporation from the surrounding ocean, insular topography affected the daily weather even more. The overall frictional effect of the land on the winds meant that the prevailing easterlies were strongest on the windward (Atlantic) sides of the islands than on the leeward sides. That was, of course, the main reason that the region's principal port towns all had been sited on relatively sheltered leeward coasts during the days when sailing vessels had provided the sole means of interisland transportation. Castries, Kingstown and St George's often sweltered in the summer because the mountains blocked the cooling breezes. The volcanic highlands of the three Windwards, all with generally north-south axes, also represented orographic barriers lying at right angles to the prevailing winds, thereby forcing the moisture-laden air to ascend, cool adiabatically and reduce its ability to hold water vapour; the resulting heavy rains at the high elevations—up to 150 inches per year in the mountains of St Lucia and St Vincent—thereby contrasted sharply with Barbados' drought prone lowlands. Although the uplift and turbulence creating the rains resulted directly from the ascendance of moist air along the volcanic mountains' windward slopes, these conditions often carried over to the islands' leeward sides so that the heaviest rains on each of the three high islands commonly occurred on their upper leeward slopes.[6]

Beyond the obvious effects of the large-scale topographic effects on local winds and rain, a variety of more subtle yet important influences prevailed. It had taken the earliest European settlers little time to notice that if they erected their own houses on slightly elevated ground, they would likely receive cooling breezes, such as from the offshore winds that at night blew out to sea as the land cooled off. At intermediate and high elevations, winds were often stronger than at lower elevations, especially where deforestation had occurred and the winds were uninhibited by a lack of dense foliage. But stiff sea breezes at the littoral could be desiccating, and they usually prevented the planting of sugar cane to the water's edge because they often created a mist of salt spray. These conditions usually prevailed along the coasts of St Philip and Christ Church on the southern end of Barbados and along the ragged southern edge of Grenada where xerophytic and salt-tolerant desert vegetation was common.

As one climbed into the hills and mountains of the Windwards, the chance of heavy breezes and rainfall increased with increasing altitude and the temperature correspondingly decreased at the rate of roughly 3°F for every 1,000 feet ascended. So at the highest elevations of these three islands, the ambient temperatures were about 10° lower than at sea level. Unhealthy fevers and 'airs' were thought to abound in these chilly surroundings especially at night and high death rates among highland villagers often were attributed vaguely to these conditions. Similarly, discomfort and disease among soldiers stationed in the West Indies often were attributed directly to the cool air surrounding the barracks above the capital towns; a typical soldier in the mid 1880s was said usually to "remain in the town to the last moment, and then hurry up the hill to be in time for his Tattoo roll call, and to encounter the cool, though in his heated state, deadly air, which sooner or later produces chill and fever".[7]

The Socioclimatology of the late 1800s

By the late nineteenth century, the British commitment to the tropics was heavily laden with theoretical and applied geographical knowledge, much of it founded on the obvious climatic differences between the tropics and mid latitudes. These differences, further, were often thought to be intertwined with differentiations in racial and social characteristics, development capacities and human virtue itself. The obvious influences of Darwinian evolution on late Victorian thinking inevitably found their way into considerations of tropical development. If individuals and species evolved and 'progressed' in response to the demands imposed on them by their physical environments, one did not have to go far to extend these same ideas to human societies. And although relationships among human beings, their activities, 'progress' and climatic variables were as infinitely complex as they are one century later, this complexity seems not to have reduced the confidence among influential British thinkers and writers that these relationships were subject to universal laws, whose mechanisms could eventually be delineated. In seeking to understand these mechanisms, it is perhaps needless to point out, racism and social oppression became the late nineteenth century handmaidens of applied 'science', a partnership that has been exposed by many writers since.[8] This intellectual alliance, moreover, was of more than theoretical importance to the peoples of the southern Caribbean in the late 1800s because it influenced local colonial policies and even local laws.

British attitudes toward the sugar bounty depression itself, and how it would affect the people of the Caribbean, needed to take into account the geographical character of the region. That, at least, was the idea forwarded by the Earl of Carnarvon in the House of Lords in May 1884. His assertion was a curious suggestion that the British imposition of industrious attitudes could save Caribbean peoples from the indolence naturally forthcoming from a bounteous physical environment. The British owed:

. . . a certain duty to the large negro population and the other ignorant and helpless inhabitants of the islands in question . . . [because] the negro certainly was very indisposed to work if he could possibly avoid doing so. It had been said that a negro who occupied an acre of land in the West Indies could, in one single month, provide sufficient food for himself and his family for a whole year besides making a certain amount of money. Eleven months of the year were consequently given up to idleness.[9]

His assertion had thereby tapped into a line of self-serving conventional wisdom in Western thought that extended back at least to classical Greece. From Hippocrates to Montesquieu, regional differences in climate had vaguely yet authoritatively been identified as prime determinants in influencing differences in human development, invariably explaining the relative primacy of the particular writer's people or ethnic group versus the relative inferiority of others. It is by no means surprising, furthermore, that, as nineteenth century British colonization involved the subjugation of tropical, non-European peoples, climate came to play a powerful, explanatory role in justifying the British domination of these peoples. Those who had attended meetings of the Ethnological Society of London in 1861, a quarter century before the Earl of Carnarvon's statement, had heard the society's president, John Crawford, explain that there was a close connection between climate and race. In Africa, according to Crawford, "the races of man . . . correspond with the disadvantages of its physical geography". Three months later, James Hunt provided an explicitly comparative perspective on peoples and climate. In the tropics, according to Hunt, "there is a low state of morality, and . . . the inhabitants of these regions are essentially sensual". Those inhabiting "temperate regions", in contrast, were advantageously blessed by "increased activity of the brain".[10]

These socioclimatic interrelationships, geographically delineated only verbally by Crawford and Hunt, had been mapped more explicitly a few years earlier by the American Josiah Nott. His world map of "zoological realms" included humans as well as other fauna, each realm possessing humans similar in "physical and intellectual characters" and "disconnected from all other races". Nott was not optimistic that the varying "species of man" could be "assimilated to all physical or all medical climates". Such adaptations, according to Nott, were merely aspects of "a hypothesis unsustained by a single historical fact, and opposed to the teachings of natural history".[11]

It is immaterial as to whether British colonial administrators of the late 1800s completely agreed with, or even knew about, Nott's writings but instructive that his writings were similar to important intellectual influences on those same administrators. Different human groups, it was thought by many, never could make complete adjustments to "unnatural climates". So European colonization policies would have to be indirect. According to the influential British writer Benjamin Kidd in 1898, the white man in the tropics "lives and works only as a diver lives and works under water" because "[n]either physically, morally, nor politically, can he be acclimatized in the tropics". Yet a European administrator, directing "people . . . separated from him by thousands of years of development" performed his duty "in the name of civilization".[12] This same line of thinking was obvious in a published booklet designed to acquaint prospective British settlers to the West Indies in 1904. Any white men planning to travel to St Vincent, for example, should not contemplate agricultural work there because all such work was "performed by the coloured natives, who can stand the tropical sun better than white men". Similarly, in Grenada "the heat does not allow the average European, bred in a climate similar to that of the United Kingdom, to undertake field labour with advantage". And young European men in Grenada sometimes fell victims to excessive drinking because "the loneliness of the life and the heat of the climate conduce to the habit, which some find it difficult to overcome".[13]

The widespread acceptance that whites were biologically unable to acclimatize fully to tropical climates reinforced, very obviously, labour systems in which whites performed non-strenuous supervisory roles and people of color did the work. It also provided a scientific justification for absentee ownership and part-time commitments to tropical colonies by British citizens whose real 'home' would always be in the United Kingdom. Yet by the late nineteenth century, a world full of evidence contradicted these views. In April 1898, L.W. Sambon, an Italian medical doctor, spoke to the Royal Geographical Society in London and cited many examples of successful white farm labour in the tropics, pointing out that Dutch settlers in Africa and the East Indies had prospered for many generations. Although some of the discussants disputed Sambon's views—suggesting, for example, that whites might adapt to the tropics only after four or five centuries—none of them offered rejoinders to Sambon's contention that the acclimatization issue really masked longstanding policies of social oppression in tropical colonies:

The belief that the white man cannot work in the tropics . . . is certainly proved by facts . . . The truth about the labour problem is that white men will not work; they go to the tropics with a fixed resolve to gain wealth by coloured labour, which only too often is another word for slave-labour.[14]

Despite the eventual debunking of the climate-race interrelationships by Sambon and others, these ideas persisted in the eastern Caribbean into the early twentieth century, a persistence that had now taken on a somewhat new explanatory twist. Prior to Darwin, the suggestion that a global array of interrelated climates, races and patterns of human behavior were 'natural' and 'God-given' had been common. But how, exactly, could varying climates produce indolence among (dark) tropical peoples and energy, creativity and thrift among (light) peoples of mid latitudes? By the late 1800s, these socioclimatic imperatives now involved an intermediate agro-biological step between climate and people and an explanation similar to the one that had been articulated by the Earl of Carnarvon in 1884. Put simply, the notion rested on a supposed tropical fertility that provided an abundance of cultivated foodstuffs with almost no effort. Innumerable reports from and about the British Caribbean in the late nineteenth century portrayed an Eden where a slow-moving local populace was surrounded by boughs of edible fruit and where initiative and industry, discouraged by the easy and bounteous local climate, had to be introduced by British administrators, whose own virtuous natures had been inspired by a quite different atmospheric ambiance: "There are few days in the year in England when it is really pleasant to loaf, and the streets of civilised cities are not tempting to recumbent meditation."[15]

The myth that tropical bounty reduced human striving had been popularized in mid nineteenth century Britain by the British writer Thomas Carlyle, a close personal friend of Professor Froude and whose ideas are unmistakable in Froude's book about the Caribbean four decades later. Carlyle, writing only a decade after British slave emancipation, described the situation in the Caribbean where the region's physical fertility overrode European notions of economics now that the local populace was no longer harnessed into productive work by the institution of slavery:

The West Indies, it appears, are short of labour; as indeed is very conceivable in those circumstances. Where a Black man, by working about half-an-hour a-day (such is the calculation), can supply himself, by aid of sun and soil, with as much pumpkin as will suffice, he is likely to be a little stiff to raise into hard work! Supply and demand, which, science says, should be brought to bear on him, have an uphill task . . . Strong sun supplies itself gratis, rich soil . . . almost gratis; these are *his* 'supply'; and half-an-hour a-day directed upon these, will produce pumpkin, which is his 'demand'. The fortunate Black man, very swiftly does he settle *his* account with supply and demand:—not so swiftly the less fortunate White man of those tropical localities . . . He himself cannot work; and his black neighbour, rich in pumpkin, is in no haste to help him . . . In Demerara, as I read in the Bluebook of last year, the cane-crop, far and wide, stands rotting.[16]

It is less important to offer a smug dismissal of Carlyle's pseudo-scientific combining of physical geography and economics at mid nineteenth century than it is to underline that Carlyle-type thinking and pronouncements permeated official correspondence and even public policy in the Eastern Caribbean of the 1880s and 1890s. Time and again planters and officials offered that the fruitful local climate was intimately interrelated with the minimal economic needs of local working peoples. Two examples among many serve to illustrate the point. A jailbreak in Castries, St Lucia, in December 1888, was said to be caused by prisoners' complaints over reduced rations. The subsequent investigation of the incident brought a formal accusation against the colonial surgeon Dr Dennehy of carelessness in meting out the jail diet. Dennehy responded early in 1889 that he had been ordered to reduce the diet which was consistent with scientific thinking because he was "aware that, in the tropics, a much lesser quantity of food was required to support life than in cold climates".[17]

In the next year, Governor Hely-Hutchinson of the Windwards articulated a Carlylesque justification for reducing public expenditures in the islands and abolishing expensive and needless bureaucracy. In assessing the varying attitudes toward poor relief in the three islands, the governor found an array of relief policies, payments to doctors and various committees dealing with the issue. Hely-Hutchinson proposed a severely reduced local poor relief programme for the Windwards, a proposal based essentially on local human geographical circumstances:

There is very little pauperism in the islands. Food, of the kind that the labouring class prefer, is cheap. Fuel except for cooking, is unnecessary: and warm clothing is not required. I see no reason whatever for the establishment of a Machinery of Boards to deal with the administration of outdoor relief, and I concur in the proposal to abolish the Poor Law Committees in St Lucia.[18]

Those pointing out the fallacious nature of portraying the West Indies as a pristine and bounteous tropical paradise were not nearly so numerous or influential as the administrators who followed the conventional socioclimatic wisdom. Yet neither did contrary observations go unnoticed. C.S. Salmon, the colonial administrator admired by Froude's nemesis J.J. Thomas, laid bare the absurdity of the happy tropical labourer image by discussing the economic realities of the British Caribbean. Writing at the beginning of the region's sugar bounty depression, Salmon pointed out that the popular impression "about the industries followed by the people of our West Indian colonies is not a correct one". Rather than the region's economy being "purely agricultural" involving "little work" by the labourers who enjoyed an existence in which "food can be almost picked up by the wayside", Salmon underlined the quasi-industrial character of West Indian sugar production which was "not a less elaborate process than that . . . followed in many of our factories". Addressing the socioclimatic axiom that the natural abundance of the tropics made life easy for those dwelling there, Salmon was devastatingly clear, considering:

it as impracticable for the negro of our West Indies to count on nature to help him in the way of food as for the modern Englishman to look for acorns and nuts as a supplementary diet. I have found it necessary to say this because of the false impression abroad, due to statements made by people who know better, but who seemingly cannot avoid saying again how easy it is to live in the tropics, simply because it has been always said.[19]

In debunking the reigning geographical wisdom of the time, neither Salmon nor anyone else denied that the tropics were indeed climatically different from the mid latitudes. Although the English had occupied their Caribbean colonies for two and a half centuries, the islands continued to provide astoundingly different experiences with nature than did the British isles. White planters of Barbados and the Windwards in the 1880s and 1890s maintained a brisk correspondence with entomologists at Kew Gardens, sending them odd insect specimens for identification in return for advice concerning crop protection from these same insects. Further, not only did the tropical climate encourage insect species differentiation, but it also seemed to underpin volatile insect growth rates at particular times. After the 1898 hurricane destroyed many of the birds on St Vincent, for example, unprecedented swarms of caterpillars on the island caused considerable crop damage.[20] In September 1903, also on St Vincent, the island's administrator rode along the windward coast that had been reduced to a moonscape by the island's volcanic eruption there only eighteen months earlier. Although the path itself was still a foot thick in "cindery material", there already were "fine stools of cane" along the way and some places where "vegetation is now luxuriant", wondrous testimony to the exuberant fecundity and resilience of the tropics.[21] And there was always the possibility that climatically induced tropical plant diseases, such as the 'blight' or 'scale' that affected Grenadian agriculture late in 1900, would ruin everything; the disease had reduced Grenada's agriculture for two years, attacking avocados, oranges, guavas, cashews and cacao alike, and if left unchecked it seemed likely to "result in absolute ruin to planters—and, consequently, to the island".[22]

As with the causes and cures of tropical plant diseases, the origins and preventive measures for diseases affecting humans also were imperfectly known in the late nineteenth century. In the West Indies and elsewhere, European doctors associated particular environments, such as marshes and various kinds of soils, with fevers and the "malarious" vapours that had caused them.[23] The commentary by the seasoned colonial administrator, Sir Harry Johnston, about central Africa in the late 1890s is instructive in portraying the state of general knowledge of the origins and transmissions of human diseases at that time and the crucial causative role played by local climates:

I take it that there are germs in the soil—I have often thought perhaps it is because of the land having lain fallow so long, never having been chastened by tillage— there are germs in the soil and water which are peculiarly fatal to Europeans, and which to some extent are also harmful to the indigenous inhabitants of the country . . . there are many parts of the tropics where the climate causes not only ill health in Europeans who go out for temporary purposes, but also a certain deterioration in the children born there.[24]

Given this relative ignorance about such a vital issue, the question as to whether the physical ambiance of a particular locality was healthy or not often was addressed by slogans, decrees or public pronouncements by insular colonial officials. These strenuous attempts by local officials or planters to portray their particular islands 'healthy' were not simply exercises in self-flattery or local pride because an island's health record had major economic implications. The healthiness of the climates of particular places was assessed routinely by the Colonial Office to determine whether or not, for example, local planters could apply for indentured Indian labourers. And a local outbreak of smallpox or yellow fever led, more often than not, to quarantine declarations and avoidance of infected ports by international ship-ping firms, recurring sanctions dreaded by local planters whose activities, of course, focused entirely on external trade.[25]

When St Lucia was recommended as the site for major harbour renova-tions and as the principal coaling station in the eastern Caribbean, the rumoured unhealthiness of Castries and its environs became much more than an issue involving local health. The harbour works themselves were be-gun in late 1885 and completed in mid 1891, although St Lucian authori-ties spent much of their time during this period attempting to convince outsiders that—contrary to rumours spread by representatives of nearby is-lands—the local climate was healthy for European troops who eventually would be stationed there to defend the harbour. In response to a query about St Lucia's 'healthiness' from the British Parliament in 1886, the St Lucian Legislative Council answered with voluminous death rate tables showing St Lucia ranking favourably with nearby islands as well as with Eu-ropean cities, asserting that in the past quarter century "the salubrity of the island has progressively increased by reason of the clearing of forests, [and] the drainage or filling up of low lands and swamps all over the country".[26]

In that same response the St Lucian authorities noted that, unlike on their own island, yellow fever regularly visited Barbados. St Lucia and par-ticularly Barbados were entangled in an intense competition in these years over which place was healthier, wrangling with important economic impli-cations at stake. Before British troops were transferred from Barbados to St Lucia in 1891, for example, Acting Governor Broome of Barbados pro-claimed his island "an extremely sanitary tropical Military Station", in con-trast with St Lucia. Broome reported further that "An experienced and im-partial person of high standing in the West Indies has stated to me that 'if there is a place in the world fitted to be the grave of the British Soldier it is St Lucia'." Colonial Office officials in London dismissed Broome's observa-tions about the comparative states of health in the two islands with conde-scension and an airy authority that far outdistanced the state of medical knowledge at the time. Their endorsement dismissed Broome's remarks as "in the First place a little behind the time [and] in the second place some-what hysterical".[27]

As the twentieth century began, communicable diseases in the islands became progressively identified with microorganisms and their vectors—principally with the mosquito which had long been considered important in the spread of disease—rather than as a direct result of the 'climate'. Old ex-planations and old preventive measures, however, still persisted along with new discoveries. The turning over of the earth was still occasionally blamed with the releasing of 'germs', so that digging and strenuous agricultural work was, as in the past, an activity invariably assigned to black workers or black soldiers, rather than whites, because blacks were said to be relatively immune to the disease-producing germs, vapours and airs.[28]

Climatic Variability

On the third day of their visit to Barbados, on Friday 19 February 1897, the members of the visiting royal commission interviewed the island's colonial secretary. G. R. LeHunte had served the crown for nearly twenty years in Dominica and Fiji before coming to Barbados in 1894. He explained that he had arrived in Barbados at the beginning of the "great drought in 1894–95", although climatic conditions had improved in the two years since then. The only thing that had saved Barbados from catastrophe during the drought, according to LeHunte, was that imported American foodstuffs had been cheap during the period. These imports augmented drought-induced shortfalls in local food crop cultivation and meant that black Barbadians were not forced to emigrate any more than they usually did.[29]

Figure 3.1, which is based upon data taken from the relevant Barbados *Official Gazettes*, illustrates that the Barbadian drought of 1894–95 was by no means an undifferentiated period of rainlessness. Calendar year 1894 was, obviously, remarkably dry. But 1895—whose crops suffered from the pronounced aridity of the previous year—was actually wetter than normal. And 1895's late summer and autumn, always the rainiest time of the year because of the eastern Caribbean's hurricane season, was much wetter than usual.

The Barbadian precipitation data from 1894 and 1895 help to dispel the notion that tropical climates are monotonous repetitions of enervating heat reduced daily by a sudden late afternoon rainstorm. Much more important, these data show that yearly 'averages' for rainfall in the eastern Caribbean are, if not meaningless, statistics that actually reveal very little about the region's local climatic conditions.

Europeans contemplating visiting or even moving to Grenada, for example, were advised in 1904 that Grenada's rainfall, at 152 inches per year in some places, was "very heavy" in contrast to England's 26 inches. But Grenada's heavy rains were skewed toward the end of the calendar year, and the island's bright, dry weather in February and March contrasted sharply—

as it still does, of course—with London's gloomy drizzle during those same months. The distinct seasonality in the eastern Caribbean's climate also was noticeable in temperature variations. Although Barbados' temperature rarely rose above 90°F and rarely dropped below 65°F, the 'cool season' from Christmas until May usually saw diurnal temperatures ranging from 82°F to 68°F. And Europeans residing in Barbados soon learned what the island's black peoples already knew, that the nights and early mornings in the cool season—especially when the weather was damp—created a noticeable chill and that long-sleeved woolen garments were useful items of clothing after dark during that time of year.[30]

Climatic seasonality, in fact, influenced the socioeconomic rhythms of the eastern Caribbean in the late nineteenth century much more than it did in mid latitude yet industrial Britain. In the islands, the reaping of the sugar cane crop from January to June and the associated local production of raw sugar contrasted sharply, as it always had, with the economically slow-moving period at the end of the year. Locally vital subsistence crops and minor cash crops also had their own seasonal characteristics. Barbados' small amounts of sea-island cotton were harvested at the same time sugar cane was reaped, and breadfruit, yams and sweet potatoes usually were ready for harvest a month or so before the cane was cut and were harvested through the cane reaping season. Mangoes ripened in the summer months, somewhat before avocados, papaya and soursop fruits were ready for harvest. Local health, disease rates and death all had distinct seasonal characteristics as well, with the cooler and drier early part of the year considered healthiest. Available demographic data bore these generalities out. The 4,986 recorded deaths in Barbados in 1899, for example, were distributed as follows by calendar quarters: first, 1,075; second, 828; third, 1,259; and fourth, 1,806.[31] Of course the cane harvest in the first months of the year put more money into working families' pockets so that more foodstuffs could be purchased than in other months; so the positing of a facile season-death relationship would be inappropriate, although the wage-generating cane harvest itself was geared to seasonal climatic rhythms.

The dry early part of the calendar year was a direct contrast to the late summer and autumn when the heavy rains came. Shipping was curtailed during the rainiest weather, as it had been in the days of sailing vessels. And travel in small vessels was always dangerous from July to November. This was the time of year when parallel banks of gray-black rain clouds rolled toward the islands from the east, yielding lashing sheets of rain at their stormiest. The rainy season also brought very intense, and thus agriculturally less valuable, precipitation for the growing crops because of high rates of runoff and the concomitant possibilities for flooding.

Colonial administrators vaguely associated local prosperity and good times with beneficial rains, but reports sent to London about local rainfall amounts usually focused on heavy rains and the damage they caused. Hardly a summer or autumn month went by in the late nineteenth century that Colonial Office clerks in London did not receive a report of damaging torrential rains in the Eastern Caribbean. The situation in St Vincent in late November 1896 did not recur every year there, but neither was it uncommon. The island had received steady rainfall for a week, saturating the soils and filling the stream banks. Then a downpour in the early hours of 28 November caused banks to overflow throughout St Vincent, and yet another intense rainstorm the following morning replenished the already swollen rivers on the windward side of the island. The resultant flood devastation in the Georgetown area was "almost indescribable". The pipes for the recently installed water works were dislocated. Five houses were swept away by floodwaters. Two children were drowned. Elsewhere on St Vincent acres of crops were ruined and newly constructed canals in the northern part of the island destroyed. Altogether twenty-five Vincentians died from the torrential rains and the flooding they had caused, twenty on the windward coast where the heaviest rains had fallen.[32]

St Lucia had undergone a similar situation two years earlier. Heavy rains fell from dusk until dawn on 12 October 1894, pouring no less than 14 inches of rain down onto the island! The rains caused only minor damage in Castries but devastation elsewhere, mostly in other settlements on the leeward side of St Lucia. Six wooden houses were washed out to sea at Canaries. A similar fate befell thirty-six "wood or wattle dwellings" at Soufrière; in the mountains above Soufrière a landslip buried a mountainside dwelling, killing three children. In the village of Choiseul and environs an unconfirmed report had 200 houses blown down by accompanying high winds. Throughout the island, "outhouses" (either kitchens or toilet sheds) collapsed. St Lucia counted eleven dead in the storm's sodden aftermath.[33]

Eastern Caribbean climatic extremes sometimes occurred, incredibly, in such close temporal proximity to one another so as to make a mockery of annual 'average' weather data. They also bedevilled local cultivators and everyone else, because all residents of the region depended, at least indirectly, on the timely arrival of precipitation. And when rainfall intensity or rainfall amounts were too early, too late, too much or not enough, local uncertainties that had been increased by the external market conditions were intensified. Grenada in the late 1890s, where a falling price for cacao had reduced the exuberance of recent years, provides a climatic case in point.

Grenada suffered drought for most of 1894, a condition 'materially affecting' local prosperity. Then on 28 September an extremely heavy rainfall "caused the rivers in the parish of St Andrew's to swell with extraordinary violence, carrying away a considerable area of cultivated land and doing great damage to bridges and causeways". The next few years were very rainy in Grenada, 1896 and 1897 exceptionally so with important local damage attributed to heavy autumn rains. In 1896, 201 inches were recorded at Grenada's mountainous centre, the weather being particularly severe in the latter half of November when, on the 15th, the river embankment at Gouyave was damaged by flooding from heavy rains. Two weeks later, 6 inches of rain fell in two hours in St Patrick, demolishing the river embankment at Belmont and destroying local crops. In the following year (1897), Grenada experienced record floods which destroyed riverbanks and almost completely washed away the stone bridge at the mouth of the Gouyave River. But by 1899 the excessively wet years of the recent past had turned sharply drier. Grenada had received only 47 inches of rainfall by the end of September, relative aridity that threatened to wither the young cocoa pods. And the 1899 corn crop on Carriacou, on which locals depended in part for survival, is said to have failed owing to the dry spell.[34]

The topographic configurations of the volcanic Windwards always influenced the spatial distribution of the autumn rainfall. The ascendance of rain clouds and associated atmospheric turbulence around the islands' volcanic highlands led to the highest rainfall concentrations in the mountains and also helped to create the region's most sensational storms. Lightning and thunder were common in the mountain rainstorms, and pounding rainfall found its way quickly into highland streams that, in turn, emptied into rain-swollen rivers in the latter months of the year.

Beyond the orographic effects that mountainous terrain exerted on rainfall patterns, there was nevertheless a randomness in the local distribution of passing rain showers that was very unpredictable. Topographic barriers could deflect rain-bearing clouds in many different directions, and the wind patterns, though generally from the east, were similarly fickle. Local planters, at least in Barbados, seem to have adapted their typical landholding patterns to the unpre-dictability of the rain, an adaptability that helps to explain in part an 'inefficient' characteristic of Barbadian land use. It was generally agreed that the common landholding pattern in the United King-

Figure 3.1. Monthly Rainfall at Dodds Botanical Station, Barbados, 1894–95 (measured in inches)

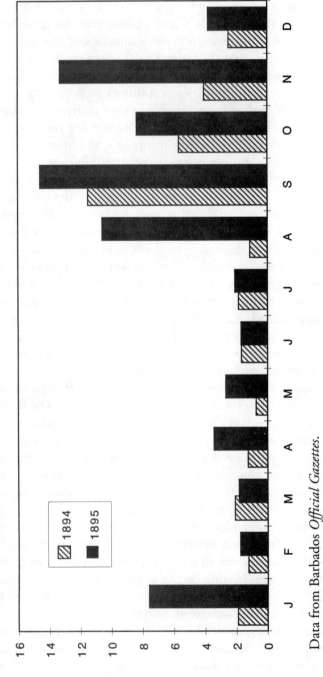

Data from Barbados *Official Gazettes*.

dom was for the owner of an estate to concentrate his holdings in one large unit, to have one's territory 'within a ring fence'. In Barbados, in contrast, small and medium-scale planters often owned discontinuous holdings, and, in some cases, it meant duplicating the overhead expense of providing milling equipment on more than two pieces of ground. Part of the reason for this distinctive characteristic of Barbadian land tenure was the difficulty in purchasing large, contiguous tracts of land on an island that had been parcelled out to planters in the seventeenth century before modern milling techniques led to the efficiency of larger estates. Yet part of the Barbadian pattern of scattered estate holdings that persisted into the late 1800s came from "a desire to catch the advantages of rainfall on some of their estates, if not in this parish then in that (for the rainfall is curiously variable in the several districts)".[35]

Yet a strategy of scattering landholdings in response to spatially random rainfall patterns was futile during prolonged periods of drought when little rain fell anywhere. Extended periods of aridity were (and are) common in the Eastern Caribbean and, other than hurricanes, the most grievous climatic hazards in the region. Speaking very generally, the probability of drought in the eastern Caribbean is most common on low-lying islands which have no mountains to trigger rain showers. Drought prevalence also increases in the region with latitude. So on relatively flat and northerly Antigua drought recurred with sufficient frequency so as to imperil local agriculture, the principal reason that the members of the 1897 royal commission chose not to recommend a system of central sugar cane milling to resuscitate Antigua's sugar cane industry as they eventually did for Barbados.[36]

Although Antigua was notorious for its drought prevalence, Barbados was not far behind. Barbados' dense human population, furthermore, was intimately dependent upon local provision crops for subsistence, a dependence supplemented with imported food; but workers' wages—which bought food imports—were directly dependent on drought-influenced sugar cane. So when drought occurred on Barbados, local officials dreaded the possibilities of increased lawlessness. The enhanced possibility of local 'risings' were therefore discussed actively during prolonged dry periods. Regular and more abundant rainfall, on the other hand, reduced local tension. The calendar year 1896, for example, was considered quite a favourable one on Barbados in terms of limited amount of criminal activity on the island. Favourable (non-drought) climatic conditions had helped greatly because home-grown vegetables were abundant and cheap so "as to reduce the cost of living to a minimum".[37]

The effects of drought were particularly insidious in the parishes of St Lucy and St Philip, flat lowlands lying at the extreme northern and southeastern ends of the island, where rain-bearing winds passed over parched village tenantry grounds and sugar cane estates, driving black Barbadians toward brackish water holes. During the drought period in 1894 and 1895, the incidences of local 'potato raids'—whereby hungry villagers 'raided' estates whose potato crops were ripening—increased sharply in these parishes and others, thereby reinforcing the perceived relationships between drought and criminal activity among the black Barbadian populace. But worst of all was the incidence of hunger-related disease in these areas during periods of drought. The ghastly (and curiously Malthusian) description of low-lying St Philip by the parish doctor during the 1894–95 drought painted a stark and desperate situation:

This terrible mortality of 44 per 1,000 took place without the occurrence of any special epidemic of disease and is due almost entirely to the weak ones being crowded out of existence in the fierce struggle of life. True we have had an immense amount of bowel complaint . . . chiefly the consequence of insufficient and improper food. Probably we feel the pinch of hard times in this Parish first and most severely owing to the wide belt of windward sea coast . . . which even in the most seasonable years is little more than arid waste and quite insufficient to support the teeming population on it.[38]

The official correspondence between Barbados and London did not always dwell on the social ills created by drought but more often concentrated on the effects aridity had on the island's main cash crop. The dry conditions of 1894, for example, complicated local efforts to combat a damaging root fungus that imperiled the local sugar cane crop. Because of the "unprecedented" aridity on the island it had become difficult to determine whether young canes had root fungus "as canes suffering from drought and root fungus have a somewhat similar appearance". Barbadian officials also seemed directly concerned with seeking a deeper understanding of the effects of drought as well as its ultimate causes. That is, at least, the impression left by the proceedings of the island's Forestry Committee in 1899. The committee considered ideas that had been put forward as early as 1885 by Daniel Morris—the royal commission's agricultural expert—regarding the relationship between deforestation and climate. Morris had emphasized, among other points, that excessive deforestation dried up streams and springs, did little to inhibit the effects of flooding, and always put local agriculture at extreme risk. Barbados' Forestry Committee, acting on Morris' ideas, recommended that the island's "wastelands" be reforested, a recommendation that was not implemented to any degree.[39]

Relationships between deforestation and its resultant climatic effects had been noted in the English Caribbean since the seventeenth century. Deforested hillsides meant that heavy rains no longer nurtured tree growth but were, suddenly, pounding erosional events that now sent massive quantities of topsoil into the sea. Deforestation also meant that (non-existent) protective forest canopies neither ameliorated climatic extremes nor allowed the proper development of insular soils. Local acknowledgement that deforestation intensified the effects of drought usually came from the small and low islands of the region, but by the late 1800s these concerns were extended to rainy St Vincent as well. In 1895, St Vincent's Lieutenant Governor A. F. Gore, in condemning the clandestine felling of trees for charcoal production in St Vincent's interior, asserted that the "deplorable waste has not affected the rainfall, but there can be no doubt that if a stop is not shortly put to this destruction, there must be a material falling off". Gore continued that as the forest cover was removed from St Vincent's mountain slopes, the removal would produce "a general decrease in the volume of water of the small ravines and numerous streams and rivulets . . . [which] . . . would to a large extent affect the productive powers of the soil".[40]

Black residents of the eastern Caribbean had much less interest in whether recurring drought was caused by atmospheric conditions, deforestation or a combination of the two, than they were in attempting to cope with the harsh economic conditions caused by prolonged aridity. A principal means of coping was emigration to seek wages elsewhere that drought conditions had reduced at home. By the late 1890s this drought-induced trait of periodic migration was so commonly known among working-class Barbadians that officials of the Colonial Office considered integrating it into a regional calculus of attempting to match labour with jobs. At the depths of the 1894–95 drought, Barbados' Governor James Shaw Hay sought to regularize "some proper system of Emigration for our surplus population" during drought episodes and similar cataclysms. The Colonial Office endorsement, noting the resilient character of mobile Barbadians, thought that the Barbadian migration trait might even help offset bringing additional indentured labourers from India into the region. "If the sugar industry of the West Indies is to be further depressed", thought London officials, it would be "desirable to introduce as few Coolies as possible . . . Barbadians would much more readily find other occupation if the worst came to the worst."[41]

Barbados was not the only place in the region where drought was thought to have created positive group personality traits via climatically influenced economic necessity. Carriacou's denuded, cut-over appearance was due in part to the island's earlier deforestation for sugar cane cultivation. By the 1890s this same land now was devoted to cotton, corn, peas and small stock, but Carriacou still provided firewood to nearby islands, mainly Barbados. And it was well known that the recurring dry periods, whose effects were intensified by deforestation and the grazing pressures exerted by the livestock on the island, drove Carriacouan men elsewhere as a matter of routine. The resultant 'industrious' nature of men from Carriacou led to Trinidadian planters preferring them to labour immigrants from other islands. And the substantial, well-kept wooden frame houses on Carriacou's arid slopes were considered much better than the average peasant's dwelling on Grenada. The Carriacou houses, moreover, seemed to symbolize that island's migrating men's collective ability to earn money elsewhere as well as their propensity to send or bring the money home in order to improve what they had temporarily left behind.[42]

The Great Hurricane of 1898

Two years after the start of the sugar bounty depression, a brief, but intense and damaging, hurricane visited St Vincent. In the predawn hours of Monday 16 August 1886, there were heavy rains in the Bequia channel south of the island. Then the full fury of the storm came at dawn, its force concentrated in the southeastern section of St Vincent. The schoolhouse at Calliaqua was 'thrown off its pillars' and demolished. High seas accompanying the storm washed away at least one building in Georgetown and 'broke down' some others. Crops were ruined throughout the southern half of St Vincent. In Kingstown, heavy winds coming from the northwest were followed by high winds 'from all points of the compass' that uprooted trees in the botanic gardens. That was a bit before 6 a.m., when the barometric pressure in Kingstown fell to 29.20 inches of mercury. By 7 a.m. the 'glass' began to rise rapidly and was up to 29.70 inches by 8 a.m., although rain poured down and high winds continued until noon.

Some reports immediately afterwards suggested that no one had been killed, but a final inventory of the hurricane damage enumerated five dead. There also had been 1,163 houses destroyed or damaged, affecting an estimated 5,700 Vincentians. The overall damage caused by the hurricane was reported at £6,460, and a bit more than half of that was paid into a relief fund composed of donations from nearby colonial legislatures and planters on St Vincent. The hurricane seemed a particularly cruel blow in light of declining prices for sugar cane—and thereby reduced plantation work—as well as the poor prices for arrowroot. In the aftermath of the storm, Governor Walter Sendall of the Windwards called for radical economic changes on St Vincent, suggesting that the hurricane might be a catalyst for the formation of a class of smallholders that would replace the island's sugar cane planters. Such an arrangement would reduce Vincentian labourers' fleeing the island to seek work elsewhere after a cataclysmic weather event and allow them to develop a variety of agricultural products "in many different directions [unlocking] that boundless fertile capacity which is inherent in the soil".[43]

Destructive as it was, the 1886 storm in St Vincent was not a major hurricane. Nor was it entirely different in intensity and overall effect from the heavy rainstorms that pounded the Windwards nearly every autumn. Barbados and the Windwards, more importantly, had not really suffered a major hurricane for well over half a century, not since the great hurricane of 1831. Sometime after midnight on 11 August of that year, an enormous hurricane had hit Barbados, smashing the vessels moored in the harbour. The high winds had levelled nearly all the buildings in Bridgetown, leaving piles of debris—not only of wood but also of stone and masonry—throughout the city that were 4 and 5 feet high. Survivors reported that Barbados' landscape had undergone a dramatic transformation, literally overnight, from a verdant, manicured garden to a brown wasteland. Similar reports came from St Vincent a few days later, as the hurricane's trajectory apparently had carried it westward causing similar damage there.[44]

In the last years of the nineteenth century the hurricane of 1831 was a fading memory, recalled by only a handful of very old people. And the absence of a severe hurricane for decades, more significantly, had provided a false sense of security for planters and others in the eastern Caribbean who reckoned that the region was now well south of the hurricane track. Their reasoning came from the reports each autumn of hurricanes passing north of Barbados and the Windwards as well as news of occasional hurricanes damaging Jamaica, far to the north and west. Yet the track of the 'gale' of October 1894—which eventually caused the heavy rain damage in St Lucia—had passed south, not north, of Barbados, diminishing the credibility of those who had attempted to wish away the island's hurricane vulnerability. The storm's occurrence also had been underappreciated because it had not done great harm to Barbados' infrastructure, ruining only a number of the workers' small wooden houses.[45]

Those who thought they knew better used the passage of the 1894 gale to warn that Barbados and, by extension, the Windwards were "liable in any year to be visited with disaster". These warnings were, in part, products of an ever more sophisticated system of gathering and disseminating weather information. During 1894 daily temperature and rainfall data were observed and collected in Barbados at Commercial Hall in Bridgetown, the Dodds Botanical Station and at Ragged Point on the eastern side of the island where the wind and the "state of the sea" were recorded. These data were then forwarded monthly to the US Hydrographical Department in Washington. In late summer and early autumn, Barbados' geographical location made it "an extremely valuable observing station, especially during the season when hurricanes may be expected. On the first intimation of the approach of a cyclone, its position and direction would be telegraphed through the Islands, and to . . . Washington, which is in constant communication with its stations on the American Coast."[46]

Despite the modern weather information system recently put in place, Barbados reported little advance warning of the massive hurricane that struck the island in the late afternoon of Saturday, 10 September 1898. The immense storm ravaged the southern part of the island, its intensity greatest between the hours of 6 and 10 p.m. At the latter hour a 75 mph gust of wind blew down the wind velocity gauge in Bridgetown. Earlier in the evening the barometer had fallen to 29.4, but then began to rise again, although hurricane-force winds blew until midnight. The storm not only brought incessant sheets of rain, but Barbadians witnessed an almost surreal and lengthy succession of lightning flashes made all the more frightening because the roaring winds had drowned out the accompanying thunder.[47]

On 1 February 1982, Aletha Grant who was then 100 years old and lived in Bridge Cot Village, St George Parish, Barbados, still had vivid recollections of the 1898 hurricane:

The day began bright and sunny. It was Saturday. I had worked at the estate all day and walked home in heavy rain. I stopped, and a shopkeeper gave me a bag to put over my head. When I got home our cow Rose was gone. It was raining with lightning and thunder. My mother said 'What about Rose?' I went outside, and only the slack rope was left where Rose had been tied. The next day, after the storm, we found Rose still alive in a nearby gully. The rain had killed lots of fowls. Lumber was strewn about so that everybody's house was mixed up with everybody else's.[48]

Aletha Grant's observations in her home village were similar to those re-corded in written records for the entire southern half of Barbados. Governor Hay reported that the rain had continued to pour down on Sunday, and it was not until Monday that damage could be assessed, even qualitatively. The police gave an immediate estimate of 10,000 workers' houses destroyed and 50,000 Barbadians homeless. The devastation was worst in Christ Church parish where nearly "all the labourers' huts are levelled to the ground, the owners sitting in a dazed condition beside their water-soaked effects". At the waterfront in Bridgetown, most of the merchants' lighters—normally used to haul imported goods from freighters moored at Carlisle Bay—had been lost, and a number of sailing schooners were wrecked.[49] Bridgetown itself was an unrecognizable jumble of downed telephone poles and wires and wrecked houses, a place that appeared to be "a city of the dead". Although the urban area had been devastated, the homeless rural people's first impulse was to rush to town for food and shelter. The Barba-dian authorities responded by sending mounted police to rural centres, giv-ing them a free hand to occupy all standing buildings and to commandeer food, regardless of the cost, so as to prevent a crush of refugees on the city that could not even provide for its own inhabitants.[50]

Continuing due west, the hurricane hit St Vincent with almost as little advance warning as it had provided for Barbados. The curator of the St Vincent botanic gardens, Henry Powell, had noticed the barometer fall to 29.8 on the afternoon of 10 September (when the storm had begun to pound Barbados), and he telephoned warnings around St Vincent, although it is doubtful that the general populace was fully alerted. The barometer continued to fall on Sunday morning, at the height of the hurricane on St Vincent, until it reached 29.5. The massive storm made the 1886 hurricane in St Vincent appear as mere 'child's play'. And the few old Vincentians who remembered the Great Hurricane of August 1831, reported that the 1898 hurricane was "in every way far more destructive".[51]

Probably the eye of the 1898 hurricane passed directly over St Vincent. The wind blew hard beginning just after daybreak on Sunday, and by late morning it blew furiously from the northeast. A brief lull at midday was fol-lowed by hurricane intensity winds from the south all afternoon. The mas-sive winds and rain left wreckage and despair throughout St Vincent, the worst damage on the windward side of the island. The planted crops, which had suffered from a pronounced drought early in the year, were mostly washed away, with particular damage to the breadfruit trees that marked vil-lage settlements along the coastal road. The entire island seemed suddenly

2. Calliaqua, St Vincent, after the 1898 hurricane
Collection: Foreign and Commonwealth Office Library, London.

littered with boards from what had formerly been the labourers' dwellings, and the few items of clothing, furniture and personal belongings from the houses were now strewn over the remains of the countryside's vegetation. Within a few hours on that Sunday an estimated 20,000 Vincentians—fully half of the island's human population—had lost their houses, and three-quarters of all Vincentians needed food. Two hundred on St Vincent had been killed by the hurricane. As had happened in Barbados, rural peoples on St Vincent rushed to town, and officials in Kingstown—which had itself been devastated—tried their best to cope with the milling crowds. The overall visual effect of the hurricane's devastation of St Vincent was described three weeks later by the captain of HMS *Intrepid*, the island appearing as if it had "been fired through. Utter desolation prevails everywhere. Hardly a green spot is to be seen. Where before all was verdant and beautiful to look upon, the towns and villages as viewed from the sea have the appearance of having been bombarded."[52]

From St Vincent, the hurricane veered northward, bringing heavy rains and high winds to St Lucia. Damage was particularly severe on the leeward side of the latter island. A downpour started early on 11 September and brought nearly 20 inches of rain in twenty-four hours to Soufrière, where the river that flowed to the sea "became a wide and deep torrent, and caused the principal damage". Landslips in the highlands washed away provision grounds. Hardest hit on St Lucia were the small producers' cocoa trees which had just begun to bear well following the damage they had sustained during the gale of October 1894. From St Lucia, the storm continued in a northerly direction, causing widespread damage as far north as the British Leewards. Although the storm was there reported as only a 'gale', it brought an estimated 20 inches of rain to Nevis and then to St Kitts, washing away roads on the latter island and covering others with fine-grained ashen soil that the rain had carried down from the mountains.[53]

On Barbados and St Vincent, the two islands hit hardest by the hurricane of September 1898, the storm's direct impact lasted for months. Damage on Barbados had been most severe in the southern parishes, although the hilly districts of Scotland and St Peter parish were hit hard as well. Without adequate shelter, tens of thousands of black Barbadians pieced together makeshift shelters from scraps of lumber and slept in rain soaked garments, sometimes on the bare earth. The damp living conditions, together with meager foodstuffs that often were half cooked, led almost immediately to an outbreak of diarrhoea and dysentery that devastated the human population of the entire island, not just in the southern districts. Disease affected everyone on Barbados—the planters as well as the workers—and it 'carried off' a large number of the very young and very old. The quarterly death statistics for Barbados during 1898—1,194 deaths in the first quarter, 1,118 in the second, 1,962 in the third, and 3,141 in the fourth quarter—provided grim numerical evidence as to the ultimate toll in human life taken by the storm.[54]

Immediate relief on Barbados was limited. Some local funds provided emergency relief. The grassroots friendly society system on the island was severely overtaxed and of little help given the magnitude of the hurricane damage, and a number of the societies' headquarters buildings had been blown away. The government arranged for some Barbadians to emigrate to British Guiana, and a trickle of those impoverished by the recent hurricane travelled to the South American colony. But local enthusiasm for government sponsored emigration was dampened since black Barbadians, even under these severe circumstances had "a rooted hatred to leaving their island", a seemingly odd response by the same peoples who had routinely emigrated to British Guiana by their own volition for decades.[55]

The human populace of all of St Vincent suffered in similar ways as did those in the southern parishes of Barbados. The storm had left dead animals and vegetable debris that clogged small drainage channels all through St Vincent, thereby creating 'stinking cesspools' around the island. Gastric diseases therefore abounded, and it was not until hastily organized crews cleared the debris and subsequent heavy rains flushed out the streams that St Vincent could even begin a return to normal. But the hurricane had wiped out local food supplies, and Vincentians resorted to chewing cane stalks to supplement their diets. In the Leeward villages of St Vincent, children were routinely put to bed without food or given a lump of salt to suck on, conditions persisting for nearly a year after the hurricane. And as in Barbados, a high death rate on St Vincent followed the hurricane. In 1898, 1,356 Vincentians died, 400 more than the annual average for the other years of that decade.[56]

British warships brought emergency food shipments to St Vincent for months. In January 1899, 1,300 people still were receiving meals, supplies and blankets from makeshift dispensaries around the island. The likelihood of looting or similar disturbances on St Vincent after the hurricane possibly had been prevented by the presence of British sailors, and some feared that lawlessness would erupt after they departed, an eventuality that never occurred. As on Barbados, St Vincent's officials corresponded with larger British colonies nearby in hopes that these other places could become migration

3. Barrouallie, St Vincent, after the 1898 hurricane
Collection: Foreign and Commonwealth Office Library, London.

destinations for those Vincentians hit hardest by the storm. And also as on Barbados, working-class Vincentians seemed loathe to emigrate, at least under official sponsorship. After the hurricane, fifty-one Vincentians travelled to British Guiana and 398 to Trinidad: "From subsequent reports it appears that the St Vincent labourers in Trinidad proved very unsatisfactory, and only a few remained there for any length of time."[57]

At the same time that planters and labourers in the eastern Caribbean were digging out from the hurricane, seeking lumber and food, and enumerating lost livestock and ruined equipment, insular colonial officials were preparing aggregated financial estimates of these same losses. Accordingly, officials began to request imperial funds to rebuild their particular islands' economies almost as soon as the wind ceased to blow. Immediate aid came from local agencies, and in the next few weeks island governments were allowed to draw limited amounts from the banks to rebuild labourers' houses. Then after two months of collecting information and estimates concerning losses from the hurricane stricken islands, the Colonial Office announced what relief funds would be allocated. Barbados was to receive a "free grant" of £40,000 from the imperial exchequer to cover expenses pertaining to "relief, rehousing, and repairs of public works". St Vincent received a £25,000 grant for the same purposes. Also, loans to the governments of the two islands for £50,000 each were aggregate sums designated to be lent to individual planters in amounts of no less than £50.

Governor Alfred Moloney of the Windwards was pleased that the grant was allotted to devastated St Vincent, but he had been denied both a requested free grant of £5,000 for St Lucia and a planter loan for the same island. Moloney's concern over the denial of St Lucia relief funds was based on the devastation that the island's small-scale cocoa producers had sustained. Hundreds recently had begun to produce cacao on highland plots purchased from savings that they had earned by migrating to the gold fields in French Guiana. Now these labourers were said to be demoralized, having lost crops and soil to the storm without relief from either the local or imperial governments that had in the recent past encouraged their small-scale farming activities as a viable alternative to plantation agriculture.[58]

The hurricane of 1898 had thereby thrown into even higher relief, in St Lucia, and in the economically depressed region as a whole, the already immediate question to what kinds of agriculture would be best for the region, an issue carrying with it the possibility for major land-use changes. The 1897 royal commission had, only months earlier, concluded that the possible demise of local sugar cane industries might best be met in some of the islands by a change to small-scale agriculture. Further, they had recommended St Vincent as a target for land expropriation eventually to benefit black smallholders. In March 1898 the imperial British Parliament had followed these recommendations by voting to appropriate "£15,000 for settling smallholders in St Vincent".[59]

Despite these developments and the storm, St Vincent's sugar cane industry was not dead, at least in some officials' minds. On 1 November 1898—one and a half months after the hurricane—Joseph Chamberlain, the Secretary of the Colonial Office, informed Moloney by telegram that he was considering a central sugar factory for St Vincent, and he solicited the governor's views. Then in late February 1899, representatives of the West India Committee of Great Britain visited St Vincent to determine whether there was sufficient local interest and investment capital for constructing a central cane-grinding factory and an auxiliary small-gauge railway system on the windward side of the island.[60]

But Moloney, influenced by the royal commission's conclusions and the parliamentary grant, was already pushing hard for a break-up of the island's plantocracy and the establishment of small-scale landholders on St Vincent. He apparently reasoned that the 1898 hurricane had provided an opportunity toward that end, just as the 1886 St Vincent hurricane had encouraged Governor Sendall to urge a widespread system of smallholders for the island. Three weeks after the 1898 hurricane, Moloney invited Daniel Morris—now based in Barbados—to assess the post-storm conditions in St Vincent. Morris came on 8 October and took a cursory view of a sample village area on the leeward side of the island. Then, claiming pressing office duties in Barbados, he returned to Bridgetown. Morris came back to St Vincent on 18 October, surveyed conditions on the windward side of the island, and wrote a report to London recommending that the local government acquire several specified estates for parcelling out among small-scale cultivators.[61]

Then, on 28 October 1898, Governor Moloney of the Windwards—citing the damage done by the hurricane and also Morris' subsequent reports—introduced a draft bill to the St Vincent Legislative Council for a law "to authorize the acquisition of land for the establishment and location of small holders". So Moloney, inspired by the geographical clean slate that devastion had produced, already had initiated legal action in favour of smallholders when the Colonial Office asked his opinion about resuscitating the island's sugar cane industry with the establishment of a large grinding mill. The storm's devastation, he might have told them, had provided unprecedented opportunity for changes; Moloney had come to St Vincent from Grenada four days after the hurricane of 1898, and shortly thereafter he had telegraphed to London his dour assessment of the damage and the way the island should be rebuilt. Of the over 7,000 houses that had been enumerated in the 1891 census, according to Moloney, no more than 1,000 (damaged) houses were left standing on St Vincent. All others were "in ruins, flat, or blown away". Most everyone on the island had lost all his possessions. Moloney concluded that "St Vincent has to be rebuilt and its future must depend on its cultivation, which can be best done by having the people freshly established on their own patches."[62]

As discussed in the chapters that follow, the 1898 hurricane that so inspired Governor Moloney's commentary (and subsequent planning activism) did not provide the impetus for a transformation in the pattern of local land ownership throughout the eastern Caribbean as it did in St Vincent. Nor were the effects of the tropical climate, despite the cynical and pseudoscientific mythology forwarded by certain Europeans, the same everywhere in the region because the islands were so very different. Drought in the lowlands of some islands was paralleled by heavy rains in the highlands of others. Seasonality also played important roles. Further, extremes of aridity and wetness often affected the same place within brief periods. Yet, a common wind blew across the arc of the Lesser Antilles. It influenced local settlement patterns and sailing routes since earliest colonial days. As it approached the eastern Caribbean, this wind carried with it water vapour and the resultant rainfall that replenished streams, ponds and swamps, and eventually found its way back into the surrounding ocean. The human use and misuse of the waters of the eastern Caribbean in the late 1800s is the subject of the following chapter.

Chapter Four
The Waters

Governor Sendall had taken precautions to avoid the kind of public gathering that, despite his plans, occurred anyway. He had instructed the captain of the HMS *Icarus* not to put ashore in Kingstown, St Vincent, with his special passenger, the deposed West African king, JaJa of Opobo, on Saturday 9 June 1888; Saturday was of course St Vincent's market day, and Sendall feared that the presence of so many rural blacks in town would lend to undue commotion when JaJa appeared. So JaJa's arrival was timed for 11:30 a.m. the next day, 10 June, an hour that coincided with Sunday morning church services. The timing of JaJa's strategically delayed arrival had, however, been leaked to the black Vincentian populace. Thus, despite the Sunday morning hour, a "crowd of considerable dimension", bursting with anticipation, assembled at the waterfront and also along Bay Street. When JaJa appeared with his son, Sunday, and a single attendant, the crowd burst into loud cheers, and they attempted to follow his coach for an opportunity to see or even to touch the African king who was quickly whisked away. JaJa himself seemed pleased by his impromptu reception on St Vincent, even if the governor was not.[1]

JaJa (a name used by his European rivals) had been born an Ibo slave named Jubo Jubogha. As palm oil replaced slaves as the principal West African export in the 1860s, JaJa was one of a number of former slaves to establish themselves as palm oil traders/rulers along the African coast, taking advantage of a general breakdown in the old sociopolitical hierarchy of West Africa that had facilitated the slave trade. JaJa founded the Kingdom of Opobo in 1870 in what is now south-eastern Nigeria, and by the mid 1880s he had established himself as the most powerful individual in the Niger delta palm oil trade. He soon eliminated other African rivals, often with brutal methods, and he traded directly with British palm oil dealers to avoid middlemen. His activities eventually conflicted with expanding British interests in the region; although he had, with suspicion, accepted the status of British protectorate for Opobo in 1884 and had earlier supported the British in the Ashanti war, JaJa was arrested by the British in 1887 and found guilty at a subsequent trial in Accra for thwarting free trade in palm oil. The British then exiled JaJa far from where he might influence British expansion in West Africa by sending him to St Vincent in the far southeastern corner of the British Caribbean.[2]

Governor Sendall originally had planned for an even more isolated destination than St Vincent. When the Colonial Office contacted him in April 1888, alerting him that JaJa would leave Accra for the Caribbean on 8 May, Sendall responded that perhaps Baliseau, in the St Vincent Grenadines, or maybe Carriacou, would be appropriate places for JaJa's internment. But London considered these very tiny places inappropriate because they feared accusations of sending JaJa to such a remote location that he would be denied proper medical care, and they also wanted him under adequate surveillance.[3]

The Colonial Office's perceptions of the Grenadines as the ultimate isolated islands in the late nineteenth century seemed accurate indeed. The few official reports about these places all seemed to deal with the malaise of abandonment and the problems of tiny island size, whether they were the results of drought that had shrivelled crops in the few subsistence gardens or perhaps the problems of combatting disease that a returning sailor had brought home. In May 1894, Governor Charles Bruce of the Windwards travelled through the Grenadines for a week, stopping at Carriacou, Union, Mayero and Bequia before arriving in Kingstown. The small islands' residents all had lamented the lack of proper medical care, inadequate water supplies and limited postal facilities, symptoms of inhabiting remote islets surrounded by ocean water. Bruce's written report of the problems faced by the inhabitants of the Grenadines was tersely endorsed and summarized by one London official who simply pencilled in the margin, "poor little islands".[4]

Not that St Vincent was all that large, and the crowd of black Vincentians that turned out for JaJa's arrival was not unlike the throngs that assembled at dockside in any of the small West Indian capital towns of the time to witness important departures or arrivals. These gatherings were, among other things, symptoms of insularity. Most Vincentians, as in nearby islands, had never been beyond the eastern Caribbean, and their limited contacts with the outside world were represented by the comings and goings via the surrounding water, events usually limited to the dock facilities in the capital towns which also were the islands' only real ports. The sea lanes leading to and from the islands, moreover, were controlled by metropolitan shipping lines and the British navy. This external control became most evident when local events required a show of force. Such a show would be necessary three years after JaJa's arrival when the *Buzzard* arrived at Kingstown to quell the possible violence in November 1891. And this show of force, very obviously, was another event that would be played out at the water's edge.

Yet the ocean surrounding each of the islands and travel via water represented, by the end of the nineteenth century, a growing source of opportunity for the common people of the Caribbean rather than a barrier and an ambient medium reinforcing external control. In testifying before the 1897 commission, Conrad Reeves of Barbados advocated a system of inter-island communications that, not incidentally, eventually became one of the commission's principal overall recommendations. Cheap and frequent steamer service among the islands, according to Reeves, would bridge the distances between them and thereby provide greater opportunities for those in Barbados and elsewhere who found themselves "in poor circumstances" and who might ameliorate those circumstances by going elsewhere. Reeves also pointed out that such a system might bring into production the "unoccupied and cultivable land" lying idle and isolated because of a lack of proper communications.[5]

Even without the kind of frequent, scheduled steamer services Reeves had in mind, travel abroad from each of the islands was becoming more common. Labour migrants, mainly men, had been travelling away and returning since emancipation half a century earlier, their travels accomplished via sailing vessels but increasingly as deck passengers on steamers. And as the bounty depression of the 1880s and 1890s relentlessly reduced opportunities at home, more and more began to drift away from the small islands. Yet long-distance travel among the common people of the small islands was still the preserve of young men, and the information they—either individually or collectively—passed on to friends and relatives who stayed behind was doubtless selective, self-serving and embellished.

It is also likely that those migrants did relatively little to reduce the natural isolation of the tiny insular societies of the eastern Caribbean at the end of the nineteenth century. Rather, their stories rendered distorted portrayals of the opportunities and dangers that existed beyond the surrounding waters. These portrayals, moreover, became incorporated into local island cultures, thereby influencing local behaviour. The exaggerated image of Panama during the French canal construction project of the 1880s as a source of untold riches provides a case in point. Early in 1887, a young Vincentian man was arrested in Panama for thievery. Authorities there re-

4. Kingstown, St Vincent, waterfront, *ca.* 1900
By permission of the Syndics of Cambridge University Library.

covered several stolen items from him along with a letter from his mother back home, urging him to return to St Vincent but "he must not do so until he can bring *plenty of money*".[6]

This insular mystique about what lay, or was thought to lie, beyond the surrounding waters, combined with the obvious interest most Vincentians maintained in their shared African heritage, doubtless help explain their extraordinary anticipation of JaJa's arrival and their attempts to see and talk with him once he had arrived in St Vincent. JaJa was quartered initially at a house formerly occupied by the police inspector. There he received a steady stream of visitors, black and white alike, although he craved more intimate companionship than that provided by ephemeral callers who wished to touch him or to hear his accent. Within a month of his arrival in St Vincent, JaJa, who complained ceaselessly about the drafty, cold house he occupied, was reported to desire "female property" and "gave great offence to a young girl here by the cash offer and other terms he proposed".[7]

The rest of JaJa's Caribbean exile was a lamentable progression of deteriorating health, broken promises and disillusionment. In late August, JaJa wrote an unanswered letter to Queen Victoria, complaining that he now was in exile and a "political prisoner . . . what I have done to merit such treatment I know not, but . . . I have been deprived of my country, my markets and my freedom . . . contrary to the spirit of the British nation". By the following May, JaJa, now assumed to the about seventy years old, had developed pneumonia and was spitting blood. And his physical condition mirrored, and was perhaps exacerbated by, his social isolation. He became withdrawn, notably sullen, and began to associate only with a few black Vincentians. At one point he attempted to bribe a local sea captain to take him to the United States. In early 1891, complaining of failing health and, sadly, asking to return home to die, JaJa was transferred from St Vincent to Barbados. That summer he was allowed return passage to West Africa via the Canary Islands. JaJa died en route at the Canaries, and his body was returned to Opobo for burial.[8]

The fascinating story of JaJa's exile at isolated St Vincent in the late 1800s could be categorized in one of several ways. Students of pan-African identities would perhaps consider it an illuminating historical link between the slave era and the present. Comparative colonial historians might see it as symptomatic of the relative ascendance and decline of varying tropical components within Britain's overseas empire. Geographers might focus on the event's insular setting, including its maritime connections both near and far. The latter emphasis highlights water, the subject matter of this chapter.

The juxtaposition of land and water is, of course, the enduring geographical essence of the Caribbean, yet water is an often neglected geographical category, usually receiving little emphasis when compared with climate and land. In the eastern Caribbean of the late nineteenth century, both sea water and fresh water were crucial and contested elements of the human geography of the region.

Runoff, Streams and Swamps

Rainfall becomes surface water when it reaches the exterior covering of the earth, a process that varies considerably from place to place and which depends mostly upon the nature of the covering or surface material itself. On Barbados, precipitation is first intercepted by the leaves of sugar cane plants or by the leaves and branches of other cultivated and non-cultivated plants, or it falls onto exposed soil or pavement. Because of the island's relatively porous coralline rock, an estimated 20 percent of the rain falling on Barbados eventually seeps into underground reservoirs; in the Scotland district in the northeastern part of the island, a lower percentage percolates into the ground because of that hilly region's clayey soils. Streams are uncommon on Barbados, occurring only in the few places where the soil is underlain by impermeable rock, and the so-called Constitution River in Bridgetown is essentially a channel for urban runoff.[9]

Rain in the Windwards falls onto a much different surface than on Barbados. Rain usually is broken up by the leaves, branches and vines of these high islands' forest canopies and absorbed by the roots, grasses and soils on the forest floors. It often seeps into the subsoils and rocks that lie deep under the forests, eventually surfacing as springs of fresh water at lower elevations and then ending up in the small but fast-moving streams and rivers that discharge into the surrounding oceans. But the real differences between Barbados and the Windwards in terms of varying surface water or groundwater flow are differences in slope. In contrast to the gentle, undulating surface topography of Barbados, water catchment areas in the Windwards are small and steep. And when these catchment zones are saturated, streams swell rapidly to the bank-full stage. According to Charles Risk, the superintendent in charge of Grenada's public water supply in the 1890s: "The natural formation of the island is such that during rainfall the slopes . . . pour the water they receive into the streams and feeders of the larger rivers which are swollen up . . . rapidly causing floods."[10]

In both Barbados and the Windwards late in the nineteenth century, the islands' natural coverings had been greatly altered—dramatically so in Barbados—during the region's two and a half centuries of European colonization; these alterations, in turn, had influenced the flow of surface water. Barbados' original forest cover had been largely replaced by sugar cane by the end of the seventeenth century, and earliest commercial planters complained of related soil fertility reductions there. But the dense foliage, complex root system and ground covering provided by sugar cane in Barbados, combined with the island's low relief, provided a cultivated buffer against excessive soil loss, at least in the months when sugar cane was growing. Alterations in the forest cover of the Windwards, in contrast, led to massive erosion. If steep slopes were denuded or altered, soil quickly moved downslope; deforestation also altered the paths for running water which, in turn, influenced the timing of peak flows at lower elevations after heavy rains, all leading to greater local flood discharges.

By the late 1800s the relationships between deforestation and surface water flow in the Windwards were obvious. Clearing upland slopes for cacao and food crops in the 1870s was held accountable for disappearing highland springs and also diminishing streamflow. But it was during the late summer and autumn, when streams overflowed, that deforestation's effects were most obvious. The rainstorm of 30 September 1895, that visited northern Grenada, quickly filled the island's steep, tiny water channels and then led to floods in which "roads, bridges, and telephone lines were swept away", a catastrophe attributed directly to the increased runoff that had been created by the "denudation of the forest land". Similar events in the next two years caused Governor Moloney eventually to call for a preservation system for the highlands of the Windwards, a proposed scheme involving forest commissioners and government rangers to patrol the mountains: "It is deplorable to see the manner in which the wholesale denudation of the Grenada highlands of their forests is proceeding. Large areas along the mountain slopes, up to their very summits, have been and are being laid bare with a total ignorance or disregard of the consequences."[11]

These changes in Grenada's highlands—not only forest removal in general but also the relatively recent appearance of water drainage channels to enhance the growing of cacao—now meant that seasonal flooding on the island had become annual, predictable occurrences, not simply occasional hazards produced by nature alone. Only two weeks after Moloney had written to London proposing widespread conservation efforts, major rain-fed flooding hit Grenada again. Downpours during the night and morning of 6 and 7 December 1897, transformed the Gouyave and St Mark's rivers into raging torrents that overflowed their banks, washed out stone bridges and destroyed buildings in the coastal villages of Gouyave and Victoria. The governor observed that these tiny communities had suffered directly from islandwide, not local, changes, and he proposed that village flood damages be repaired with colony-wide funds derived from "extra taxation by an increase of the export tax on cocoa".[12]

The hazards of excessive runoff and raging rivers were not confined to Grenada. Inhabitants of all the Windwards combatted annual river flooding. Authorities in St Vincent cited recent infrastructural improvements there in the early 1890s—the construction of new bridges and culverts and the strengthening of the banks of the Mesopotamia River—designed to control and channel excessive runoff. These preventive measures were necessary to ensure even minimal pedestrian locomotion among neighbouring coastal villages. The drowning death of a nine-year-old girl from Belair, just east of Kingstown, in late November 1897, when the Warrawarrou River overflowed after heavy rains, was a tragic reminder that these preventive measures were ongoing necessities to protect even children walking to and from school.[13]

It was not simply running water causing increased hazards during heavy rains but also solid—sometimes massive—debris that hurtled down stream channels and hillsides. A year earlier to the day that the Belair schoolgirl had drowned in the southern part of St Vincent, pounding rains in the northern part of the island had "completely altered" the inaccessible area known as the "Carib Country" as "roads, bridges, houses, and acres of land, cultivated and uncultivated, were swept away, and 25 lives were lost". Much of the Carib Country damage came from recent deforestation as the channelled and overland water flows carried with them "thousands of enormous trunks of trees".[14]

In each of the Windwards, similar landslides and landslips associated with heavy seasonal rains were common; landslips were and are frequent in all tropical areas where steep slopes become saturated, and individual slides can involve the movement of entire hillsides, resulting in massive destruction of forest ecosystems that take decades to regenerate. And Windward cultivators often have suffered immeasurable agricultural losses owing to landslides and landslips.[15] Despite the 1896 losses in the Carib Country, landslips were less common on St Vincent in the 1890s than in Grenada or St Lucia because of the generally high ashen content and porosity of St Vincent's soils. In contrast, northern and western sections of Grenada, with clay-rich soils, were very susceptible to landslips. Further, during and after the 1898 hurricane, the extensive damage to St Lucia was more because of landslides than running water. In Castries and the botanic garden, only a few trees were lost, but elsewhere on the island massive landslides created long-term destruction:

The steep hill sides, surcharged with water, slid away in all directions carrying away plantations, houses, roads, and bridges, leaving rock and rubbish behind . . . A promising cocoa crop was in great part completely swept away . . . So complete was the disappearance of many fine plantations that even where the soil has not been entirely washed away a delay of from 5 to 10 years in the re-establishment of the trees is inevitable.[16]

Nor was Barbados immune to occasional landslips. In September 1901 "heavy and continuous rains" at Boscobel, in the far northern end of St Andrew parish, where clayey soils slope toward the Atlantic Ocean, saturated the ground. A one-mile square area of land began to slide toward the sea, taking houses and people with it. The effects included a breaking up of the land surface, opening of fissures and deep cracks in the soil, and a filling of drainage channels and subsequent disruption of local drainage patterns. Eighty houses were destroyed in the Boscobel landslip and 500 persons rendered homeless.[17]

The Windwards' streams did not always overflow, and they were routinely used by island residents. Highland dwellers used stream water for washing and drinking, and the larger rivers were valuable sources of fresh fish. Although it would be impossible to assess quantitatively the nutritional value in local diets, the means of fishing was of sufficient importance to attract official attention. Of particular interest was the so-called mountain mullet (*Agonostomus monticola*), a traditional food resource for rural blacks, one of several species that could move between fresh and saltwater. In the early 1880s, Lieutenant Governor A.F. Gore amused himself while inspecting local estates by fishing some of the St Vincent rivers, and he found these mullets "like grayling, excellent eating". Gore was concerned that these fish were disappearing because of the poisoning of mountain streams by local blacks, an activity nearly impossible to curtail because of the inaccessible terrain. In November 1885, Vincentian police seized small-mesh nets of some of the fishermen after local authorities complained that streams and estuaries were being overfished. A decade later, the fish component in the diets of black Vincentians was regarded as a crucial preventive element in warding off "the ghastly hand of starvation which only an abundance of vegetable products and a coast teemful with fish are keeping from many a door in this Colony".[18]

The St Vincent planters still crushed their canes using small, antiquated watermills into the late 1890s. Gravity flow from mountain streams was channelled into 'little troughs' on lower-lying plantation lands, and the running water powered grinding machinery. The Vincentian planters, notably Alexander Porter, were obviously aware of the virtues of modern, steam milling techniques that would have produced a higher quality product. But they preferred water power, citing not only the prohibitive costs in building modern milling plants in a depression period but also their freedom from having to pay for imported coal. Early in 1895, Professor J.B. Harrison, the government analyst of British Guiana, visited St Vincent to assess the island's sugar cane industry. Harrison commented positively on the well-worked fields, but he lamented the "deplorably backward state" of sugar manufacture, noting particularly the deficient grinding power of the water mills and the resultant low quality of the raw sugar produced in the factories.[19]

The insistence by Vincentian planters of clinging to this outmoded method of crushing canes led to occasional conflict between them and government authorities over the control of local waterways and local water supplies. During much of 1886, recurring incidents involved the Porter plantations' interception of the water that fed Kingstown's piped water system. On some mornings, Kingstown residents could depend on adequate water pressure for only about half an hour owing to the diversion of water in the hills above the town by sugar estate owners. This predicament left scores of people crowding around each of Kingstown's twenty-three standpipes and an angry urban populace short of water for drinking, cooking and washing. Governor Sendall then came to St Vincent to arrange to purchase water rights from Alexander Porter, a protracted negotiation that lasted for months.[20]

In the late 1800s in Barbados and the Windwards, a key distinction between rural and urban lifeways was the ready availability of piped water in the capital towns. Most rural peoples, in contrast, continued to depend on ponds, wells, streams, springs and fresh water tanks. The control and availability (or lack thereof) of adequate water supplies in urban centres were thereby vital public issues that affected all town dwellers.

Bridgetown residents had had the luxury of piped water since the early 1860s, although they had been without water for three weeks in 1880 ow-

5. Women washing clothes, Grenada, *ca*, 1900
By permission of the Syndics of Cambridge University Library.

ing to a landslip near the springs that fed the water system; alternative wells and underground streams had been tapped to supply the Bridgetown piped water needs in subsequent years, and an altercation between two Barbadian water companies, not unlike the one that had pitted Porter vs. St Vincent officials a decade earlier, led to the local government taking over Barbados' water supply system in 1895. Castries, St Lucia, suffered periodic piped water shortages in 1893, in part because of the demands for fresh water from coaling ships. The anxiety St Lucian officials felt over the possibility of an "alarming . . . water famine" led to elaborate planning for an improved water system for the town. And, given the importance that nearly everyone associated with local water supplies, it is little wonder that the residents of St George's, Grenada had, in 1885, been so intolerant of Mr Risk's inebriated incapacity to keep the town's water standpipes flowing.[21]

A central issue in the dispute between the Barbados water companies was over the 1894 contract for rural areas. The Water Supply Company already had provided some of the rural districts with piped water for several years, and the Bridgetown Company now wanted the contract too. Yet the introduction of piped water into the island's rural parishes occasionally worsened—rather than improved—rural conditions; during the 1894 drought in Barbados' St George parish "the trickling standpipes [were] altogether inadequate", representing, as much as anything else, angry foci of local discontent by attracting "frantic and disorderly crowds who frequently tear and pommel each other in their struggles to obtain the precious fluid". Most Barbadian villagers, however, continued to depend on ponds and wells, water sources increasingly (as medical knowledge improved) associated with poor sanitation and related diseases. In 1897, Dr C.E. Gooding visited a typhoid victim at Perry's Tenantry in St Philip Parish. He found the boy's mother washing his bedsheets—soiled with typhoid excrement—in a pond where other women washed clothes and children played. "It is needless" concluded Gooding "to go further to seek the source of infection."[22]

But residence in Bridgetown did not guarantee relief from water-borne diseases, and poor sanitation in some city areas made living conditions there worse than in the country. In 1884 the Bridgetown area immediately south of the Constitution River had "a great many privies with pits in which the sewage is allowed to collect for months" meaning that the inhabitants of the small wooden shacks packed into tiny land plots suffered from occasional typhoid and rampant diarrhoea. The river itself did little to drain and cleanse the urban area. Quite the opposite, near the Victoria bridge there often was "nothing but a tidal swamp, being a receptacle for all kinds of foecal matter, filth, garbage . . . frequently collected and retained for a considerable time by the small shrubs along its banks . . . on still nights when there is no breeze . . . the smell is almost unbearable".[23]

Although typhoid bacilli could, and occasionally did, contaminate Barbados' underground water aquifers, the more impervious soils in parts of the Windwards meant more standing water there. Sir Rupert Boyce, dean of the Liverpool School of Tropical Medicine, contrasted Barbados' "ideal porous soil" in 1910 with Grenada's "stiff clay soil" which underlay the latter place and explained a "whole island threaded with streams . . . and here and there a marsh", conditions leading to clouds of mosquitoes and the prevalence of widespread malaria in Grenada. The freshwater streams elsewhere in the Windwards—in part because of unhygienic practices by the local human populace—provided the media for other water-borne diseases; yet it is uncertain whether or not schistosomiasis, a disease of the intestines and urinary tract caused by trematodes of the genus *Schistosoma* and for which St Lucian freshwater streams are known late in the twentieth century, was introduced to the island before 1900.[24]

What seems to have been fact about St Lucia, however—a fact nevertheless disputed by the local authorities because of dreaded quarantine sanctions—was that the stagnant surface water in the streams draining the Castries area was a perfect disease vector habitat. Yellow fever broke out at the army garrison near Castries in November 1901, and five deaths, probably all from yellow fever, were recorded that month and the next. Neighbouring colonies placed St Lucia under quarantine, although coaling operations continued at the St Lucia harbour with precautions taken to prevent contact between ship crews and coal carriers. Early in 1902, Dr George C. Low of the London School of Tropical Medicine, arrived in St Lucia. With the help of military authorities, he eliminated stagnant waters around military barracks. But handling civilian matters was more difficult.

Low's description of Castries left little doubt as to why it was considered a disease-ridden town. The Castries River, according to Low, was "in the dry season a sluggish filthy stream" with "many backwaters and pools full of vegetation . . . Native huts crowd its banks and. . . excrement and other filth is freely deposited in it. *Anopheles* larvae were several times found in it." Of particular note was the "very dirty swamp" in front of the botanical gardens at the end of the harbour. Low categorized it a haven for mosquito breeding and identified the disease vectors as well: "Here are many pools abounding in *Anopheles* larvae. The breeding grounds of the *Culex taeniatus,* the yellow fever mosquito, and *Culex fatigans,* the spreader of filarial diseases are legion."[25]

Low also noted the unhealthy social environment in Castries, speaking out against the merchants who were attempting to connive with local authorities to "suppress facts" about the yellow fever and thereby avoid both the responsibilities of cleaning up Castries and accepting quarantine sanctions. St Lucia's administrator, Harry Thompson, offered a rebuttal to Low's report on 23 April 1902, describing the "monstrous task" it would be to rid Castries of mosquitos. Then on 24 April, Thompson sent a confidential memo to London suggesting that Low's report (and similar reports by other doctors) about St Lucia's unhealthiness were actually anti-St Lucia propaganda from those who favoured keeping Barbados the principal British garrison in the region. Thompson appended varied health data with the report to argue that "St Lucia is indeed healthy", and he suggested that the negative reports about St Lucia, in light of an existing pro-Barbadian conspiracy, "is hardly to be wondered at". Thompson's death by heart attack, four days after he submitted the April 24th memo insisting on St Lucia's healthy environment, could hardly have reassured London that the reports he had tried to discredit were fabrications![26]

Harbours

Dr Low's report would have hardly been a revelation to residents of Castries. Anyone with a sense of smell would have attested to the foul, stagnant waters of St Lucia's capital town, although he probably would have attributed these conditions more to the harbour itself than to the filthy streams spilling into it. Castries residents for years had dumped their household sewage directly into the Castries River, into the other small streams draining into the harbour or into the harbour itself from piers. The waters of the harbour—on the leeward side of the island and surrounded by land on three sides with a narrow outlet to the open sea—circulated only minimally. So a sludge of human waste and associated debris settled at the eastern end of the Castries harbour, immediately adjacent to the town. For decades, when ocean-going vessels came too close, this "putrid matter was stirred up which became most offensive to the neighbourhood", and there had been local recommendations, as early as the 1840s, that the harbour be dredged.[27]

But the impetus for the major transformations of the harbour at Castries in the 1880s—to include major dredging operations—came not from local sources but from British military decisions. A royal commission in 1879 had recommended the consolidation and fortification of two major imperial coaling stations in the West Indies. Jamaica was the logical choice for the northern and western part of the region. And the Castries harbour with its deep inlet that could be defended from land fortifications above it and also large enough for ocean-going steamers to anchor and turn, eventually was designated the coaling station of the south. Grenada also had been considered defensible but had little room for coaling operations, and Barbados could not be defended easily.[28]

On 16 February 1884, Governor William Robinson met with the members of the St Lucia Legislative Council to consider borrowing funds to improve Castries' harbour so that it could become the British navy's southern Caribbean coaling centre. The council considered the financial estimates for the project prepared by Sir John Coode, a British engineer, that ran as high as £70,000 for dredging, dock and wharf construction "for the largest Trans-Atlantic Steamers". Most council members were enthused about the project's possibilities, suggesting that improved harbour facilities would help economically and thereby compensate for St Lucia's lacklustre sugar industry. Others thought that local harbour jobs might prevent the island's best workers from drifting off to Panama. The Council eventually passed unanimously the raising of a loan by issuing debentures in England for £40,000, a sum to be devoted only to "the thorough dredging of the Harbour and the necessary repairs to existing wharves".[29]

Within a few years, overruns had pushed the project's cost to £70,000, although the harbour renovation itself—begun in November 1885—was now well underway and had changed Castries nearly overnight from a sleepy backwater to a bustling industrial panorama featuring men and machines working on land and water. Dredging machines, built especially for the project, were removing the rock and coral barriers that remained in the harbour, and the dredges' engines belched clouds of black smoke that hung in a gray pall over the town. A professional staff of foremen and divers had come from England for the project, and they supervised the activities of over 200 black labourers. Besides the dredging, the most conspicuous activity in the harbour transformation was the laying of concrete pilings for a new 650-foot long wharf. Massive concrete cylinders each were laid 40 feet below the waterline to anchor the wharf; the first of these cylinders had been laid in mid September 1885, and fifty-eight had been put in place within the ensuing year. By mid 1885 the Castries waterfront already featured piles of coal that had been brought to fuel the ships and dredges so that visitors to St Lucia were afforded incongruous scenes of "cocoa-nut palms growing . . . out of coal stores, and gorgeous flowering creepers climbing over the workmen's sheds".[30]

Castries residents had, understandably, been concerned that these massive dredging activities would foul the atmosphere with the odors of stirred up sewage. Their immediate fears were, however, unfounded because the dredging had occurred sufficiently far out in the water so that the only material removed had been coral and clay. Yet the harbour project's completion in mid 1891 did little to quicken the problem of sluggish discharges of sewage from Castries streams into the ocean inlet. If anything, the problem had been magnified, not so much because the physical conditions had changed but because more ships and therefore more visitors—both military and civilian—were now calling at Castries. Further, the Castries area now housed a British military detachment to protect the coaling station. From all reports, the troops were less fearful of enemy encounters than they were of the "abominable stench" that came from Castries and the frequent fevers many of them suffered and attributed to the unhealthy environment.

A flurry of correspondence among the local authorities in St Lucia, the Colonial Office and the War Office in the early 1890s focused on the contamination at the eastern end of the harbour. On hot and still days, the stench from the harbour's mouth was simply "overpowering", leading to a light-headed malaise among those exposed to it. An obvious, but extremely expensive, solution to the problem was to design a new sewage disposal system for the entire Castries area. During 1892, local officials began to concentrate the town's sewage at predesignated points and to have it taken out by sail-powered barges and poured into the open sea. This arrangement lessened the immediate problem by mid 1893.[31]

Despite the stink of Castries' dockside, the harbour renovation and the establishment of the coaling station had put considerably more money than before into local circulation. Labourers' wages boosted merchants' shops, and the influx of soldiers into St Lucia meant more business than before, an important consideration during the sugar depression. But the construction project's wages had been short term, and the siting of the coaling station and ancillary army quarters had apparently attracted wage-seeking 'riff-raff' from nearby islands that increased crime noticeably in the Castries area. According to one St Lucian police magistrate, the coaling station and garrison had "brought . . . camp followers from Barbados with their auxiliary scum . . . Hardly a schooner arrives now from that Colony without . . . Barbadians on board. And . . . there is more English spoken about our streets at present than heretofore." A number of labourers from the British Leewards also had come to work in St Lucian sugar factories, and they, as well as some of the Barbadians, ended up as coal carriers on the St Lucia docks.[32]

Castries' face was physically transformed by the siting of the coaling station there. Sometimes the piles of coal at dockside, and even along the waterfront streets, were so high that they obscured views of the town's buildings and even the roofs. And although some of the coal-carrying jobs went to transients, the majority of the carriers were St Lucian women. When ships were in port, roughly 500 coal carriers were occupied, three-quarters of them women. Usually they assembled under a single foreman or 'crier', and then, upon command, they scrambled for coal baskets. Then they each would carry baskets of coal (weighing over 100 pounds) on their heads up steep wooden inclines to the ships. Each carrier received 2 cents for five baskets carried, and a day's work brought about 3 shillings. The carriers usually were paid in coal tickets or coal tokens, currency accepted by the merchants, and even the market women, in Castries.[33]

Some of the black artisans coming to St Lucia from Barbados for the harbour project doubtless had had experience on a roughly similar effort on their home island. From 1889 to 1893, a massive, 240-foot long dry dock facility was constructed at the Pier Head in Bridgetown. Each side of the dock was delimited by concrete retaining walls that enclosed individual sections composed of 20-inch square greenheart beams. The construction originally was to last for two years, but the time was doubled because the excavation was flooded by spring tides. By 1897 the completed dock attracted hundreds of ships each year, including those of the Royal Navy stationed in the Caribbean. The construction project also had provided short-lived jobs for hundreds of black Barbadian artisans and labourers whose livelihood opportunities were reduced by the sugar depression. When the dry dock needed repairs in 1895, a near riot ensued caused by work-hungry men; 500 clamored for 200 jobs, causing a crush that had to be controlled by a guard of forty police, including mounted horsemen.[34]

Neither St George's, Grenada, nor Kingstown, St Vincent, had elaborate harbour facilities. In both places ocean-going steamers were unable to proceed directly to local wharves because of shallow waters. People and produce therefore were lightered back and forth between ship and shore. Nonetheless, by the early 1900s both the Royal Mail Steam Packet Company and also Pickford and Black's Canadian line serviced both places, calling two or three times per month. The steamer *Orinoco*, representing the latter company, ran aground and suffered damage on Grenada's southern coast on 2 November 1900, an event helping to inspire the construction of a lighthouse at Point Salines four years later, a structure equipped with a "white light of the Fourth Order, visible for twelve miles". The nature of the harbour traffic in both islands reflected their locations at either end of the Grenadines. Every Saturday morning flotillas of canoes and small schooners from the smaller islets and also from the coastal towns of the leeward and windward coasts of Grenada and St Vincent arrived with vegetables, eggs, small stock and a variety of other products for sale.[35]

Migrating, Sailing and Smuggling

Although most human inhabitants of the late nineteenth century Eastern Caribbean had never travelled farther than their home islands—or, at most, no farther than the closest nearby places—the brisk, informal traffic in small boats carrying people and goods connected individual islands to their nearest neighbours. The daily movements in tiny vessels along the chain of the Grenadines between St Vincent and Grenada, were paralleled by larger craft that sailed regularly from the Windwards to Barbados and Trinidad. Fortnightly "shipping intelligence" reports in the local newspapers often carried the names of schooners and sloops as well as the number of 'deckers' aboard that had arrived, or departed, in the past two weeks. Occasionally, the few items aboard these small craft were inventoried by customs officials if they suspected smuggling. One representative case among many involved the sloop *Faith* from Trinidad, seized in Grenada in October 1894. The Grenadian customs officials found on board the "two Dutch stoves, one parcel nails, one tin nails, one jar confectionery, two pairs ladies' boots, one pair duck trousers, one piece print, one piece red cotton, and one flannel shirt".[36]

Official records of travellers' departures and arrivals were not aggregated annually and doubtless such records would never have captured the entire volume of the interisland traffic in people. Yet one observation, for the first five months of 1888 for St Vincent, indicates that something approximating a population equilibrium was maintained by the circulation of people on small boats throughout the region. This description also suggests the futility in attempting to classify these human migrations in any meaningful way:

I find, according to the departures and arrivals of passengers published in the Government *Gazette*, that, for the five months ending 31st May last, there were 841 departures and 906 arrivals, but not being able to ascertain the purpose for which the passengers leave the Island, I am unable to furnish an analysis of the numbers who leave as Emigrants, Immigrants, Traders, Pleasure-Seekers, Derelicts, and Refugees. But taking the concurrent numbers of departures and arrivals as a criterion, it is evident that a large percentage of the people who leave here for the neighbouring islands, and particularly Trinidad, do so for the purpose of trading in Live Stock, Starch, Farina, and other commodities, and not from a state of indigence.[37]

The informality and unpredictable character of this interisland small vessel traffic detracted from its possible contribution to the economic development of the region. At least that was the opinion of St Vincent's acting administrator in 1897; he deplored the uncertainties faced by Vincentian livestock producers who attempted to ship animals for sale to either Trinidad or Barbados via the "miserable sloops". After endless delay, these small-scale producers often lost everything, experiences that obviously discouraged production of crops or animals for export. Officials tirelessly condemned the captains of small vessels for overloading them. Schooners and sloops travelled from island to island packed with people and animals. One such case involved the small sailing schooner *Advice* that in May 1898, arrived in St Lucia from Barbados badly weighed down, a common and dangerous practice: "The voyage between Barbados and St Lucia is frequently extremely rough and by no means free from danger for the small intercolonial craft which are notoriously often overloaded."[38]

Sailing in the other direction from St Lucia was no safer. The channel between the northern end of the island and Martinique was notoriously choppy and also subject to blustery winds blowing directly in from the Atlantic. These conditions prevailed in the channels between the other islands as well, creating hazardous passages for sailing craft. Added to these ever-present dangers were the uncertainties of the occasional southerly or westerly waves and swells that damaged small craft at sea or even those lying at anchor in the village inlets of leeward coasts. And the risk of death by drowning for those travelling aboard small sailing vessels struck by sudden wind storms was not confined to the hurricane season of late summer and autumn. On the morning of 10 June 1897, a cyclone ran from southeast to northwest across the northern end of St Vincent. The sloop *Alma*, returning to Kingstown from St Lucia, capsized, and two passengers drowned. The storm also washed a man overboard from the sailing sloop *Carib* as it was trying to leave Rabacca Bay.[39]

The sailing vessels themselves were constructed on local beaches by the men who sailed them, small sloops and larger schooners crafted from local lumber. The beam or width in each of the vessels was usually about one-fourth its length and the depth of the hold half the width, although these proportions were not followed rigorously as no written plans or blueprints guided construction efforts. The vessels' capacity ratings were as low as 10 to 20 tons, and they were powered by the wind that filled their tattered canvas sails. The small wooden boats were the probable descendants of the sailing vessels that had carried freedmen from island to island in the days immediately following emancipation, and construction techniques had been transmitted by fathers to their sons. The black seamen who commanded these vessels were considered reckless, independent and unafraid of taking their boats out in "the wildest weather". Most ship captains were "illiterate", a condition that local officials acknowledged in granting them a certain latitude in sometimes relaxing shipping regulations so that these seamen could transfer goods and peoples from one coastal location to another. Their formal illiteracy also meant a near absence of maps or charts. The seamen sailed the familiar waters of their own islands where they knew the locations of rocks, shoals and treacherous currents. But their travels farther afield, to Trinidad and Barbados, were all the more dangerous because they depended on dead reckoning to reach their destinations.[40]

Those involved in sailing and maritime activities in Barbados and the Windwards were variously identified as "seamen", "mariners" and the like in the population censuses of the late nineteenth century (Table 4.1). Although their numbers were small relative to the island populations as a whole, these men had extraordinary (if informal) social and economic status within the black societies of the Eastern Caribbean. Their prestige was derived from their activities outside the rigid land-based hierarchies of field labour and wage work. And their daily activities, of course, took them far

from the islands themselves, separating them physically from insular colonial domains. Others travelling with them from one island to another on
small sailing vessels—the hucksters, labour migrants, refugees, pleasure
seekers and others—were obviously dependent for their safe passages on
these men who demonstrated considerable physical and intellectual skills in
guiding boats safely through stormy conditions and interisland passages.
And courage was an obvious requirement for all seamen in coping with the
dangers involved in maritime activities.

Boat captains and crews also had to be wary and mindful of supernatural influences. The sailors often personified the sea as a fickle woman, subject to immediate change as she was influenced by the (male) wind; but she
also was intolerant of any evil actions by those who rode on her surface.
The Sea Devil often exerted his authority as well by taking human lives.
Sailing men were thus obligated to take preventive countermeasures to protect themselves and their passengers and vessels while at sea by practising
obeah related acts of magic and sorcery. So a supernatural aura, beyond the
prestige seamen enjoyed from their hazardous daily activities, further enhanced their reputations within these small, insular societies in the late
nineteenth century.[41]

Although colonial authorities usually took a relaxed attitude toward
these seamen and their vessels, the informal movement of people from one
island to another became activities of official concern during outbreaks of
disease. Officials who, under different circumstances, might unwittingly
publicize their own ignorance about how diseases were transmitted on their
own islands, usually were quick to apply quarantine sanctions against
neighbouring islands and to reinforce these rules by prohibiting the arrival
of small vessels suspected of coming from those places. In 1888, smallpox
on Martinique led to the attempted enforcement of quarantine sanctions in
the British Windwards to prevent sailing vessels coming from the French island. The attempt was largely successful except at Islet Ronde, a small fishing quay north of Grenada, where smugglers brought, among other things,
smallpox that resulted in twenty local cases of the disease.[42]

Whereas quarantine was employed only sporadically by colonial officials, and—as in the case of St Lucia's yellow fever outbreak at the turn of
the century—resisted locally at all costs, smuggling via the small sailing
craft in the islands was a ubiquity that required continuous vigilance. The
1882 royal commission dealing with government finances in Jamaica and
the Windwards summarized the prevalence of smuggling in the Wind-

Table 4.1 Fishermen in The Windwards

Grenada	Boatmen and Fishermen	Mariners
Town of St George's	69	48
Parish of St George	44	6
St John	78	1
St Mark	41	11
St Patrick	52	9
St Andrew	32	23
St David	8	4
Carriacou	18	234
Total	**342**	**336**

Source: N.J. Paterson, compiler, *Grenada . . . Census of 1901* (St George's: Government Printing Office,1902 p 37 Table 26)

St Lucia

	Seamen and Fishermen
Castries-Town	203
Castries-District	27
Anse-la-Raye	27
Soufrière	54
Choiseul	32
Laborie	8
Vieux Fort	41
Micoud	14
Dennery	14
Gros-Islet	88
Total	**508**

Source: Alex. Clavier, "Report on the Census of St Lucia . . . 1891", *St Lucia Gazette* (29 January 902), p 49, Table 13.

Table 4.1 Continued

St Vincent

	Fishermen	Mariners	Ship-wrights	Fish Pot makers
Kingstown Police District	35	239	39	4
Calliaqua P.D	5	16	2	0
Windward P.D.	2	4	0	0
Leeward P.D.	49	41	0	0
Grenadines P.D.	27	134	C23	3
Total	118	434	64	7

Source: C.O. 264/13/ *St Vincent Official Gazette, 1881*

wards, and the difficulty in controlling it. In discussing the raising of import duties on which local government officials depended heavily, the commissioners acknowledged that such a strategy would doubtless increase the flow of contraband, benefiting those involved in illicit trade rather than the officials. Even in normal conditions, the commissioners lamented, smuggling among the islands was so common that there were noticeable differences in revenue receipts "in accordance with whether the sea was rough or smooth".[43]

It hardly needs emphasis that formal colonial rules collided with the informal transportation of goods among islands so that the definition of what was and was not 'smuggling' depended on one's point of view. In some cases, the delineation of customs boundaries between islands, with the intent to limit unauthorized trade, was absurd. Until 1898, for example, colonial officers actually had tried to curb traffic between Petit Martinique (under Grenada's jurisdiction) and Petit St Vincent (under St Vincent). The islands were less than half a mile apart, the families of both places intertwined, and they routinely exchanged visits to carry household items back and forth, including fresh water in times of drought. In 1895 Governor Moloney 'liberalized' trade and migration restrictions between Petit Martinique and Petit St Vincent. Until then, at least formally, a resident of the latter island wishing to visit the former was supposed to acquire a permit in Kingstown, St Vincent—a 30-mile voyage away—in order to do so![44]

But the traffic in contraband was more than a nuisance self-imposed by metropolitan bureaucrats attempting to extend customs regulations over a string of tiny islands where people and goods were always in motion. The excise taxes in rum, for example, brought in several thousands of pounds in revenue annually to each colony. Accordingly, officials were vigilant in attempting to stop tax-free shipments of rum. The establishment of coastal patrols in St Lucia in the early 1890s seem to have paid off in inhibiting smuggling rum and other items from Martinique that had been carried on for years; St Lucia's consumption duty collected in 1875 had been only £7,206, a figure that increased to £15,455, by 1894. These data, of course, reflected heavy volumes of contraband, not simply a rum bottle or two sneaked to or from a particular island. In November 1887, for example, Captain Denton and a party of police constables from Kingstown captured a cache of 1,500 gallons of smuggled rum at Union Island in the St Vincent Grenadines.[45]

Part of that same police operation, however, subsequently ran into trouble, demonstrating the organization and muscle of the smugglers themselves and suggesting that they, rather than ephemeral police forays, really controlled trade in the Grenadines. On the way back from Denton's raid at Union Island, Corporal John and two constables seized the sloop *Echo* and began to haul her to St Vincent. They were forcibly halted en route by the captain and crew of the *Swan*, taken to Carriacou, detained for twelve hours, and then set free. Authorities issued an alert for the "pirates" who had captured the police and then called the HMS *Ballard* from Trinidad for assistance. Upon arrival in Carriacou, the *Ballard* commander found the *Swan* abandoned and the *Echo* nearly sunk off a sandbar. Warrants were issued for the arrest of two of Carriacou's notorious smugglers, but that was futile because they had disappeared. The revenue officer of Carriacou, a Mr Isaacs, is said to have treated the entire affair "rather gingerly".[46]

Small coastal steamers augmented the sailing vessels by the 1880s and 1890s, hauling people and goods from place to place. The steamer routes and schedules were, moreover, sufficiently regular that government officials of St Lucia in 1889 allowed the small ships' agents to convey letters and cards (at a rate of a penny apiece) to destinations around the island independent of the regular postal services. Travel aboard these small, steam-powered vessels was uncomfortable, a consideration Conrad Reeves emphasized to the 1897 commissioners when he suggested regularly scheduled steamer services by larger ships among the islands. Three years earlier, as only one example, Governor Bruce had had to travel from Grenada to St

Lucia aboard one of the small coasting steamers, the Royal Mail Steamer being held in Trinidad because of a yellow fever quarantine. Bruce complained of no meal service on the small boat, although it is doubtful he had much appetite owing to the heavy weather and choppy sea aboard these "small vessels without keels".[47]

In general, however, steamer travel of any kind to and from the islands usually was considered qualitatively different from travel via small sailing vessels. Larger steamships had been in the West Indies since the 1830s, and they always had represented a mode of externally controlled, long-distance conveyance of goods and peoples differing from the short local journeys aboard sailing vessels. And although some men and women from Barbados and the Windwards in the 1880s and 1890s still travelled seasonally on sailing schooners as far as Trinidad for wage labour, most went as deck passengers on steamships. Seasonal migrations to Trinidad had been established at emancipation and, by late in the same century, these movements had become routine; the confederation disturbance in St Vincent in late 1891, for example, really had been an outburst against, among other things, a rumoured ban against labour emigration.

But the malaise created by the sugar bounty depression was beginning to push individual and collective migration trajectories farther from the eastern Caribbean than ever before. Individual Barbadians, who for decades had travelled to British Guiana for cane harvesting, by the first years of the 1900s had extended their travels to Suriname, Brazil, Ecuador and even to the headwaters of the Amazon in eastern Peru. And the Windward islanders also had lengthened their journeys farther than ever before in working for the French in Panama. J.A. Froude, in the late 1880s, described the "tens of thousands" of West Indian islanders who had emigrated to Panama and recounted his experience at Dominica as black deck passengers "swarmed" aboard the steamship on which he was a passenger to travel to Central America:

The vessel which called for us at Dominica was crowded with them, and we picked up more as we went on. Their average stay is for a year. At the end of a year half of them have gone to the other world. Half go home, made easy for life with money enough to buy a few acres of land . . . Darien has seized their imaginations as an Eldorado.[48]

Froude indeed seems to have understood the motivations of the labour migrants who travelled from the Windwards to Panama, men and women whose migrations and returns were intimately bound up with the conditions in their home islands and whose movements were beginning to reduce the isolation that insularity imposed. Thousands travelled away and returned in the depression decades to earn money elsewhere to buy land plots at home. Part of the testimony of the treasurer of St Lucia to the 1897 royal commission, for example, explained that French-speaking emigrants from his island had brought and sent home nearly £70,000 worth of gold from Panama between 1885 and 1890. Then, after the French had withdrawn from Panama, St Lucians had begun travelling aboard steamers to French Guiana to act as general labourers and 'bearers' in the goldfields there. "No account has been kept of this emigration", the treasurer explained. But he continued that "One thing is certain, that a large proportion of . . . [the migrants] . . . are successful, and return to the colony with substantial sums of money." He further pointed out that St Lucians returning with money from the South American colony used it to pay off debts, purchase land, make deposits in local banks, improve and build "dwellings in the several towns and villages", and that their success abroad combined with obligations at home reinforced their continuous movements back and forth from French Guiana.[49]

Probably the longest journey by any group from the Eastern Caribbean in the depression decades was in July 1892, when roughly 350 islanders travelled to Africa for wage labour, a testimony not only to desperate local conditions but also to the opportunities that steamer travel now represented. The contingent of fifty-one St Lucians, four Vincentians and the remainder mainly Barbadians had been recruited for railroad labour in the Congo Free State and advanced thirty shillings each before departure. They travelled east from Bridgetown aboard the steamer *McGarel* to the Canary Islands. From there they boarded a German steamer and proceeded south along the West African coastline. After reaching the mouth of the Congo River and reacting to rumours that they were about to be enslaved, the West Indians mutinied, but they were subdued by Belgian soldiers, sent upriver for railroad work, and never heard from again.[50]

Sea Fishing

Dr J.E. Duerden, curator of the Museum of the Institute of Jamaica, delivered a very different kind of paper at the West Indian Agricultural Conference in Barbados in January 1900. His presentation was an assessment of the region's marine resources, an issue acknowledged as understudied yet potentially important for the British West Indies. Duerden reviewed the high costs for imported salt fish as a subsistence staple into the region and pointed out the associated "anomalous condition that the West Indies are small islands, surrounded by wide seas inhabited by large numbers of edible fish". He further suggested that the local fishing industries were in dire need of development; at present they were "mainly in the hands of the natives, and . . . conducted without much organization, capital, or enterprise". A key problem, according to Duerden, would have been familiar to those who subscribed to the 'bountiful tropical environment' notion that helped explain West Indian indolence: "The prices realized for fresh fish are generally high, and a few days' labour is sufficient to provide the fisherman for the remainder of the week with the few necessaries of tropical life." Duerden's article was later discussed approvingly in the influential British journal *Nature* which emphasized that a closer understanding of the British Caribbean's "economic zoology . . . might be the means of placing the depressed colonies in an improved position . . . thereby lessening their constantly recurring charge upon the mother country".[51]

Those British visitors to their West Indian colonies at the turn of the century might have been similarly inclined to the view that the region's marine resources represented an obvious and potentially valuable food source, waiting only to be tapped by modern fishing techniques. Such an outlook would have been reinforced by a cursory trip around any of the islands when fish were in season because they would have seen village women and children crowded around docked fishing boats that had returned from the sea in late morning, usually with fresh fish to sell. In St Vincent the great prevalence of edible jackfish (*Selar crumenophthalmus*) beyond the immediate coastal waters was even thought—consistent with Duerdon's assertion— to reduce villagers' economic drive. Early in 1898 rumours abounded in Vincentian villages that the local government was about to give, rather than sell, local lands to black workers who were said to be "content to idly wait with a breadfruit in their laps and a jackfish in their mouths for the day of spoliation".[52]

But harvesting fish from tropical waters was not the same as cultivating subsistence crops, especially when densely settled island populations had to eat every day. To be sure, fishing in the islands had long traditions. A limited number of slave fishermen had trolled the reefs and inlets of every island. And by the late nineteenth century, fish doubtless supplied the major source of protein in some of the fishing villages of the Windwards. Yet fish availability was seasonal and preservation techniques limited to occasional drying. These factors seem responsible for traditionally relegating local fishing activities to the 'natives', who could be counted on to provide fresh fish in season (and to absorb the risk associated with fishing) but not to sustain fully the islands' human populations.

Since eastern Caribbean fishing was dominated by small-scale fishermen in the 1890s, the activity rarely found its way into local production or export statistics from any of the islands. Fishing statistics were available only for Barbados. The 1897 commissioners learned that about 1,250 men and an estimated 250 market women, were involved in Barbadian fishing. They were estimated to have earned altogether £19,500 annually, but two-thirds of that income came from flying fish which were usually unavailable in any numbers during the late summer and autumn months.[53]

Nearshore marine habitats of the region were not unrelated to terrestrial insular conditions. Mangrove swamps and seagrass beds near the shores filtered suspended sediments from land-based runoff. This filtering thereby protected the reef ecosystems and also the dozens of fish species on the reefs, many of which grew to maturity in the brackish waters around mangrove vegetation. Fishermen in rowboats—and even canoes "on the old Carib pattern" in Dominica and St Vincent—set fish traps and used nets and lines for reef fish, notably hinds, parrotfish, triggerfish and angelfish as well as for snappers and groupers farther out on the banks. At a greater distance from the shore, the migratory oceanic pelagic fishes, whose life cycles were not associated with bottom habitats, attracted fishermen who manned the wooden sailing vessels that had sails, small holds and crews of up to three or four. Major pelagic species—which accounted for perhaps two-thirds of overall fish catches in the Windwards—included dolphin, tuna, kingfish, bonito and skipjack far out at sea and also jacks, ballahoo, spratt, dodger and robin closer to shore. Spiny lobster, conch and sea eggs (especially on Barbados) were routinely sought and collected along the islands' littorals.[54]

Fishermen (see Table 4.1) could be found in all of the islands. In the Grenadines, fishing (next to smuggling) was perhaps the most important local economic activity, especially on Bequia. Barrouallie, on an inlet along St Vincent's leeward coast, was the centre of that island's rural fishing activities. Fishermen from St Lucia were extremely skilled and thought by others to have special, sorcery related powers helping to explain their extraordinary success. Barbadian fishermen caught snappers far from shore in late summer, selling them in the Bridgetown market for 8 cents/pound.

But the flying fish season was the most exhausting yet lucrative for Barbadian fishermen. The operation known as 'driving' the flying fish began before dawn each fishing day when boats departed from the coastal villages of the southern and western littorals of Barbados and ventured to between 5 and 12 miles offshore. Then the crew lowered the mast and sails so the vessel could drift with currents and winds. Then baskets containing partially decomposed carcasses of flying fish and also nets containing trapped, live flying fish were trailed in the waters. The flying fish attracted by each of these techniques were then caught by baited lines and hooks. The flying fish following these 'scenting' or 'washing' techniques occasionally attracted, in turn, hungry dolphins (probably a general term for various cetaceans of the genus *Delphinus*) that then became easy prey for the fishermen. Individual fishing boats commonly had catches of over 1,000 flying fish in a day, and a figure as high as 5,000 was not unknown. The crew divided the catch—one-third usually going to the boat's owner—which they then sold on shore at the rate of 150 fish for one dollar.[55]

The flying fish season in Barbados lasted from December to July, with the highest volume of catches in April and May. And the seasonal character of sea fishing throughout the eastern Caribbean affected local village diets, reinforcing the traditional 'hungry time' of late summer and autumn. In those months, heavy rains in the northern part of South America also led to enormous quantities of murky, sediment laden, fresh water being discharged from the Orinoco and Amazon Rivers. This massive rainfall runoff phenomenon of the northern hemisphere's late summer explained a skimming of low-salinity and recognizably greenish water (called 'Orinoc' by fishermen in Grenada) over the saline ocean water around the Windwards. When this seasonally obvious and low-salinity water was present, affecting the water as far north as the St Vincent Grenadines, neither pelagic nor near-shore fishing was an productive as in other times of the year.[56]

Village activities, livelihood routines and local economies in the eastern Caribbean of the 1890s were influenced by the seasonal character of off-shore fishing. The flying fish markets in Barbados were active in the first months of the year when the fish were plentiful and cheap. Another example was from St Vincent and St Lucia where local fishermen routinely sailed out to harpoon blackfish (*Globicephala macrorhynchus*), whose flesh was highly prized in local fish markets. Known elsewhere as the pilot whale, the blackfish obviously was not a small creature; adults reached lengths of up to 20 feet and weighed as much as 3 tons. Schools of up to 100 blackfish frequented the waters off the Windwards. Although blackfish landings were made in every month of the year, the highest number of catches were in September, at the same time that breadfruit was ripening and becoming abundant on land. Windward fishermen maintained a metaphorical explanation of their high success rate in late summer when the blackfish's seasonal lack of wariness led to its tendency to swim near the surface: "Any time breadfruit in tree, blackfish a fool."[57]

The most remarkable activity accomplished by fishermen of the eastern Caribbean at the time—the pursuit and hand harpooning of whales from small wooden boats—was a distinctively seasonal activity as well. Besides taking blackfish, men of the Windwards occasionally landed sperm whales (*Pyseter catodon*) and killer whales (*Orcinus orca*)—locally known as 'whitefish'—throughout the year, the presence of these whales in the Windwards' waters often explained as an attraction to nutrient and plankton-rich conditions created by ocean upwelling. But the seasonal presence of the humpback whale (*Megaptera novaeangliae*) in the waters off the Grenadines apparently was because the blubber of young whales afforded insufficient protection in the cold winter oceans of high latitudes, and the warm, nutrient-rich waters of the eastern Caribbean thereby represented ideal calving grounds. In any case, the seasonal migrations of the humpback whale were very evident at the turn of the century and also provided the conventional explanation of the origins of the local whaling industry:

In this channel [between St Vincent and Grenada] from January to May, the humpback whale . . . loafs on his way to the colder waters of the North Atlantic. For years the New Bedford whaler has been lying-in among these islands to pick up crews, and it is from him that the negro has learned the art of catching the humpback.[58]

American whalers had worked the region since the early nineteenth century with their peak activity in the 1860s when they produced upwards of a thousand barrels of whale oil a year in the Grenadines, an activity that declined precipitously in the 1870s. While they were in the islands, the New England seamen took on local men as crew members—principally as harpoonists and lookouts—who sailed elsewhere with the Americans and then returned with enhanced sailing and fishing skills. Less romantic whal-

ing related activities, such as boiling fat from blubber in large metal caul-
drons, was also a technique Americans apparently passed on to locals.
Grenadine fishermen established their own permanent whaling station in
Bequia during the 1870s and also one at tiny Petit Nevis in the next decade.
There they constructed their whaling boats that were modeled after Nan-
tucket-type craft introduced earlier by the Americans. The vessels were
about 25 feet long with v-shaped hulls and two different sails. The frames
and ribs were of local white cedar with pine imported from North America
for planking. Sailcloth, nails and rope for the vessels came from England.

It took eight men to beach one of these whaling vessels, although the
crew itself usually numbered six. The hunts for humpback whales usually
headed east from Bequia, so that hauling carcasses back to shore would be
aided by the wind-driven ocean current. The harpoonist, standing in the
prow of the vessel, launched his hand-held 'iron' into the whale's body after
the rowers had positioned the vessel close enough to the whale. If the hunt
was successful, the journey back to shore could be as dangerous as locating
and killing the whale had been. Dead whales sometimes took in sea water,
causing them to sink, and night passages hauling whale carcasses were occasionally accented by squalls and even shark attacks.

Whaling crews from Bequia usually butchered their prey at the littoral,
allowing ocean water to buoy some of the heavy carcass while they peeled
unwanted portions from it. They diced the blubber into small cubes before
reducing it to oil through heating. A single humpback whale, depending on
its size, yielded up to 1,500 gallons of oil, a commodity the whalers usually
stored in wooden casks. Whale oil export data routinely appeared in the annual reports for St Vincent in the late 1800s, usually being valued as several
hundred pounds per year. In islands as small as some of the individual
Grenadines, these monetary sums were important. In March 1893, Governor Hely-Hutchinson travelled through the usually impoverished Grenadines where things seemed brighter than usual. "The whaling season is an
exceptionally good one and has in great measure helped to make things
more prosperous", the governor proclaimed. Prosperity seemed particularly
evident at Canouan where "already some 74 barrels of whale oil had been
obtained."[59]

Butchering crews usually worked on isolated beaches and inlets because
of the stench of rotting whale flesh. Whereas the oil was destined for export, the meat or 'beef' from the whales was prized by local peoples. Either
the whalers themselves or the market women to whom they sold the whale

flesh cut the meat into strips and then salted and dried these strips. This 'corning' process helped preserve the meat for as long as two weeks, making it all the more attractive as a dietary supplement to a starch-heavy diet of local vegetables. The unmistakable presence of whale flesh in the open-air markets of the Windwards in the first few months of every year was perhaps most obvious in St Vincent, and it provided an olfactory experience similar to that in the beachside butchering areas, as an excerpt from a March 1897, Kingstown newspaper makes clear:

The whale nuisance is so much in evidence at this time of the year that it hardly needs our feeble voice to call attention to it. It is a nuisance which it is impossible . . . to wholly prevent, but surely an attempt might be made to minimize the annoyance which it causes to those who do not appreciate its unpleasant odour. During the whaling season the stalls of the Kingstown market which is situated in the heart of the town are covered with whale-meat in all its stages of putrifaction, the smell of which is most disgusting.[60]

The whaling men of the Grenadines were accorded extraordinary prestige within the local black societies, an understandable cultural response toward those who—like other mariners of the region—stood apart from the local and regional agriculture based social hierarchies. The perilous activities in each step of local whaling activities required courage. An obvious requisite for whalermen was physical strength. And an undue personal display of sentiment or attachment, even to one's families, could lead to sudden grief and sorrow because of the precariousness of a whaler's existence. Death by drowning was a distinct possibility every time a whaling boat left the shore. A traveller among the small islets north of Grenada at the time noted "One often sees a notice like this: 'May 1st 1909.—A whaleboat with a crew of five men left Sauteurs for Union Island; not since heard of.' "[61]

Of course all of the fishermen of the region, not only whalers, faced daily risks of being capsized and drowned, and every coastal fishing village harboured memories of those family and friends who had "gone bottom". A fisherman daily faced the impersonal elements of nature either alone or with a small group of friends. He coped not with tyrannical estate managers but with the Sea Devil and other forces beyond his control. His familiarity with varied elements of magic and his possession of good luck charms were therefore survival skills of a special kind.

Since official accounts and records, beyond whaling, of small-scale fishing activities in the late nineteenth century Caribbean were so rare, it was

6. Folk-whaling in the Grenadines, *ca.* 1905

(*From F. A. Fenger, Alone in the Caribbean (New York: George H. Doran Company, 1917).*)

only during an extraordinary event, such as a storm, that these otherwise mundane activities were thrown into high relief. The gale of 12 October 1894—the same storm that had shaken Barbadian complacency that the island was south of the hurricane track—provided an example. The storm uprooted trees, destroyed or severely damaged 400 workers' houses, and it arrived so suddenly that it caught a number of Barbadian fishermen at sea. An estimated twenty-two boats with a total of sixty-one men and boys were carried by high winds north and west of Barbados, some as far as 100 miles distant. A French vessel that had been moored at Barbados picked up sixteen of the stricken fishermen at sea and landed them at Martinique, but seventeen were lost forever.[62]

The gale also blew several of the fishing boats from Barbados carrying an estimated twenty-seven Barbadian fishermen all the way to St Lucia. Then within a week St Lucian authorities assembled the itinerant storm victims and sent them back to Barbados. Upon his return to Bridgetown, Nathaniel Hoyte—one of the survivors of the unplanned visit to St Lucia—described the experience to the Bridgetown police. Hoyte's matter-of-fact account could not mask an experience that was an odyssey involving fright, rescue, bravery and comradeship:

On Friday 12th October I went out with three men in a boat 'Turtle' belonging to M. Bascomb to catch red fish. We moored the boat about five miles from land. The gale came on and the boat broke the mooring line and drifted. The land was hidden by mist and we could not see in what direction to steer. We hoisted a little of the mainsail, but it was soon split by the gale. We came across a Moses (the Barbadian term for a type of near-shore rowboat) with three men. One of them Rufus Morris had a peg leg. We took them aboard and let their boat drift. Night came on and we lowered sail. At sunrise there was no land in sight. We then made what sail we could and about 2 o'c (Saturday) we sighted land. Soon after this heavy clouds set between us and the land and hid it from us. We kept our course and sighted land again about 5 p.m. At nightfall we lowered sails again and at sunrise on Sunday morning we had again lost the land having drifted during the night. We put up sail and in 3 hours sighted land again, after which we never lost it. At 6 p.m. we got to Castries where we found the 'Walcott' with her own crew and three men whom she had rescued from the 'Mabel'. Early on Friday morning we had caught a red fish but from the weather we could not cook it until Saturday. We then made up a fire on the ballast roasted the fish and ate it. We had some fresh water. When we reached Castries on Saturday evening we were taken to the Police station where the 'Walcott' men already were. Next morning passed and on Friday we heard that 4 more boats had arrived at Vieux Fort. They proved to be the pilot boat 'Mischief' with Hurley and a boy named Edwards and 3 fishing boats with the two Winters and 9 other men. They all came to Castries by Steamer and we left for Barbados in Schooner 'Topaz'. . .[63]

The ordeal of the Barbadian fishermen being cast adrift in October 1894 and then finding refuge on St Lucia provided experiences that increased their first-hand knowledge of this island. The distinctiveness of that mountainous and foreign place, furthermore, probably reinforced, at least subconsciously, the reality of their Barbadian identity. The patois-speaking villagers they probably saw and heard in Castries were certainly different from people at home whose lives were centred around the sugar estate tenantries. These island differences that formed the basis for insular identities had been obvious since emancipation when men and women began to travel freely from one island to another and then shared their experiences once they returned home. Yet, by the end of the nineteenth century, as greater numbers of fishermen and others travelled from place to place on vessels powered by both sail and steam, these differences were experienced by increasing numbers of travellers and returnees. Sea travel had provided the opportunity for residents of particular islands to accumulate a storehouse of information about the people they had observed and met from elsewhere.

Whereas travel across the ocean waters provided the basis for new inter-island experiences, the channelling of fresh water on particular islands late in the nineteenth century narrowed access to a common resource. Newly urban and upwardly mobile populations, whose access to supplies of fresh water was the basis for the maintenance of their sanitation and personal hygiene, placed greater expectations on civil authorities for reliable water supplies and appropriate drainage control. In St Vincent, competition between planters and these authorities over water supplies reinforced animosities that were decades old. In all of the islands, fresh water supply, whether piped, flowing in streams or falling in the form of rain, was the lifeblood of the economic activity of these populations which was centred on agriculture. And most commercial agriculture, as discussed in chapter five, was confined to the islands' lowlands.

Chapter Five
The Lowlands

The overall contrasts between the lowlands and the highlands in the eastern Caribbean late in the nineteenth century were as obvious as they are today, one century later. Especially in the Windwards, where lowlands gave way to highlands and vice versa, stark differences in human geography between the two zones were well known: the lowlands were measured, commercial, accessible and, most important, under white control; the highlands were remote, rugged, overgrown and the locus of black subsistence activities. These impressionistic yet meaningful local contrasts were even considered indicative, at least on occasion, of the vigilance necessary by representatives of the British Colonial Office if they were to bring lasting civilization to their tropical colonies, even these small Caribbean islands they had owned for many decades. In commenting on the relatively large extent of the mountainous Crown (government owned) lands in St Vincent, the royal commissioners of 1882 warned specifically of environmentally detrimental deforestation activities there by black charcoal producers, but more generally that highland squatters were likely to "relapse into a semi-savage state, to the injury of the whole community".[1]

Caribbean altitudinal contrasts however had been accorded only minimal official significance in the past by British Colonial Office administrators, whose habit of referring to flat wall maps, either to explain or to plan local land use, led to a decidedly spatial bias in their discourse about land use differences. In a memo describing Vincentian land hunger early in 1890, for example, Governor Hely-Hutchinson explained that white landowners' holdings choked off possibilities of black settlements because the planters' holdings "form . . . a ring round the island".[2] Seven years later and as "peasant proprietary" momentum was building, Governor Moloney of the Windwards mused in a significant way that inappropriate recognition of the interrelationships between highlands and lowlands in the past might be rooted in land law originally framed for the British countryside itself. Moloney made the point while discussing the recent denudation of the forested highlands of Carriacou, an activity proceeding without regard for the erosional consequences affecting landholders at lower elevations. Moloney understood that the Swiss, for obvious reasons, always had accorded the owners of valley lands special rights against wanton destruction of mountain lands above them. In contrast, according to Moloney, English law, in a "sad and unjust omission . . . gives no right to the owners of low lands to prevent deforestation of the upper lands".[3]

As the bounty sugar depression intensified and extended itself into the 1890s, differences between highland subsistence zones and lowland commercial areas in the British Caribbean became ever more obvious, at times overshadowing abstract geographical principles imported from Britain. The 1897 commission's testimonies did much to reveal the productivity of highland subsistence refuges and their importance to local peoples. But the differences between high islands and low had had official recognition at least two years earlier when a delegation of dignitaries from Barbados, accompanied by three "members of the artisan class", left Bridgetown on April 1895 to determine the suitability of interiors of some of the Windwards as emigration destinations for Barbados' 'excess' population. The sojourn itself had little lasting effect, Windward officials being unenthusiastic about receiving Barbadians (and the Barbadian artisans returning home after seeing some of Trinidad's dark, isolated forests). Yet regional inter-island geographical distinctions were highlighted and publicized as a result of the journey. The delegation's comparative observations about the high country of St Lucia and low-lying Barbados during the depression were particularly intriguing. In both places, it was noted, the sugar depression had reduced cultivation and labourers' livelihoods. In the highlands of St Lucia, however, resultant wage reduction "does not necessarily mean distress, because the means of living . . . are provided on every hand". In low-lying Barbados, in contrast, "the case is different. With a super-abundant population the struggle for bare existence is . . . very keen, and at such a time as at present painfully acute; starvation is only avoided by extended poor relief and emigration has become an absolute necessity."[4]

Bounding the Lowlands

The edge of the sea, of course, marked the lower limits of the lowlands. That boundary, as discussed in chapter 3, was, on occasion, noticeably fluid, especially during the heavy storms of late summer and autumn when high winds drove ocean waters inland. And on occasion the ocean boundary could be even more treacherous. On 18 November 1867, an earthquake off the coast of Grenada was accompanied by a sudden drop in sea level. What followed was a surge of water, causing the land-sea boundary to fluctuate several feet in the late afternoon and creating waves that both damaged several buildings fronting the Carenage at St George's and inundated cane fields as far north as Gouyave.[5] In normal times, the flatter estate land—acreage closest to the sea—was best for crops, although salt spray or 'sea blast', as around Barbados, southern Grenada and along the northeastern littoral of St Vincent, was detrimental to crop cultivation.[6]

Much more important was the boundary between lowlands and highlands because usually that was the delimitation between privately held lands below and government Crown Lands above. In the summer of 1897, the administrator on St Vincent asserted that that island's lands could be categorized rather easily between those that could be "successfully cultivated" and those cultivated only "with difficulty and risk", a division that had "been sharply drawn by nature" because of St Vincent's precipitous interior slopes and "the very shifty nature of the soil". This geographical dichotomy was in direct contrast with the situation on Grenada whose clayey soils had provided "cultivable land . . . accessible almost everywhere".[7] Three years later, R. B. Llewelyn, the administrator on St Lucia, suggested bluntly that lands there were either "cultivable" or "worthless". And the latter category was based mainly on elevation: "The lands that may be considered worthless are those at a great altitude, say above a thousand feet, and those far distant from the coast or from roads."[8]

It hardly need emphasis that men, not nature, drew boundaries in the islands and that prior assumptions about 'natural' boundaries between highlands and lowlands and the agricultural potential of each zone were always subject to change. The earliest planting of cacao in Grenada, for example, had taken place in the highlands, and it was assumed the crop would not prosper elsewhere. But when higher prices for cacao and decreasing prices for sugar pushed cacao into lower elevations in the 1870s and 1880s "it was found that cacao trees bore even better crops in the lowlands".[9]

Speaking very generally, boundaries between privately held lands and interior Crown Lands separated accessible areas from inaccessible zones in the eastern Caribbean in the late 1800s. In Barbados, where there were no Crown Lands, accessibility was never an issue except during exceptionally heavy rains. And when the subject of transportation arose on the island it usually ended up as a testimony to Barbados' excellent road system. A.H. Verrill was almost lyrical about the island's overall accessibility:

Everywhere on Barbados stretch perfect roads, like broad white ribbons across hills and dales of green, and, for those who prefer a railway journey . . . there is the 'Barbados Light Railway', a fascinating toylike railroad that carries one leisurely from Bridgetown to Bathsheba across the island with frequent stops at plantations and tiny hamlets.[10]

One reason Barbados' overall accessibility was so appreciated was the comparative inaccessibility of the interiors of the nearby Windwards. In early 1898 in St Lucia the path over the mountains from the Cul-de-Sac area to the Mabouya Road (connecting Castries to Dennery on the windward coast) was "almost impassable" and always so in bad weather. Two years later the road has been improved and named the "Goldsworthy Track" (for a recent administrator), and the government claimed that this improved communication link had tapped heretofore inaccessible yet fertile lands. But this exuberance bore little relation to the continuing inaccessibility of much of the rest of St Lucia from Castries because of the poor road connections. Early in 1900, as only one example, government spokesmen expressed concern that many men of the island were being hired away by unscrupulous labour recruiters for work in the goldfields of French Guiana. Those St Lucians fortunate enough to return created morale problems throughout their local districts because they lived for a while in 'riotous dissipation' with the money they had earned, then they returned again to the South American colony. These vague, moralistic assessments of St Lucian labour migration actually reflected the remoteness and associated lack of familiarity that the St Lucia administrators had with outlying villages of the island because all of their information came not from direct observation but from the local priests as to what was occurring in village districts.[11]

The proposed 1895 Barbadian emigration scheme, whereby 'excess' Barbadians would be sent to be Windwards, accorded special significance to the upper boundaries between plantation lands and interior Crown Lands in places like St Vincent, St Lucia and Dominica. These hillside boundary zones were considered ideal settlement areas by the emigration committee, representing "base lines" from which Barbadian settlers could "work back into the Crown Lands" in the Windwards.[12] But the upper boundaries of estates were not always strictly delimited on the ground. And in St Vincent, the vague character of the boundaries between estates and Crown Lands provided a legal precedent—one originally established during slavery—that allowed planters in the late 1800s to exert strict socioeconomic control over neighbouring black settlers.

Although the 1,000-foot boundary between Windward Island estates and interior Crown Lands was a rough rule of thumb, not all estate lands extended so high, and if they did they usually were not cultivated to that elevation. A list of Alexander Porter's estates in St Vincent compiled in 1897 provides a representative guide to the boundary elevations for estates on that island because Porter's twenty-one estates, located throughout St Vincent, included more than one-quarter of the island's cultivated lands. The average low boundary for Porter's estates, several of which started at sea level, was slightly less than 100 feet above sea level. The average upper boundary was about 750 feet, although Porter's Richmond estate, partially cultivated in sugar cane and arrowroot and 22 road miles from Kingstown along the leeward coast, extended up to 1,500 feet above sea level.[13]

Caribbean land boundaries in the decades after slavery had carried with them, of course, momentous social significance. The boundaries between estates and mountain lands or between estates and village lands had, since slavery days, represented oppression versus freedom to black working peoples and security of tenure to planters who had invested heavily in buildings and machinery. And owning, or even controlling, a piece of land in Barbados, the Windwards, or elsewhere among rural black peoples in the British Caribbean in the 1890s carried with it a sense of pride, dignity and satisfaction not to mention the economic wherewithal to counter planter oppression.[14] By the 1880s and 1890s, especially in Grenada and St Lucia, some plantations had begun to sell off portions of their lands, and small scale settlers also had established plots adjacent to previously existing estates. The spatial result of these changes were similar to what B.W. Higman has described for Jamaica at the same time, land-use patterns representing "a complex creole mosaic, the . . . landscape being composed of intermixed large and small holdings, some laid out on strict geometric principles and others following the natural contours of the land".[15]

The plantation-smallholder mosaic was not as evident in Barbados as in the Windwards. Although small freehold areas existed in Barbados, the prototypical village settlements there were the plantation tenantry zones adjacent to and controlled by individual sugar cane estates. Yet boundaries within the Barbadian lowlands—especially those between parishes—were very important to individual black Barbadians. Parish vestry boards taxed individual landholders for funds to pay for, among other things, local medical relief and poor relief dispensed by parish medical officers. And in more than one case malnourished and sick individuals were directed to proceed (on foot) to distant almshouses in the next parish when local officials had determined or suspected that they resided outside their particular parish boundaries.

Keeping track of the trends in land tenure changes in Grenada—where the increase in smallholders meant a continuing division and subdivision of both previously existing estates as well as heretofore unclaimed Crown Lands—was a daunting problem for local authorities. The confusing land tenure picture there often thwarted the attempts of magistrates to collect house and land taxes. Grenadian smallholders increased their bewilderment by moving their small, wooden-frame houses in order to avoid tax payments, a ploy that rendered tax collection "largely ineffectual, there being considerable arrears and a great deal of friction between those indebted in . . . tax and the officers by whom the law was enforced".[16]

Land boundaries and divisions were even more complicated on St Lucia where squatting was commonplace, not only on Crown Lands but also on lands that had been abandoned by previous owners. Nor was the distinction between privately held land and adjacent Crown Lands entirely clear. Late in 1886, the St Lucia government offered Crown Lands for sale west of Micoud on the island's windward coast; this relatively low-lying area, locally called Jacquin Lands, was attractive to a number of the St Lucians who had returned with savings from Panama. But the owner of nearby Mondesir Estate, Alexander du Boulay, claimed that the Jacquin Lands had actually been a "dependency" of Mondesir for years. Subsequent litigation honoured du Boulay's claim, a legal process that lasted for six years.[17] Complexities in St Lucia's land tenure, moreover, lasted into the early twentieth century and were often attributed to the enduring stamp of earlier French colonization. A local land commission in 1903 concluded that differing metropolitan surveys of the island at different times and a longstanding tradition of interior settlement had created uniqueness in St Lucia where "ungranted and vacant . . . lands intermingle closely with private land and therefore a continuous and uniform Crown boundary line cannot exist here as in the neighbouring Colony of St Vincent whose interior lands were never settled".[18]

Although St Vincent's rugged interior had indeed been less settled than St Lucia's, the boundary between private and Crown Lands in the 1880s there was by no means clear cut; rather, it was complicated by a similarly layered colonial history that characterized the other British Windwards. After St Vincent had been ceded from France to Britain in 1763, a survey of the island was undertaken by Chief Surveyor John Byres, and the 'Byres

Plan' was completed in 1776 (Figure 5.1).[19] The plan (1) delineated the boundary between low-lying arable land and the interior Crown Land that was very "mountainous and uncultivable", (2) designated large portions of the northern and northeastern sections of St Vincent as given "to the Charibs by the Late Treaty in 1773", and (3) indicated a coastal perimeter of "Three Chains" (nearly 200 feet) that normally was controlled by contiguous estates but which could be usurped by the St Vincent government for coastal fortifications and defence facilities.[20] Most important was that the written legend on the face of the Byres Plan itself specified quasi-legal relationships between St Vincent's plantation lands at low elevations and the contiguous, mountainous Crown Lands higher up; although these adjacent Crown Lands were "uncultivable" they could not "otherwise be disposed of but to such [contiguous] Planters without injuring them . . . they are therefore considered by us as appropriated to the Use of the Planter contiguous".

Crucial to understanding St Vincent in the 1880s, the 1776 Byres Plan was still being used there as a legal precedent to enable Vincentian planters to control those black labourers who inhabited hillside plots immediately above the coastal estates. In 1887, Governor Sendall explained to the London Colonial Office that, in the decades immediately after emancipation, slaves' descendants had been allowed to cultivate subsistence crops in the mountains "upon the sole condition that they sold their surplus labour to the planter". With the passage of time, and even though many estates had changed hands, a typical lowland planter of St Vincent in the 1880s, with the aid of the Byres Plan, had thereby come to "usurp more and more of the rights of ownership over lands [above coastal plantations] which had in many cases come to be regarded as part of his estate". And very often "rents came to be charged for the privilege of occupying and cultivating the land".[21]

Sendall's clarification regarding Vincentian land peculiarities had followed the relatively minor 1886 hurricane. The storm had provided him an opportunity to speak out about how important St Vincent's potential peasantry would be for the island's future. This inspiration, moreover, had not been his alone because in 1885 the Colonial Office had favoured a general survey of St Vincent so that small grants of Crown Lands could be made to former estate workers, indicating a shift in land-use that would be "of the utmost importance . . . [to] . . . the prosperity of St Vincent".[22] And the emphasis on a small-scale 'peasant proprietary' for St Vincent of course reflected the shift in British economic thinking after mid nineteenth century

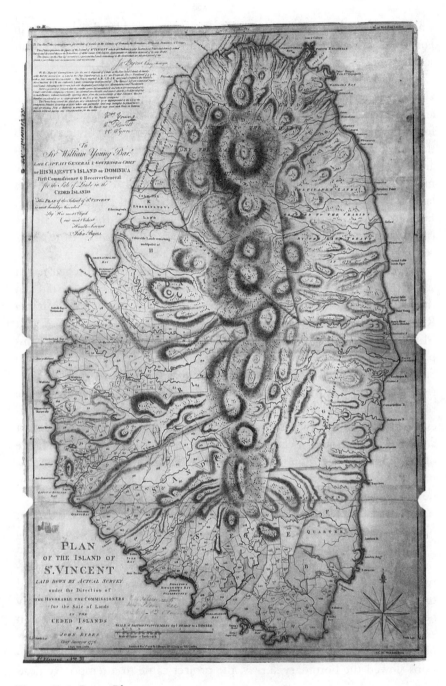

Figure 5.1. Byres Plan

which had also favoured, among other things, smallholder development in Jamaica in the 1870s and 1880s where land was being taken over by small-scale settlers.[23]

In November 1885 Sendall had forwarded to London a proposal from Commander R. Hughes, the acting protector of immigrants in Grenada, and a former government surveyor in the Cape Colony. Hughes proposed, for the princely sum of £3,500, a complete land survey of St Vincent, a job that would be complicated because of the need to disentangle old boundaries. The following June Sendall wrote to London suggesting that a more modest survey, one delimiting the "interior boundary" between private lands and Crown Lands, would be just as practical and far less expensive. Early in 1887, St Vincent's Legislative Council approved the survey of the island's interior boundary, and in February, James F. Mitchell, a British surveyor, arrived in Kingstown to initiate the project.[24]

In March and April, under dry and sunny conditions, Mitchell began surveying the Crown Lands boundary above Alexander Porter's estates in the northeastern quadrant of St Vincent, in the vicinity of the Tourama River and directly east of the Soufrière crater. Porter complained that Mitchell's boundary was farther downslope than on the Byres Plan, a complaint not upheld. By August the survey line had been extended north to Sandy Bay and plans made to extend roads from the lowlands into the interior Crown Lands. At this point Porter demanded compensation for the roads, an appeal similarly denied. Porter, never a favourite with local officials whom he often tried to bully, had opposed the survey from the start and had led the other Vincentian planters to condemn it as a frivolous waste of tax money. At one point, an official at the London Colonial Office, apparently tiring of Porter's obstructionist rantings, simply dismissed his pronouncements as "stupid".[25]

The St Vincent boundary project moved on, a government activity that obviously carried with it much more social import that simply drawing a line on the ground. In March 1888 the local government had requested funds for Crown Lands rangers to patrol and adjudicate land disputes between planters and peasants in the far northeastern corner of St Vincent and to prevent squatting there. By early 1889, the surveyed interior boundary between plantations and government lands extended for 18 miles with an estimated forty yet to survey. Then, as Walter Sendall was replaced by W.F. Hely-Hutchinson as Governor, and as heavy weather and planters' objections slowed the boundary survey, the project came to a temporary dead end. In May 1890 Hely-Hutchinson called in the government surveyor from Trinidad, a Mr de Labastide, to check the mapping work that Mitchell and two associates had accomplished since 1887. De Labastide, noting that the work had been done at seven different scales and on perishable paper that had become frayed and worn, pronounced the entire project "worthless".[26]

That summer de Labastide himself set to work in order to traverse the roads on St Vincent and to establish a boundary line. But four years later, the island's director of surveys noted that the land hunger of potential small-scale settlers in St Vincent still had gone unsatisfied because of (1) the inaccurate surveys of the recent past, (2) the recent illness of a draftsman, and (3) "the most recent usable map of the island is dated 1776".[27] By mid 1897, after the royal commissioners had come and gone, the interior boundary for much of the island finally had been surveyed and a plan sent to London, showing only the far northern and far southern ends of the island unsurveyed. Yet the boundary saga on St Vincent persisted into the early twentieth century; the owner of Camden Park estate in June 1901 had "begun to demand rent" from black settlers cultivating highlands nearby, a demand based "on the old original map of the island known as 'Byres's plan', dated 1776".[28]

On either side of the St Vincent boundary line issue, both literally and figuratively, were the rival claimants for the island, white planters and black workers. And even within the constraints imposed by the legal extension of the Byres Plan, black cultivators claimed their rights to rent land. Lowland planters customarily extracted rents—usually paid monthly—from black squatters above the estates, enlisting police magistrates to collect the fees. Some rent-seeking planters scoured the hills above their estates for squatters, occasionally claiming that their domains stretched all the way to the other side of the island. Black settlers, on the other hand, occasionally asserted usufructuary rights to these rented lands. When planter C.E. Cloke purchased an estate on the northern end of St Vincent in 1886, he evicted members of a nearby village consisting of seventeen mud huts who responded (unsuccessfully) that their several years of rent payments entitled them to stay.[29] And on a number of Vincentian estates there always were a few renters who tilled the same land their fathers had occupied "and in many cases . . . erected permanent houses and planted permanent products" as if the land were their own.[30]

But these few cases hardly satisfied the majority of the black populace who, seeing neighbouring estate lands lying idle because of low sugar prices, had no land of their own to compensate for declining wage possibilities. So when active discussions and rumours began in the 1880s about land being made available on the island, and when actual surveying began, delegations of potential black landholders petitioned officials for land, some of them exhibiting "considerable impatience" over the issue. Even the near riot in Kingstown late in 1891 was in part attributed to land hunger; the governor was convinced that the reason the assembled throng directed their anger against the government was because they were "persuaded that the Government is contemplating nefarious schemes against their welfare . . . [a feeling] . . . mainly attributable to the fact that the land, speaking generally, is in the hands of a small and privileged class".[31] And even when the land issue began to turn in favour of potential smallholders after the royal commissioners had visited St Vincent early in 1897, frustrated blacks were displeased over even minimal legal necessities in obtaining plots. At a well-attended meeting at Barrouallie in January 1898, Governor Alfred Moloney had to explain that potential settlers would have to buy their land plots, thereby countering the rumours of agitators that land in the neighbourhood was to be given away.[32]

Blacks could be forgiven for their frustrations over legal impediments slowing land tenure changes on St Vincent because legal ploys represented the planters' principal defensive strategies to head off change. With Alexander Porter leading the way, the planters objected routinely to the surveying in the 1880s and 1890s, such objections often delaying the survey for up to three weeks depending on the weather. Sometimes planters filed legal complaints, and then when public hearings were to take place, they would be 'called away' to other locales such as the neighbouring Grenadines.[33] Delaying tactics notwithstanding, Vincentian land tenure complexities—as in the other Windwards—often were bewildering and posed their own obstacles to surveying a boundary between private and Crown Lands. In January 1888, the island's administrator, Captain Denton, visited the northern end of the island to assess agricultural activities there in light of Crown Land recently becoming available. He travelled north in a shallow-draft boat, reported a bit of squatting in the neighbourhood, and was impressed with one individual's cocoa holdings. He also described briefly the entangled "control" of one block of land there: "Owia is an arrowroot estate, owned by some persons residing in England of the name of Littledale, and is leased by them to a Mrs Mackie, who in her turn has mortgaged her interest to a firm of London merchants named Anderson."[34]

Sugar Cane

The 1897 Royal Commission had, of course, focused precisely on the economic malaise caused by the steep drop in sugar prices. So the research, questionnaires, testimony and all else associated with the commission—as well as nearly all of the other correspondence between London and the Caribbean colonies in the depression decades—dealt with the region's sugar cane industry first, and everything else trailed behind. On most of the islands, as far as the planters were concerned, sugar was simply the sole economic   activity.

In answer to a written questionnaire submitted by the 1897 commissioners, planter Henry Hale of St Lucia made the point succinctly: "Sugar is the only product which gives employment all the year round for a large number of men and women. All other industries employ small numbers and only at long intervals. Added to this the abandonment of the sugar industry involves the loss of £10,000,000 invested in machinery."[35]

Among Barbados and the Windwards, although the cultivation of sugar cane was by far the most important economic enterprise in the aggregate, the activity itself was concentrated in the lowlands of Barbados, St Lucia and St Vincent. In the former, the growing of cane and initial processing of sugar came as close as possible to monopolizing an island's economy. In response to a printed questionnaire from the 1897 commission regarding the likelihood of "distress" on Barbados in case the sugar industry failed, the planters and government officials there provided the following written answer: "In the event of a general failure of the sugar industry, distress would be universal. *Everything in Barbados depends immediately or ultimately on that industry.* No other industry known to us would afford employment for the dense population."[36]

The production of sugar cane in Barbados and elsewhere was, very obviously, tied closely to external markets, and local cane cultivation transcended particular islands in other ways too. Local agricultural officers and island sugar chemists, for example, compared cane cultivation techniques, plant types and diseases from one island to another, comparisons hardly ever made in relation to subsistence crops. Professor Froude in 1886, moreover, saw in Barbados' intense cultivation of sugar cane a key to the island's 'Englishness', in comparison with its neighbours:

Barbadoes is as unlike in appearance as it is in social condition to Trinidad or the Antilles . . . every square yard of soil is cultivated, and turn your eyes where you

will see houses, sugar canes, and sweet potatoes. Two hundred and fifty years of occupation have imprinted strongly an English character . . . in pleasing contrast
with the conquered islands which we have not taken the trouble to assimilate. In
them remain the wrecks of the French civilisation which we superseded, but we
have planted nothing of our own. Barbadoes, the European aspect of it at any rate,
is English throughout.[37]

In the same year Froude was making his observations, The Reverend
J.H. Sutton Moxly, the chaplain at the British garrison in Barbados, remarked with less exuberance but more insight of the island that "There are
few places in the world in which so much depends on the success or failure
of one industry as in this island." He further suggested that cabled sugar
prices from London to Barbados determined the "social barometer of the
place, a fall or rise of one-fourth a cent in the price of sugar per pound causing a corresponding fall or rise in the cheerfulness of the community".[38]

The external control over Barbados' sugar cane industry explained the
island's internal human geography. Roads, settlement patterns and port facilities all were located to facilitate the growing of sugar cane and the expor-
tation of raw sugar. The island's dense human population was necessary, in
Barbados' antiquated system of sugar production, for the purpose of carrying out all of the steps in local sugar production, from initial field prepara-
tion to the eventual loading of hogsheads of sugar aboard ocean-going vessels, and every other step in between. Barbadian sugar production thus
depended on its high human population density and vice versa; when J.W.
Root in 1899 rejected glib suggestions about the abandonment of Barbadian cane cultivation, he was simply reiterating what others had said in different ways, "There is absolutely nothing to take its place."[39] The organization of the island's labour force, moreover, was directed towards maximizing
sugar production, a generalization that could be extended to sugar cane
growing in the lowlands of St Vincent and St Lucia as well. Seasonality,
punctuality and routine were hallmarks of the sugar cane industries in all of
the region because field and factory activities were tightly linked and closely
coordinated. Overall social coordination and control were inevitable in the
production of plantation sugar cane as it required "careful scheduling at the
top, and the application of iron discipline at the base".[40]

Official queries about the possible results if sugar collapsed really were
unnecessary because, in the depression decades of the late nineteenth century, abysmal conditions on some plantations in the eastern Caribbean already provided grim evidence of what could happen to the region as a whole

7. Barbados cane harvest, *ca.* 1890
Collection: Foreign and Commonwealth Office Library, London.

if sugar failed altogether. In St Vincent, when Alexander Porter allowed his lands (which had been centralized to facilitate cane production) to go without proper tillage, the effect was to "deprive large numbers of labourers of their daily bread, and [to force] them either to starve or to expatriate themselves, leaving their wives and children behind them".[41] At the local level, one could easily blame Porter for his hard-hearted attitude, but the way in which the depression conditions had unfolded on St Vincent also was symptomatic of how thoroughly the insular production of British Caribbean sugar cane was controlled by outsiders, in some ways more so than ever before. According to C.S. Salmon, the regional sugar industry, which always had depended upon infusions of European capital, now could be closely monitored "by cable" by "the distant capitalist in London or Glasgow". And it was their reluctance to advance money through local merchants, not necessarily the indolence of local workers or even local planters, responsible for the dismal grassroots effects of a capital starved sugar cane industry: ". . . ruins strewed about plentifully, bad roads, seedy looking villages, an ill-clad and ill-fed population, all evidently poor, large tracts of good land left vacant, most of the cultivation negligent, native labour emigrating".[42]

Except for occasional small patches of cane that highland subsistence cultivators grew for home use and animal feed, sugar cane in the eastern Caribbean in the 1880s was, as it always has been, a lowland crop. When it was grown above the 500 foot contour in Barbados, such as in the hilly areas of St Thomas and St Andrew or above the west-facing escarpment in St James and St Peter parishes, it usually was 'ratooned', one or more crops growing from the stumps of harvested canes. In the lower areas, such as in the St George valley directly east of Bridgetown, labourers planted individual canes by hand after each harvest season (January to June), a closely supervised and labour intensive activity uninhibited by hilly or steep terrain.[43]

An accounting of the planting-to-harvest routine in Barbados in the late 1800s helps to explain why the crop was able to absorb the time and energies of such a dense human population. Ox-drawn plows usually plowed under stubble from the previous crop before labourers dug each cane hole with hand shovels. As the individual cane cuttings were planted, men and women carried baskets of animal pen manure to the fields and 'forked' this material into the cane beds. Especially after cane varieties became subjected to advanced agricultural research in the 1880s, planters who could afford imported fertilizers had these inputs added by hand to individual cane holes. On occasion, plantation managers sowed leguminous 'catch crops' of beans in the canefields that were harvested and the plants then plowed into the ground to add mulch and nutrients to the soil. After the canes sprouted and the 'tillering' of the plants provided a leafy cover that inhibited excess weeds and provided a shaded microclimate in the individual fields, labourers monitored the progress of the crop, weeding with hoes and hands.[44]

At harvest time, usually fifteen to eighteen months after the cuttings had first been planted, the fields in Barbados came alive with human activity. Black overseers, known as 'gangers', supervised the groups or gangs of (usually male) cane cutters. Young women often were the loaders of the cut cane onto ox-carts, cumbersome wooden vehicles which were the responsibility of male carters. Other women picked up stray canes while younger boys and girls were 'trashers' who did odd jobs in the fields. The many activities did not end in the cane lands but extended to the factory yards where unloaders and trashers were active and numerous. At the mill-yards children's gangs accomplished routine cleaning up and similar jobs, their activities normally supervised by older women.[45]

The intense hand cultivation of the sugar estates in St Vincent's lowlands was, according to Professor J.B. Harrison, comparable to that in Barbados. Harrison, who had had long experience in Barbados before becoming an agricultural officer in British Guiana, visited St Vincent in 1895 and was favourably impressed with the high state of hand tillage there which he termed "garden cultivation". Yet different from the coastal clays of British Guiana or even the limestone based soils of Barbados, St Vincent's porous volcanic soils retained little moisture, a physical condition that had worsened because the island's soils had not been properly maintained. Harrison considered the 'green manure' method on St Vincent useless and urged that massive amounts of pen manure be added to the island's cane lands in order to increase their capacity to absorb and hold water. He also suggested to some planters the copious use of ammonium sulphate to increase Vincentian soil fertility, although he was uncertain how helpful that advice would be for St Vincent's light, porous soils.[46]

Sugar cane growing in the lowlands of the St Lucian valleys differed from Barbados and St Vincent in important ways. By the late 1890s, estate-focused cane cultivation in St Lucia had withdrawn to enclaves surrounding the large factories in the Cul-de-Sac Valley, Roseau Valley and at Dennery, as well as Vieux Fort. Overall sugar production in St Lucia had shrunk by the late 1890s to roughly half that of the early 1880s, and some of the canes ground at the large usines on the island were being cultivated by black and brown cane farmers.

Although its output in exported sugar had been reduced, St Lucia by 1897 no longer produced the old-fashioned open pan or muscovado sugar that still came from Barbados and St Vincent. Over the previous decade, roughly thirty St Lucian muscovado estates had ceased operation, their lands taken up by small-scale cultivators. The new factories were equipped with modern machinery that turned out "vacuum-pan centrifugal sugar for the American market". And the smoke-blackened chimneys that towered above the St Lucian lowland steam factories—which housed filters, drying pans, evaporators and heating vats, all tended by European-trained sugar chemists and engineers—created an even sharper contrast than before with the island's upland subsistence communities of black hoe farmers and charcoal burners.[47]

Similar modernization had not come to St Vincent and only piecemeal to Barbados. The antique water-mills on St Vincent produced only muscovado sugar, one more indication to London that the island's future was hopeless unless the stranglehold on its economy by the island's backward-looking plantocracy was released. Barbados however presented an altogether different situation. The Barbadian sugar industry had evolved incrementally on the island for well over 200 years, and Barbadian sugar manufacturing in the 1890s, using a series of copper boiling pans or 'tayches', with workmen standing by with hand-held dippers and skimmers, had not changed appreciably since the days of slavery. But the sugar depression was squeezing everyone, and even wage reductions could not protect the Barbadian plantocracy from having to contemplate major changes.

In 1897, Barbados counted 430 sugar cane estates with an estimated islandwide total of 106,560 acres, each estate thereby averaging about 248 acres. Steam power crushed canes on only 99 of the estates, and windmills persisted on the remainder, the prevalence of wind power helping to explain why there had been so little estate consolidation and why small plantation size still was so common on Barbados. Only 6 percent of Barbados' sugar output in 1897 was modern 'centrifugal sugar', the remainder muscovado. And the many tasks in a typical wind-powered mill and its adjoining boiling house on Barbados were obvious if anachronistic symptoms of the island's dense population. Estimates were that roughly twenty-five men working (at pitifully low wages) sixty to seventy hours per week in such a factory complex could produce 10 tons of muscovado sugar. And suggestions from London that Barbados' sugar industry be modernized with central mills often were viewed as outsiders' meddling and usually with anxiety because no one could predict what might happen if such upsetting change was introduced into an island that had gone well beyond being overpopulated.[48]

Whereas the overpopulation and cumulative overdevelopment of Barbados based on old-fashioned sugar production technologies had severely restricted the island's plantocracy in adopting new techniques, these geographical constraints did not inhibit active agricultural experimentation with sugar cane plants. And in the 1880s, in response to a series of cane disease outbreaks in the West Indies and elsewhere, Barbados emerged as one of the most important sugar cane research locales in the world. At the agricultural experiment station at Dodds, the Barbadian agronomists J.R. Bovell and J.B. Harrison directed their energies in four interrelated directions: (1) testing various manures on cane, (2) comparing different cane varieties, (3) raising and cross-breeding new cane varieties from seedlings, and (4) investigating plant diseases.[49]

The scientific research accomplished by Bovell and Harrison provided new sugar cane types to be cultivated in Barbados and formed the basis for cane research there well into the twentieth century. For most of the nineteenth century the Bourbon or Otaheite cane, introduced to Barbados from the Pacific by way of Jamaica in 1796, had nearly excluded all other cane types on Barbados. Then as a series of diseases attacked the Bourbon elsewhere in the Western hemisphere, Barbadian authorities imported other cane varieties for trial tests late in the 1880s in anticipation of similar troubles there. It was not until 1890 that the Bourbon canes on Barbados were diagnosed as suffering from 'rot', probably from a fungus. Then many Barbadian planters, under advice from the researchers at Dodds, turned to another cane variety known locally as White Transparent, a variety more resistant to fungus disease. And Bovell's celebrated cane seedling research, traced back to observations that others had made on Barbados as early as 1858, involved cross-breeding new cane varieties later planted successfully in Barbados, British Guiana and elsewhere in the region.[50]

The intimate relationships between commercial and scientific interests in Barbadian sugar cane in the 1800s represented an extension of a British fascination with the eastern Caribbean's economic botany that had begun well over a century earlier. The first botanical garden in the Western hemi-

8. Windmill, St Lucy parish, Barbados, *ca.* 1890
By permission of the Syndics of Cambridge University Library.

sphere had been established near Kingstown, St Vincent, in 1766, and for the next half century the St Vincent garden played an important role in the transfer and dissemination throughout the Caribbean region of commercially useful and also ornamental tropical plants from Asia and the Pacific and from the circum-Caribbean zone as well. The St Vincent garden's directors worked closely with the botanists at Kew Gardens, and the St Vincent garden also profited from the brief French occupation of the island in the early 1780s because the local French commander arranged for the transfer of species from other French tropical possessions to St Vincent. The most famous event for the St Vincent garden was in January, 1793, when Captain Bligh, commanding the *Providence*, brought 465 breadfruit plants to the director, some of which—nourished by St Vincent's volcanic soil—began to bear fruit in less than two years.

The St Vincent garden suffered from neglect early in the nineteenth century and by mid-century could hardly be distinguished within the tangle of semi-wild tropical foliage immediately north of Kingstown. Then in the depression decades late in the century, with renewed interest in the commercial possibilities of non-sugar cane plants, new government sponsored gardens were established in several islands in the eastern Caribbean. The St Vincent garden was resurrected in 1890 by Governor Hely-Hutchinson, who had served the Crown in Fiji and New South Wales before coming to the Caribbean, and who himself was a keen observer of the local environment. The new botanic curator was Henry Powell (who would later notice the plunging barometer in his office at the botanic station during the 1898 hurricane) who within a year had nearly restored the St Vincent garden to its earlier beauty and neatness.[51]

A similar botanical garden was established near Castries, St Lucia, in 1887, its function to serve as an area for the propagation of important and existing plants of possible commercial value. And a garden also had been founded near St George's, Grenada, the year before. In the next decade the Grenada Garden's curator travelled extensively through the island, his visits to small-scale farmers reported to have beneficial results. These kinds of efforts and economic functions had been foreseen by Daniel Morris, former director of the Jamaica botanic garden and future agricultural advisor to the 1897 royal commission. Writing in *Nature* in 1887, Morris had emphasized the need, given the British Caribbean's dangerous reliance on the economic homogeneity of now-depressed sugar cane, to develop a series of local gardens and botanic stations that would cooperate in the development of new plants and thus "develop more fully than heretofore their natural resources".[52]

But the potential agricultural diversity represented by the new botanic stations was only a thin line of defence against a monolithic regional sugar industry now centuries old. And sugar's persistence had made its possible downfall all the worse. Economics, conventional agricultural wisdom and biology had thus converged in the eastern Caribbean in the 1880s in joint condemnation of sugar cane monoculture and its susceptibility to collapse. The sugar depression's lowered wages and their grim grassroots results—unrelieved by non-existent complementary economic activities—were everywhere. Longstanding European agricultural practices—not to mention the subsistence strategies followed by small producers in the tropics—similarly deplored reliance on only one crop. In 1871 Charles Kingsley had warned that the exclusive cultivation of sugar cane in the islands—and the crop's sudden and total vulnerability to drought or hurricane—violated the time-honoured practices of European agricultural diversification that condemned the farmer "who does not stand on four legs, and, if he can, on five".[53]

Now the potentially disastrous biological effects of crop homogeneity were becoming all too apparent in the lowlands of Barbados and the Windwards. The fungus disease that had been identified in Barbados' canefields in 1890 had spread over much of the rest of the island by 1893. Then in the following year, fungus disease and drought had combined so that John Bovell was unable to tell which of the two (or a combination thereof) was responsible for the sickly appearance of many of the fields. Bovell travelled to London, discussed the problems with old tropical hands at Kew, and returned with the not terribly new suggestion that perhaps "crop rotation" may save the day. Suggestions as to the adoption of non-sugar crops ranged far and wide, including one from Barbados' Governor Hay for indigo. A sugar cane diseases bill in 1894, calling for, among other things, the government monitoring of Barbadian canefields, failed in the island's planter-dominated House of Assembly. Although the well-being of Barbados' 200,000 inhabitants (99 percent of whom had no vote) hung in the balance, debate in the house bordered on fantasy. How could cane diseases brought to Barbados by an act of divine providence, ran one popular argument, be countered by mere human law?[54]

Yet men, not God, had been responsible for the creation of an agricultural monoculture on Barbados that was defenceless against drought, fungus and financial decisions made in London and New York. The island's 1894 sugar cane crop did not collapse altogether, although the volume of cane harvested in 1895 was the lowest in over two decades. Nor did the island's labouring population explode into rebellion, although the incidence of 'potato raids' and similarly organized violence and lawlessness increased noticeably in the wake of the island's 1894–95 sugar shortfall.[55]

One way to limit the spread of fungus in the canefields, according to most of the agricultural researchers at the time, was to burn the infected plants. Yet burning sugar cane stalks, or even entire fields suspected of harbouring injurious microorganisms, risked unleashing a cure much more injurious than the disease. This danger was of course the runaway cane fire, an occurrence that had been dreaded ever since sugar cane had been planted in the Caribbean. And although legislation in the sugar colonies stipulated that canes were not to be grown too close to roads and settlements, everyone knew that on a breezy day when the fields were ripe and dry, cane fires could jump roads and burn dozens of acres. Cane fires depended, obviously, on fire or ignition, but the presence of acres of undifferentiated ripe fuel—another potential curse of the homogeneity of lowland sugar cane cultivation—was the more crucial ingredient.

Burning sugar cane was not part of the pre-harvest routine to eliminate cane trash or pests in the eastern Caribbean in the 1890s. So when a committee of plantation owners met at the Planters' Club in Kingstown, St Vincent, in April 1894 and outlined a plan of burning throughout the island to reduce the incidence of cane disease there, the decision had been made from "dire necessity". Two months earlier, when Professor Harrison had visited St Vincent, he had recommended selected burning of the many canes whose stalks and stems had been attacked by fungi as well as insects. At the same time, he had warned of extensive burning of cane trash in the island's fields because it probably would reduce even further the quality of St Vincent's porous volcanic soil.[56]

Although both disease and fire represented threats that could lead to the immediate collapse of oversimplified sugar cane monocultures, burning carried with it the potential for malicious human intervention as well. The cane fire, as it had throughout the region's plantation history, helped inspire the infectious urge for the destruction of a planter's crop, and the terrifying image of a blazing Caribbean canefield symbolized more than a hint of revolt and rebellion. In any case, as the sugar cane recession deepened in Barbados, the incidence of cane fires increased (Table 5.1). The fires were said to be associated with three general causes: (1) sparks from the railway locomotives that ran east from Bridgetown through the cane lands of south central Barbados; (2) workers' carelessness with cooking fires and smoking; and (3) "those due to unknown causes but probably to acts of incendiarism".

The first two causes could be controlled, but the latter was impossible to prevent. Everyone knew, moreover, that a cane fire was one of few ways estate workers could vent their frustrations. Although a 'Fire Enquiry Act' had been passed by Barbados' Legislature in 1879, planters considered it unwise to investigate too deeply into cane fires for two interrelated reasons: first, it would provide ample opportunity for labourers to air their grievances; and secondly, it might leave the impression that cane fires were the only way to get planters' attention. As the number of Barbadian cane fires increased into the 1890s, however, their frequency and cumulative crop destruction was sufficiently serious to threaten the island's economy. For years it had been customary for planters to purchase policies with local insurance companies to cover all or part of their crop value, transactions involving premiums that were very expensive as the crop was planted but which decreased as harvest approached. The frequency of depression-induced cane fires on the island increased to the point that on 6 March 1901, Governor Hodgson met with top island officials and representatives of insurance companies who had suggested that, owing to cane fire damage, they may have "to consider their position and decide whether Insurances could be continued on existing terms or continued at all".[57]

Official attitudes toward incendiarism in the Barbadian cane lands then changed from benign neglect to attempted prevention. By late in 1901 a government sponsored system of surveillance on the island included secret patrols on horseback, random monitoring by police detectives, the transfer of police constables to new districts where they were not so well known, the distribution of handbills to school children, and the offer of monetary rewards. None of these strategies was successful because black Barbadians, even in times of acute distress, were unwilling to report one another to white planters or police officials.[58]

As with cane fires, few other characteristics of the Barbadian lowlands could be explained without reference to the island's sugar cane monoculture. Perhaps the most distressing were those associated with the pitifully meager diets of members of the black working class and their associated needs to pilfer small amounts of cane to chew or even to eat in order to supplement locally grown and imported foods. The ecological domination by sugar cane also was felt elsewhere in the region at the village level, where

Table 5.1 Barbados Cane Fires, 1891-1901

	Number of Fires	Acres Damaged	Number of Arrests	Caused by Railway	Caused by Accident	Cause Unknown (Probably Arson)
1891	170	555	5	3	47	120
1892	86	294.5	2	0	18	68
1893	71	189.75	1	0	19	52
1894	73	153	3	0	30	43
1895	142	377.75	3	0	22	120
1896	68	142.75	0	0	21	47
1897	105	253.75	1	0	51	54
1898	118	302	2	0	43	75
1899	147	498.75	3	10	45	92
1900	243	715.5	8	19	44	180
1901	189	715.75	6	33	46	110
Total	1,412	4,198.5	34	65	386	961

Source: C.O. 28/254, no. 89, "Cane Fires," 21 May 1901, p 419.

it counted most. For example, the mongoose had been introduced into St Vincent early in the 1870s to rid the Vincentian canefields of rats. By the late 1890s however the mongoose, uninhibited by the absence of predators on the island, had thrived, multiplied, refocused its foraging activities, and was actively destroying many of the pigs, chickens and even subsistence gardens maintained by black Vincentians, a perverse extension of the island's sugar cane monoculture directly into black villagers' subsistence activities.[59]

Even after it was abandoned in favour of other crops, sugar cane's legacy was often stark because it left behind erosion-susceptible landscapes where forests originally had thrived. For all of its problems and social inequities, sugar cane had anchored the soil better than the clean-row crops that had taken its place. In the Choiseul district of southwestern St Lucia, in mid 1901, sugar cane recently had given way to cotton. The subsequently high rates of sheet erosion there and the denuded appearance of the landscape around Choiseul moved the local authorities to remark that "the whole country looks a desert".[60]

The remarks from the St Lucian authorities about Choiseul and environs also point out that, although sugar cane dominated the eastern Caribbean lowlands, it was not the only crop cultivated there. As sugar cane's acreage withdrew into peri-factory enclaves in the St Lucian lowlands, some farmers there switched to cacao as well as cotton. On Carriacou, corn, cotton and livestock dominated the drought prone lowlands. On Barbados, black estate labourers grew a variety of food crops in their tiny subsistence plots within the plantation tenantries, and limited estate cultivation of yams and potatoes on Barbadian estates even led to exports of these items to Trinidad and British Guiana.[61] Less than a century after its introduction into the region, breadfruit groves dominated the dank ravines and small valleys where village lands were located. On St Vincent, appropriately, the breadfruit was so important in 1887 that "it provides in season sufficient provision for the sustenance of the labouring classes".[62]

Particular mention should be made of arrowroot (*Maranta arundinacea*), a New World root crop transferred from Amerindian to Afro-Caribbean cultivators during the seventeenth and eighteenth centuries. A perennial, growing 3 to 5 feet high, arrowroot was easily propagated by cuttings, and its rhizomes yielded a high quality starch with food and medicinal value, and it later was exported as a thickener for soups and sauces. Arrowroot was most important in the St Vincent lowlands in the decades after slavery where it thrived on the island's ashen soils and was grown mainly by small-scale black cultivators on the margins of sugar cane estates. The crop was sufficiently important on St Vincent that it was enumerated (in numbers of barrels) as an export item in the final report of the 1897 royal commission along with cocoa, spices and livestock. In the 1870s and 1880s, the success and prosperity of small-scale arrowroot producers on St Vincent had inspired several owners of large estates to cultivate it, thereby driving down the price through overproduction. Indeed, a letter to a Kingstown newspaper in 1888 warned that a major agricultural problem for St Vincent was "the mistake of putting all its eggs in the cane and arrowroot baskets".[63]

Despite the presence of other crops, however, the lowlands of the eastern Caribbean were cane lands, and sugar cane estate owners—despite the widespread advice to diversify and the warnings about sugar's imminent demise—seemed trapped in a downward spiral that they themselves were quickening. In compiling the annual report for Barbados in 1897, colonial secretary Ralph Williams offered that the neat and orderly appearance of the island was masking the "distress which underlies it". Williams pointed out that Barbados was a closely tended garden with "hardly an acre uncultivated". But a hard look at some of the buildings and plantation houses revealed the neglect, wear and loss that sugar was creating. "Of course, the secret of it" suggested Williams "is that the industry is eating up the last vestige of its capital."[64] Apparently Williams considered the Barbadian planters as having passed the point of diminishing returns, their efforts now irrationally counterproductive as they attempted to cope with unprecedented economic problems in old-fashioned ways, by driving the land harder and harder as they always had done in the past.

Human Population Density

During the four days of hearings in Bridgetown, in February 1897, perhaps the most oft-repeated comment the royal commissioners heard about Barbados—other than that of the near total dependence on sugar cane—was how crowded and dense the island's human population was. The point was all the more obvious after the commission's first stop in British Guiana where its members had been apprised of that colony's large, lightly inhabited interior, and how it beckoned further development. Of course the commissioners knew that Barbados was crowded from their own first hand experiences, their earlier hearings in London, and all that they had read in the

Colonial Office archives. But witness after witness in Bridgetown described the Barbadian labour force as "swarming" or "superabundant". These terms, furthermore, seemed understatements for an island of only 166 square miles whose human population for 1901 would be estimated at over 195,000.[65]

One needed a sense of history to appreciate fully the overcrowding on Barbados, a subject that has fascinated observers both before and since. The geographer David Lowenthal, for example, has attributed much of the explanation of Barbados' population profile to "historical inertia". During the 1897 hearings, however, Archibald Fitzdonald Dowridge, a "Master Taylor" residing in Bridgetown, combined history with outrage in describing the island's long-term population pressures. Dowridge described overcrowding in the island homes as "a notorious fact and crying shame" that was an object of copious public discussion but no official action whatever. He further offered that "Our ancestors were brought here for nearly 200 years to toil under the most harrowing conditions" for which neither they nor their descendants ever had been remunerated, although the Caribbean planters at emancipation had been paid their £20 million "merely to mitigate the form of robbery and slavery".[66]

Probably Dowridge's statement was tolerated as an angry outburst rather than appreciated for its painful accuracy. And it is difficult to know how thoroughly Colonial Office officials, including the 1897 commissioners, appreciated that Barbadian population densities, as well as those elsewhere in the British Caribbean, had been created by earlier and ongoing imperial economic strategies. It was not as if this long view was unknown in available reading materials. C.S. Salmon, the former official who had served the Crown throughout the tropics, had written in the 1880s of how postemancipation Indian immigration into the Caribbean had artificially driven down wages to the detriment of the entire region's workforce. Salmon also pointed out how the region's fragmented insularity had helped to create different population densities of workers in discrete places, often separating "the demand from the supply". Salmon's early remarks also may be regarded as theoretical forerunners to academic exchanges of the late twentieth century regarding comparative postemancipation population densities in the British Caribbean and their effects upon varying types of labour coercion.[67]

But the commissioners during their stay in Bridgetown were, after all, more interested in contemporaneous assessments of people/land relationships on Barbados and the many ways these relationships manifested themselves. Perhaps the most obvious way was simply in the appearance of the land. Only the year before, the colony's emigration committee had stated flatly that Barbados' population had now cultivated all of the island; there was no "waste land" toward which more people could turn.[68] Similar comments abounded regarding Barbados' cultural landscape. Professor Froude had provided a positive, even cheerful portrayal of the island's overworked countryside:

The soil was clean, every inch of it, as well hoed and trenched as in a Middlesex market garden . . . vegetables enough are raised in Barbados to keep the cost of living incredibly low . . . The people were thick as rabbits in a warren; women with loaded baskets on their heads laughing and chirruping, men driving donkey carts, four donkeys abreast, smoking their early pipes as if they had not a care in the world, as, indeed, they have not.[69]

Of course more serious analyses were available as to Barbados' population predicament. The island's demographic 'distress', a term used increasingly in the 1890s to describe Barbados, could simply be attributed to declining economic opportunities. The Barbados House of Assembly in 1895 had pointed out to the Colonial Secretary that "the population of the island has attained its present enormous proportions" under different economic conditions and that depression sugar prices were now unable to sustain the population as had earlier, more favourable prices. This message was also one more way the plantocracy could complain to London about bounty-fed European beet sugar.[70]

Population problems and their possible solutions aside, Barbados' overcrowdedness in the 1890s and official commentary about the high human population density had come to be associated with having broad explanatory value, even revealing the essence of Barbadian culture. Put more simply, the many people packed onto the island was thought to provide the scientific explanation for a competitive trait among Barbadians that was lacking in other West Indians. The crude, Darwinian overtones were perhaps most obvious in some of the parish medical reports that provided clinical views of Barbadian ill health, not necessarily in terms of a hemmed-in, malnourished populace, but of physical, interpersonal competition. In contemplating the high mortality rates along the drought stricken littoral of St Philip parish in 1894, the parish doctor remarked on the absence of any particular disease, claiming that "This terrible mortality . . . is due almost entirely to the weak ones being crowded out of existence in the fierce struggle of life."[71]

The crowdedness of the island influenced not only health and well-being, but it also was said to shape the Barbadian's bold personality and his characteristic aggressiveness:

Here, where two hundred thousand people dwell upon less than two hundred square miles of land; here on an island more densely inhabited than any spot in the world,—save China,—there is no place for the indolent lackadaisical, easy-going, come-day, go-day, God-save-Sunday negro of the other islands. It is a case of work or starve for every man, woman, and child, and, as the man of color has an inborn horror of an empty stomach, he chooses the lesser of two evils and works.[72]

Many similar published comments at the time reinforced the point that dense population—or, put another way, a shortage of cultivable land—was the explanatory variable that made black Barbadians tick. In a discussion among colonial officials of the Windwards in 1893, the possibility was raised that industrious Barbadians might take up the isolated interiors of those islands. St Lucia's administrator, A.F. Gouldsbury, was doubtful. Gouldsbury agreed wholeheartedly that it was "the pressure of population" that forced the Barbadian to be "industrious and hard-working while living in Barbados", but he doubted that "these desirable qualities would continue to exist to the same degree if he were relieved from the stern necessity of continuous daily toil".[73] A decade later a writer describing the entire region echoed Gouldsbury's (and others') sentiments: the Barbadian was of "a different nature to other islanders" because of his "hard struggle . . . among . . . a crowd, where the weakest goes to the wall" as opposed to cultural characteristics on "another island where land is a drug and population is needed".[74]

The supposed soporifical effect of land availability was an apparent variation on the bounteous tropical environment theme traceable to the writings of observers such as Thomas Carlyle. But in this case one did not have to appeal to the tenuous, hazy relationships among climate, environmental fecundity and human behavior. If Barbadian drive and aggressiveness were products of the need to cope with overcrowdedness—an assumption widely shared—then the opposite probably was true. In any case, that was what Governor Hely-Hutchinson of the Windwards feared in a confidential memorandum in 1890 speculating on what might happen in St Vincent if the momentum for the formation of a black peasantry kept building. It was important that the labourers be freed from the tyrannical control by the estate managers, Hely-Hutchinson surmised, but if they got their own land, they would "become lazy and indolent, [and] work as little as possible".[75]

Condescending, racist terminology framed the overpopulated Barbadian landscape issue. Throughout Barbados, black workers and their families 'swarmed', a term commonly used in the late nineteenth century to describe the movements among individuals within "tribes of men . . . subject to such periodical migrations as are witnessed in the northern grey squirrel and the Norwegian lemming".[76] Of the many children who inhabited Bridgetown with no visible means of support and who occasionally pilfered food, they "infested" the city (according to the inspector general of police in 1892) and preferred "an idle and dissolute life".[77] The many men frequenting the waterfront in the 1890s, hoping to earn a bit of money hauling freight or baggage, were invariably characterized as 'loafers' and 'idlers'. Dr F.B. Archer, the medical officer for the Bridgetown area, succinctly identified these underemployed men for the visiting royal commissioners: "They are the scum of the population."[78]

But Barbadians were not scum, lemmings or population ratios, and it would be inappropriate to suggest that every white official was indifferent to or did not notice that, despite desperately crowded conditions, many blacks on the island took pride in their houses and the upkeep of their tenantry grounds. Similar feelings also were common on St Vincent where an identity with particular village communities was "deeply ingrained" in a typical black villager there who "likes to live in a village near to his church or meeting-house, to have constant intercourse with his friends, and to send his children to school".[79] The lowlands of St Vincent, furthermore, were very densely populated with black labourers, a demographic reality that became grimly apparent when some of the Vincentian planters had begun to curtail planting in response to low sugar prices, allowing the land to lie fallow. When that happened, the villagers on St Vincent did not necessarily display the hard work that some officials felt would be forthcoming if only the labourers were pushed by necessity to the work-or-starve choice that they had interpreted for Barbados. According to Dr W. Bruce-Austin, a Vincentian medical officer testifying before the 1897 royal commissioners, much the opposite was true:

During the last few years . . . since the decline of the sugar cultivation . . . the labourer, naturally indolent, has become absolutely lazy and indifferent; he is half starved, half clothed, and sits all day on his plot of land indifferent to surrounding circumstances; his health and his character are rapidly deteriorating from sloth and starvation; he refuses to work for the small wage offered to him (15 to 16 cents a day) for what he complains is very hard labour, and declares that he would rather starve than work for that wage.[80]

Although some government spokesmen seemed sensitive to these complexities and ambiguities among lowland plantation labourers in the eastern Caribbean, the failure of black men and women there in the late 1800s to fit oversimplified geographical stereotypes confounded theoretical schemes concocted by colonial administrators. Matching 'excess' peoples with 'empty' lands, after all, seemed a sensible planning strategy. The sugar cane industry of St Lucia, for example, always was chronically short of labour early in the 1880s, and at one point the local administrator had called for the introduction of Chinese workers to solve the problem.[81]

Yet why import Chinese, or, for that matter, the Indian 'coolies' each year, from the other side of the world when nearby Barbados, as nearly everyone acknowledged, had far more people than it should? Barbadian seamen and a few emigrants already had settled in St Lucia by the early 1880s, and the harbour renovation and associated coaling activities at Castries in the ensuing decade had attracted hundreds more. Further, the Barbadian propensity to emigrate was well known. Although precise data were lacking, it was well understood that hundreds of Barbadians annually left the island to harvest sugar cane in British Guiana. Their actions, furthermore, were not difficult to understand; migration was an obvious way residents of an overpopulated island could cope with the competitive stress created by crowdedness. Encouraging or channelling Barbadian migration to the right places within the Eastern Caribbean could thereby even out people/land ratios in two places at once. The idea became very attractive during the 1894–95 drought in Barbados, when Governor Hay of Barbados convened the emigration commission with the intent eventually to send some of the Barbadians elsewhere. The Colonial Office endorsement was positive, suggesting that the scheme might have regional implications as well. "Some more effort ought to be made to replace Indian Coolies by Barbadians", suggested one London official. The strategy seemed reasonable because if the region's sugar industry collapsed it would be desirable "to introduce as few Coolies as possible . . . [and] . . . Barbadians would much more readily find other occupation if the worst came to the worst".[82]

The emigration scheme failed because, as officials would learn after the 1898 hurricane on Barbados and St Vincent, when it was not their idea "there is . . . a curious reluctance on the part of the labourers to emigrate".[83] One reason was lack of incentive, other than exhortation, to leave friends and families for inadequately known and quite different destinations from their home islands. Another was the distinct possibility of receiving cool receptions at other places. When the several Barbadian officials assessing possible nearby destinations for Barbadian settlers arrived in Dominica early in 1895 they were pleased to note "an abundance of fertile well-watered land" that was "easily accessible". The environmental amenities on that rainy and mountainous island were however unmatched by the attitudes of most of the residents of Dominica "some going so far as to tell us plainly, they did not want any Barbadian immigrants".[84]

Given Barbados' well-known population pressures and the Colonial Office's receptivity to migration schemes, it is unsurprising that Barbadian officials attempted to rid the island of some of its more unsavory elements. A law passed in 1883 by the Barbadian legislators authorized reformatory boys from the island to be sent elsewhere for 'apprenticeship' after they served local jail terms. Since their parents had allowed them to become wards of the local government, permission to send the boys away could be "dispensed with", especially in light of the "fully stocked" nature of the local labour market. Some of the boys were sent to Grenada in the late 1880s, but an attempt by Barbados' Governor Hay to send a larger number of reformatory apprentices to Trinidad in 1898 was rejected by officials in Port of Spain.[85]

Health, Mortality and Elevation

The high human population densities in Barbados' lowlands were related, in the minds of most observers, directly to ill health and high death rates (Appendix A). Several witnesses appearing before the 1897 commission reconfirmed this perceived relationship. Dr Charles Hutson, a poor law inspector in Barbados for seventeen years, attributed most of the deaths to typhoid, acknowledged that he considered the island's infant mortality rate very high, and suggested that these conditions probably would exist so long as Barbados was overcrowded. Archibald F. Dowridge augmented his remarks about crowding within workers' houses by noting that "The food of the labourer is inferior and unsuited to supply the waste of physical strength engendered by outdoor daily labour under a burning tropical sun."[86]

It was not that low elevations themselves were to blame; Hutson had told the commissioners, for instance, "I do not think that the colony is naturally an unhealthy one." But the socioeconomic characteristics of Barbados, features that the island's low-lying, fertile and accessible landscape had encouraged and sustained, were ecologically detrimental to its resident human workforce. Sugar cane had outcompeted subsistence crops, leaving the labourers as dangerously dependent on imported foodstuffs as during slavery. Plantation wages purchased imported foods so the January to June harvest season was still the best time of the year. But if drought, cane diseases, insect pests or a combination of any of these recurring hazards attacked the growing sugar cane, labourers were without sufficient wages for food imports, and often their tiny subsistence gardens had been similarly affected.

Another reason that the crop season was best for black Barbadian labourers and those inhabiting islands similarly devoted to sugar cane was that cane cuttings were plentiful from January to June, and sugar juice augmented the meager diets for cane workers and their families. On St Vincent's lowland estates, a black worker was allowed "a certain quantity of syrup for his family", and, different from the dead season of the year when wages (and therefore imported food) were in short supply, Vincentian cane workers' physical conditions were said to improve: "During the period of preparing the sugar, the labourer almost lives on the saccharine matter, and there is a marked improvement in his health."[87]

Yet the geographical perversity of food deficient sugar cane islands carried with it, along with ill health in the dead seasons owing to malnourishment, a certain social pathology at times related directly to the use (and need) of canes to supplement workers' diets. A statistical report of floggings on Barbados for 1901 showed that 685 whippings of boys (some as young as eight years old) with tamarind rods had been administered, chiefly for pilfering food from October to December when low wages and little work had curtailed food purchases and increased hunger and anxiety. Yet such punishable 'crimes' continued into the cane season as well; large-scale 'praedial larceny' in February 1902, was very noticeable, "with few exceptions . . . confined to the theft of Sugar Cane, nearly always in small quantities. Hunger as often as not is the incentive."[88]

A factor only indirectly related to topography but immediately detrimental to the welfare of lowland sugar cane workers was the duty imposed on imported food. C.S. Salmon had argued vociferously against import duties early in the 1880s, asserting that these taxes added 40 percent to workers' household food expenses. He insisted that the duties lowered standards of living and also represented a loss in estate labour power because the resultant tax burdened diet for the individual worker was "manifestly insufficient for genuine labour".[89] Barbadian officials were unmoved by such arguments from Salmon and others. The general welfare of individual workers and the financial health of the colony, went their argument, were interrelated because more food purchased meant more duty collected. Yet the Barbadian government, with its hemmed-in human population, could rely on a sizeable threshold of food imports simply because of the island's large population, even if many were ill-nourished. The worker-duty revenue interrelationship was, furthermore, groundless because duties on imports could be raised peremptorily. In June 1896, for example, duties on all imports into Barbados were increased by 20 percent despite depressed wages after the 1895 and 1896 sugar crop shortfalls had reduced overall taxation revenues.[90]

Whatever the reasons for food shortages, the lowland estate workers without access to assured sources of subsistence suffered mightily during the depression years of the late 1800s. Innumerable reports by parish medical officials in Barbados indicated outbreaks of minor illnesses, gastric and intestinal disorders, slow-healing cuts and minor injuries, all symptomatic of malnourishment. Similar conditions in St Vincent were described in 1897 by Dr W.F. Newsam, who had practised medicine there for twenty years but had seen notable deterioration only in the past decade. Unlike in 1887, when "the physique of the labourer . . . was far better than it is in these days", Newsam reported numerous Vincentian estate workers "with scrofulous ulcers, and with broken-down constitutions, the greater part of whom have ultimately to be passed on as incurable to the Pauper Asylum".[91]

The most tragic dimension of ill health in the Barbadian lowlands was the high infant mortality (Table 5.2). Dramatically more frequent than in the neighbouring high islands, babies' deaths in Barbados were not counted separately as part of official records until 1895. Yet local medical officers could not help but notice that in some years, such as during the 1894—95 drought, and in some parishes, infant mortality rates soared over 50 percent. Poor nutrition, unsanitary conditions and parental neglect (a common 'reason' cited in officers' records) contributed to the high infant death rates. The local system of poor and medical relief also bore some of the responsibility because the onus often fell upon mothers to carry feverish babies long distances for treatment:

The high death rate amongst small children is frequently referred to by our Parochial Medical Officers . . . I often note in the journals that the Inspectors refuse to call the Doctor, giving as their reason that they consider the child small enough to be carried to the dispensary by the mother . . . I think that it is by no means improbable that the exposure entailed in bringing out the little ones is oftentimes responsible for a death which might perhaps have been avoided if the doctor had been called.[92]

Overall death and morbidity rates were high throughout Barbados, but the most vivid descriptions of poor health conditions came from the dry, low-lying parishes at the extreme northern (St Lucy) and southern (Christ Church and St Philip) ends of the island. And a rough rule of thumb among Barbadian officials was that health conditions improved as a function of elevation, a more healthy ambiance found at higher altitudes. The colony's Colonial Secretary G.R. LeHunte, in summarizing the state of the island after drought stricken 1894, lamented the associated typhoid and dysentery outbreaks and explained that the arrival of the autumn rains had done little to cleanse the island. That was because those rains "were insufficient to either carry into the sea the vegetable matter washed down from the higher to the lower lands, or to drive the disease-producing germ sufficiently deep into the ground to render it innocuous". LeHunte concluded his summary with what he termed a "topographical analysis" of Barbadian death rates: these statistics had increased from 16.7 to 19.6 per 1000 in "the highlands of St John and St Andrew in the interior" whereas the overall death rate had climbed from "33.1 . . . [to] . . . 45.5 per 1,000 in the low flat districts of Christ Church and St Philip", the low-lying southern zone of Barbados having the island's highest overall death rates.[93]

Conventional wisdom that better health conditions existed at higher elevations had come in part from the long-term British occupation of the region, probably most directly from recent military experiences. British military commanders in Jamaica had recognized from at least the early nineteenth century that European soldiers' morbidity and mortality rates were significantly lower at encampments in the mountains. Even in Barbados, with little variation in its elevation, soldiers residing at the barracks near Bridgetown were periodically evacuated to Gun Hill, barely above the 500 foot contour in St George parish, in times of epidemic disease and had been taken there as early as the 1854 cholera epidemic. The European soldiers in Barbados again went to Gun Hill in October 1881 during a yellow fever epidemic in Bridgetown, although the disease apparently followed

Table 5.2 Barbados Infant Mortality, 1895-1898

Total Burials of Infants under One Year of Age

	1895	1896	1897	1898
St Michael	1,846	1,943	2,074	2,536
St Phillip	365	417	508	756
Christ Church	488	487	482	900
St George	292	351	329	613
St Thomas	291	351	278	453
St John	253	265	214	371
St James	294	274	268	460
St Peter	254	276	201	438
St Lucy	125	216	239	328
St Joseph	232	257	222	318
St Andrew	148	159	148	242
Total	**4,588**	**4,996**	**4,963**	**7,415**

Infants' (under one year) Deaths as a Percentage
of Total Deaths

	1895	1896	1897	1898
St Michael	35.3	40.1	36.7	33.8
St Phillip	34.8	42.4	34.8	35.3
Christ Church	36.0	41.3	39.2	31.9
St George	30.8	33.6	34.9	35.0
St Thomas	31.2	45.8	39.5	34.2
St John	38.3	40.0	40.1	40.4
St James	35.0	46.7	38.4	38.7
St Peter	38.6	46.0	44.2	40.4
St Lucy	53.6	41.6	41.0	40.5
St Joseph	38.3	48.6	36.0	37.1
St Andrew	31.7	30.0	33.7	29.7

Sources: C.O.32/18, Poor Law Inspector Reports, *Barbados Official Gazette*, 1898, 12 May and 15 May 1899.

them to the higher ground, and the troops then were evacuated temporarily to England.[94]

Yet the elevation-health relationships in the British Caribbean were not clearly understood, much of the conversation about health and environment in the 1880s and 1890s having to do with 'miasmatic airs' or perhaps germs imbedded in the soil and then escaping lethally when an area was tilled or deforested. 'Yellow fever' winds and even the night air itself were thought to play crucial roles as to whether or not people fell ill. The most general precaution taken to avoid disease was simply to remove oneself from the infected people or the area where the disease was evident. And the strategy of heading for higher elevations as part of this general precaution, whether carried out by individuals or groups, was scientifically correct because it distanced people from the swampy terrain, cane lands and standing water in lowland village settlements where mosquitoes thrived.

The perceived relationships between elevation and human well-being seemed most obvious on the islands where there were both lowlands and highlands. Although St Lucia authorities strenuously attempted to sanitize the island's health reputation, there was no doubting that its valleys were places of sickness, often for the Barbadians who travelled to work in and around the large sugar centrals. Yet lowland illnesses also were noticeable among the few indentured Indians in St Lucia. The report of the island's protector of immigrants for 1879 was explicit. "It may seem an idle fancy to connect discontent with bottom lands" began the report, but the facts seemed painfully obvious. When indentured Indians of St Lucia were relegated to labour in the lowlands they were attacked by fevers that "both debilitate and demoralise", rendering those affected "utterly unfit for exertions". In seeking an overarching explanation for these grim conditions, the protector of immigrants posed and then answered his own rhetorical question: "Why? The bottom lands still generate malaria."[95]

In a more general sense, higher elevations in the region were associated with more personal freedom and well-being—at least for working peoples—than were lowland zones. Comparative observations of the differences between lowland and highland settlements were perhaps most obvious in Grenada, where an economy based upon lowland sugar cane production in the 1860s and into the 1870s had become reliant on cacao production at higher elevations in the 1880s. The physical movement upwards of the centre of gravity of Grenada's agricultural economy also had involved many other changes. More land was controlled by small-scale producers. Work regimens were less regulated. Settlements were more dispersed. Individual dwellings were sturdier. George A. Gentle, Grenada's Archdeacon, who had witnessed positive socioeconomic change on the island since 1873, reported to the 1897 commissioners that this change all had been for the better. Young men and women were learning habits of decency and modesty, habits denied them in the crowded, coarse existence of the sugar cane barracks. Economic self-reliance had put former estate labourers in touch with business leaders from whom they were learning commerce and good manners. A greater respect and desire for formal education was evident. Smallholders displayed a natural interest in civic matters and public affairs rather than listlessly accepting orders as before. In describing these changes, Gentle had associated the original unfolding of these good things to the geographical shift from lowlands to highlands that had taken place among Grenada's working peoples:

The advantage to the health of the labourers exchanging dwellings in the crowded villages or in the still more crowded tenements of the sugar estates for houses standing more or less apart in their own grounds must be at once apparent; and the difference of locality would point the same way, for there was the additional change, in the great majority of cases, from the low-lying position of the sugar factories to the breezy and malaria-free slopes of the hillsides. That the labourers' health was greatly improved by this migration I have no doubt at all. . .[96]

Just as variations in health and overall human well-being were associated, in the minds of some observers, with the differences in lowlands and highlands in the eastern Caribbean of the late 1800s, so too were other geographical variables. In most cases, land values were dearer in low altitudes than they were higher up because commercial activities usually were confined to lower elevations. Yet, when commercial cacao activities began to transform the Grenadian mountains, as discussed in the next chapter, the same kinds of erosional and monocultural problems often associated with lowland sugar cane began to occur there.

The economic depression of the late nineteenth century also found its geographical expression in the tired, worn-out image taken on by the region's lowlands. The small islands of the eastern Caribbean had been informally dubbed the old islands by British officials decades earlier, at the time of emancipation. Yet, by the 1880s and 1890s the many characterizations in official correspondence of Barbados having reached its human population limit or threshold suggest that government authorities and planters alike had ceased considering that island's cane lands as infinitely elastic, always ready to accept ever more intense agricultural inputs. The availability of new and inviting tropical acreage elsewhere in the world also doubtless reinforced these changing attitudes toward the lowlands of the eastern Caribbean.

Chapter Six
The Highlands

Archdeacon Gentle's impressions about the late nineteenth century improvements—economically, socially and even psychologically—for Grenada's working peoples as they ascended from being sugar cane labourers to cacao-based smallholders, had parallels elsewhere in the region. Grenada's economic transformation was unique, but a sense of release was associated with highlands throughout the Commonwealth Caribbean. Personal freedom and the physical sanctuary represented by the insular highlands, furthermore, were bound up with local histories. In the summer of 1892, an energetic new administrator for St Vincent, Colonel I. H. Sandwith, visited and inspected various buildings, roads and public works throughout the island. He had occasion to walk along a trace running east from Chateaubelair, below the Soufrière crater, and then continuing over the island to the windward coast. Sandwith was pleased to meet fishermen of the island's leeward villages returning with empty baskets—having sold their catches to windward villagers—and he was told that livestock was occasionally driven all the way across the island on the steep pathway. One year later Sandwith again took the same trail, this time following a spur of it all the way to Soufrière's southern summit as the path had been improved so that persons could "repair to the Crater for their 'marooning' (i.e. picnic) parties in order to enjoy the wonderful and unique sights provided by Nature".[1]

Highland areas were important and pleasurable places not only for recreational or ephemeral activities. Permanent or part-time cultivation of upland plots involved "a kind of pilgrimage" from the enervating heat of the lowlands to a breezy realm where one could exercise choice and live cheaply, experiences that, taken altogether, carried with them "important therapeutic value, both physically and mentally".[2] Black peoples inhabiting highland plots even worked together more readily than in the crowded, competitive lowlands. At least that is what Governor Moloney asserted while pushing hard for the establishment of a black peasantry in the Windwards in 1899. Small-scale cultivators in Grenada's upland interior, according to Moloney, exhibited a "cheerful readiness with which they cooperate in helping one another in any task requiring united effort as for instance building or moving their wooden houses".[3]

Yet an overly romantic notion of highland freedom or an emphasis upon altitudinal conditions alone would miss the main reason why forested, upland interiors were, for many black peoples, zones of refuge and retreat. These mountainous, somewhat inaccessible and poorly understood areas were, very obviously, only nominally controlled by colonial officials. And those peoples inhabiting upland areas—permanently or even part-time— were not nearly so susceptible to being registered, counted, taxed or watched as were those residing below. So for every recorded comment of Moloney-type exuberance alluding to the positive character of highland identities, there were four or five official remarks deploring those who inhabited upland interiors of West Indian islands. Mountainous interiors shielded illicit bush rum distilleries. Escapees from city jails headed for the hills. According to the 1882 royal commissioners, highland zones represented poorly surveyed open spaces on maps, but in reality they were "the refuge of squatters and bad characters generally".[4]

Black inhabitants of island interiors, without the civilizing effect of white supervision, would lapse into the 'savage' or 'African' modes of production that was the subject of commentary heard over and over by the 1897 commissioners. When they interviewed J.E. Tinne, a colonial official and planter of British Guiana, in London prior to their voyage south, the commissioners had asked what would happen if the West Indian sugar industry failed. Tinne predicted that Guianese blacks "would become bush negroes again" much like the "savages in Surinam" whom he actually had seen.[5] In the commissioners' subsequent journey through the islands, witnesses repeated these ideas over and over to the point of projecting a highland image of an anarchic "Hayti", a primitive human condition being kept alive in various West Indian mountains, which might descend to engulf entire insular societies once the estates and other European supervised institutions collapsed.

African based beliefs and customs were indeed maintained more easily in the inaccessible and lightly patrolled highlands than in coastal towns or plantation tenantries. European officials routinely decried these practices as mountain traits, thereby identifying the highland areas as zones where superstitious blacks saw jumbies behind every tree. In making one's way through forested island interiors, an individual commonly came upon isolated gardens carved out of the forest, plots usually protected from evil spirits by animal skulls atop wooden stakes.[6] In Grenada in the 1890s, Hesketh Bell described the houses of highland blacks as closed and shuttered to ward off "loogaroos" (loup garous or werewolves) whose presence could sometimes be distinguished by faint, bluish lights in the forests. Bell dismissed such apparitions as excitable misinterpretations of peoples simply carrying lanterns through their cocoa plots at night. Yet Bell also acknowledged the wisdom of some of the "old Africans" in the interior of Grenada who understood the medicinal value of certain forest plants. Their knowledge was however so "mixed up with so many absurd superstitions and conditions, that it is most difficult to find out where the rubbish leaves off and the truth begins".[7]

Genuinely disturbing events could and did occur in areas far removed from government supervision. Official concerns over the disproportionate number of female babies dying at birth among St Lucia's black populace early in the 1880s inspired suspicions of infanticide. Routine inspections of stillborn children by district medical officers might have thrown light on the issue, although such inspections were almost impossible "in a thinly inhabited and mountainous colony like St Lucia".[8] Twenty years later, the gruesome 'Monchy murder' in northern St Lucia reinforced perceived interrelationships between savagery and geographical inaccessibility. In 1904, an old St Lucian man brought a young Barbadian boy back to St Lucia on the pretence of his becoming an errand boy. He was brutally murdered, dismembered and some of his body parts used for occult ceremonies. St Lucian officials eventually hanged three men for the murder. The murder had taken place in a remote zone of northern St Lucia and not, strictly speaking, in the highlands. Yet the chief culprit fit official highland stereotypes very well: "The ringleader in the crime was shown to have been a resident in Hayti for some years, where, in all probability, he had been brought under the influence of voodoo worship . . ."[9]

The official ignorance of the nature and extent of insular West Indian highlands was a matter of record. Late in the 1880s, tropical forester E. D. M. Hooper, of the Madras Forest Department, travelled through the eastern Caribbean and, with the assistance of local officials, assessed soils, timber and the agricultural potential of the interiors of various islands. Hooper's written reports promised to "afford for the first time in history the actual . . . conditions of the interior of several islands beyond the confines of the present areas under cultivation".[10] Yet, despite Hooper's worthwhile but very general reports, island interiors were still virtually unknown a decade later. Barbados' forestry committee in 1899 was very precise about its remaining 481 acres of timber (although much of the remaining forest's undergrowth had been removed for cane compost), but Barbados was obviously unlike the mountainous windwards. St Vincent's steep, forbidding interior had had only its outer limits surveyed. When the 1897 royal commissioners arrived, St Lucia's administrator told them the "chief difficulty" he had encountered in preparing returns for them was the absence of a reliable survey of the island. And the year before in Grenada, officials similarly lamented improper surveys and widespread ignorance about the extent of interior Crown Lands, although a commission had been appointed in 1890 to try to answer these questions.[11]

Given the lack of familiarity that most island residents had with their mountainous island interiors, it makes sense that fantasy and exaggeration naturally abounded concerning these zones. The presence of the venomous fer-de-lance (*Bothrops atrox*) in the mountains of St Lucia buttressed the island's dangerous and unhealthy image. When Lafcadio Hearn described the fer-de-lance in Martinique as "lord of the forest and the solitudes by day" who "extends his dominion over the public roads" at night, he might as well have been describing similar generalizations about St Lucia.[12] And the riot of mountain foliage and variety of botanic species obvious to anyone who ascended mountain trails brought forward fantastic descriptions of how this tropical fertility could be harnessed to fulfil human needs. Professor Froude was lyrical on the subject after his brief visit to the interior of Grenada, which he described as "a Garden of Eden" where "All precious fruits, and precious spices, and gums, and plants of rarest medicinal virtues will spring and grow and flourish for the asking."[13] These claims were not confined to academic fantasy; one wonders, for instance, how seriously London officials regarded the exaggerated claims they received in 1895 from Governor Charles Bruce of the Windwards based on a piece he recently had read in the St Lucia newspaper:

We have fertile land enough . . . in St Lucia to support . . . twice the population of Barbados. When one realizes that the plantain produces to the acre 44 times more food than the potato, and 131 times more than wheat; that the banja-yam is more nutritious, bulk for bulk, than the potato; and when one at the same time reflects that the plantain can be grown practically over the whole island; that the cultivation of the cassava is simple and inexpensive, and the returns very large; that the bread-fruit literally covers the land; that Indian corn will give three crops a year; that the banja-yam grows in wild abundance in our woods, conviction will be compelled that our claim for . . . St Lucia to support a large population solely with her own products is . . . more than mere boasting . . .[14]

Fantastic as this description was, the availability of land for working peoples—whether or not it was mountainous, sloping, inaccessible or subject to runoff and landslips—signified a physical refuge in St Lucia and Grenada that was absent in Barbados, at the other extreme. The captivity of slavery had separated most peoples from interior lands in the Windwards until the 1830s. Thereafter, access to mountain lands represented a means of coping with colonial power holders. When the members of the 1882 royal commission visited St Lucia they learned about the lamentably unreliable labour force there. A number of factors were cited, including the French background of the island, the attraction of Panama, and black indolence in general. But more provocative than these other reasons was the testimony of a Mr Devaux who was a St Lucia planter: "The labouring population are perfectly independent here; there is too much spare land."[15] Fifteen years later, sworn surveyor John E. Quinlan similarly explained St Lucians to the men representing the much more influential 1897 commission: "It is evident that the St Lucian will never be crushed or forced down . . . They have the land . . . they can never starve . . ."[16] And in 1900 in a book-length narrative/study entitled *British America*, an anonymous essayist attempted to explain why black Grenadians seemed so much more pleased and content with their lots than those on Barbados or Trinidad: "And what is the reason, we ask, for this obviously happier and more prosperous condition of things? The secret lies in the fact that the island is owned by the people . . ."[17]

Deforestation

Rather than emphasizing lowland-highland differences in the eastern Caribbean in the late 1800s, one could discuss cleared versus forested lands and, for all practical purposes, be speaking about the same contrasting areas on the ground. In general, lowlands were devoid of native forest vegetation while the forests remained in the highlands, an important if obvious landscape distinction that had originated with the first plantation clearing more than two centuries earlier. During slavery the boundary between cleared and forested land had signified much more than vegetational change because forested zones were often the haunts of maroons. And because the highland forests still were beyond daily supervision a half-century after emancipation, peoples and activities in these interior, wooded zones—judging from the written evidence from the 1800s—were regarded with official unease and distaste. This socially based disapproval was, however, often interrelated with sound environment considerations; the deforestation that led to excessive runoff and soil erosion discussed in chapter 4 was universally deplored because it created hardships for everyone.

Except at the mountain summits, interior forests of the Windwards were not examples of pristine 'natural' ecosystems. In the high country of Grenada, for example, the Mona monkey (*Cercopithecus mona*) introduced during slavery and the mongoose (*Herpestes auropunctatus*) brought in the 1870s had probably extinguished several bird species by the 1890s and were regarded as pests by upland cacao producers.[18] Walking through wooded intermediate slopes in Grenada and St Lucia, moreover, involved frequent encounters with breadfruit trees or groves of tree ferns marking earlier cultivation plots. And, despite the pronouncements about fantastically bounteous environments and descriptions of forests' miasmatic exhalations that injured humans, knowledge of the wooded highland areas was not uniformly primitive. Those contemplating the clearing of wooded zones for agricultural use were being warned increasingly that tree size and soil fertility bore little relationship to one another. And one description of species diversity in the forests of the Lesser Antilles in 1890 is not far from what one might find in a primer on tropical forest ecology one century later:

You do not find here, as in the great forests of the North, the eternal monotony of birch and fir: this is the kingdom of infinite variety;—species the most diverse elbow each other, interlace, strangle and devour each other; all ranks and orders are confounded, as in a human mob . . . Our oak, the balata, forces the palm to lengthen itself prodigiously in order to get a few thin beams of sunlight . . .[19]

A widespread rationale in favour of limiting further deforestation, and thereby restricting human occupation of island interiors, was that deforestation was claimed to lead to lessened rainfall. E.D.M. Hooper's 1887 forest report about Grenada described the denudation of the island's interior slopes to make way for cacao planting and subsistence agriculture, castigating what he saw as "wasteful" because it led to soil degradation and was also a factor in "interfering with the local climate".[20] A decade later, the 1897 royal commissioners, in summarizing their overall conclusions about Trinidad's interior, condemned itinerant squatting in the island's Crown

Lands where woodsmen felled forest trees because, among other problems, their actions usually "would injuriously affect the rainfall".[21]

Relationships between deforestation and rainfall decline had been authoritatively forwarded by conservationists within the British empire for at least a century although the precise scientific reasoning as to exactly how forest clearing led to decreased precipitation necessarily remained vague. Indeed, Sir Hans Sloane had made careful observations of soil erosion in Jamaica in the 1670s and had subsequently entertained notions about relationships among deforestation, runoff and climate change. With the global expansion of the empire, similar environmentally oriented thinking continued apace, much of this research focused on islands. Observations from St Vincent became part of the global scientific network in 1766 when the botanic garden was established at Kingstown. And twenty-five years later important conservation legislation in St Vincent had implications that extended well beyond the Caribbean. The Kings Hill Forest Act in St Vincent in 1791 recognized that forest clearance might reduce rainfall, and it called for the local government to protect the land and reduce timber exploitation. "Once made law, the Kings Hill Act constituted the first forest protection legislation in the English-speaking world based on climatic theory."[22]

The second director of the St Vincent botanic garden, Alexander Anderson, explained, late in the eighteenth century, why forest conservation was so necessary. His suggestion and similar pleas to protect woodlands, furthermore, marked something of a departure from the thinking that had animated the activities of earliest European planters and settlers in the region. The original forest areas had had to be cleared for the subsequent cultivation of cash crops. And forests in general had been considered reservoirs of unhealthy fevers and vapours. Anderson, in contrast, insisted that a necessary amount of woodland left standing would reduce heat. Further, he asserted in the same spirit of the thinking behind the Kings Hill Act, that there really was no "reasonable doubt that trees have a very considerable effect in attracting rain" because "they promote the circulation of the atmosphere". Finally, Anderson thought that Europeans who inhabited wooded zones received the benefits of dews, dampness and cool temperatures and were "far more healthy, lively and robust than the seaside inhabitants".[23]

Doubtless these late eighteenth century ideas about deforestation directly affecting rainfall mechanisms and reducing rainfall amounts had been carried forward for a century within the conventional wisdom concerning West Indian environments. But this general notion was continually subjected—as a matter of daily occupation of the tropics—to rigorous empirical testing. Planters in the Windwards and elsewhere who had experienced pounding, destructive rainstorms on recently cleared land were, for very obvious reasons, entirely justified in questioning this idea. Early in 1884, in discussing a proposed forest preservation ordinance for all of the Windwards, D. G. Garraway, a police magistrate of St Vincent's Leeward District, refuted the clearing-leads-to-drought assumption. Despite recent clearing for arrowroot patches in St Vincent, according to Garraway, the rainfall had by no means diminished over the past twenty years.[24]

Garraway and others were, however, acutely aware of how downpours affected deforested lands. So it was not that there was no relationship between climate and clearing, just that the latter did not influence the former. The point had been clarified in a lecture given by Daniel Morris in Jamaica in 1885. When Morris discussed the "relationships between the existence of a forest and a climate" to a group of Jamaican planters, he was by no means espousing Anderson's and others' notions that forest clearing somehow reoriented atmospheric circulation beyond immediate localities. Yet the overall impact of deforestation on these same localities was that the climate's effects usually were more severe than before. Forested hillsides and valleys of the Caribbean islands were buffered from climatic extremes according to Morris, but once the vegetation was removed it meant ". . . the diminution of rivers, the drying up of streams and springs, the occurrence of destructive floods, of unseasonable and prolonged droughts, the raising of the temperature of both air and soil, excessive drainage, aridity of the soil, and uncertainty of the growth of crops".[25]

In 1897 Governor Moloney reiterated the points Morris and others had made about how deforestation impoverished the land. In deploring the cutover character of Grenada's highlands late in the 1890s, Moloney cited Alexander von Humboldt, attributing to the fabled German traveller the adage that rampant deforestation left twin legacies of firewood loss and water scarcities. Moloney, on the basis of his observations in the Windwards, added that von Humboldt should have included "denudation of soil and land slides" as well.[26]

Not all of the concern over deforestation focused on clearing for crops. Perhaps even more troubling to Windward Islands officials were the activities of charcoal producers in the mountains. Charcoal burners were a shadowy lot whose activities could not be tracked using official import or export data but whose contributions played a major role in local livelihoods. Despite the occasional official nonsense that working peoples of the Caribbean needed no fuel because they lived in an earthly paradise of continuous warmth, cooking fuel was necessary and naturally scarce. Neither driftwood nor dry wood in the forests was abundant for local use. So upland charcoal producers felled trees, burned (or smouldered) the green logs in hand-dug pits under conditions of limited oxygen, and sold the resultant chunks of charcoal directly to black villagers and occasionally at local markets. Villagers then burned the charcoal in iron or earthenware braziers called 'coal pots' for their boiling or baking.[27]

Most charcoal production was accomplished for local use, although some from the Windwards went to Barbados. Stacks of firewood from British Guiana were commonplace sights on the wharf at Bridgetown, but sloops and schooners from the Windwards also carried an undetermined volume of charcoal there as well. And the combination of local needs and demand from Barbados had a direct impact on Windward mountainsides. In 1898, while assessing the character of the St Lucian countryside, Governor Moloney ascended one of the trails in the Mabouya Valley, inland from Dennery in the east central part of the island. Moloney, viewing a devastated forest area, was "shocked" by a scene caused, he was told, "by the manufacture of charcoal for export to Barbados".[28] And although this situation was apparently new for St Lucia, it had been commonplace for years in the Grenadines where the limited stands of timber on these tiny islands were routinely stripped and exported. On Bequia in the early 1880s, everyone knew that local forest destruction resulted from the export quota of firewood and charcoal which was "greater than that used for home consumption".[29]

The 1882 royal commissioners had had little good to say about charcoal making on St Vincent and actively condemned those involved in its production in their mountainous retreats above the cultivated lowlands. After the sugar cane was harvested in June or July it was "difficult to get hands for the field work" in St Vincent because the men then went into the mountains to cultivate provision crops. There they felled trees, and it was common for them to "relapse into a semi-savage state, to the injury of the whole community". Not only were their seasonal highland activities inconvenient to the lowland planters but also, according to local spokesmen, they were physically detrimental to the entire island: "The greatest harm is the unrestricted manner in which all the woods are being cut and burnt into charcoal."[30]

There is little doubt that Vincentian charcoal production was injurious to the local environment. The charcoal makers on St Vincent were concentrated in the slopes just above the most densely populated lowlands of the island. They stripped the vegetation from the hillsides above the Calliaqua and Marraqua valleys in the southeast and also destroyed much of the forest cover farther west, at altitudes up to 1,000 feet above sea level on the slopes of mount St Andrew where St George and St Andrew parishes came together. Throughout the southern part of the island the reduction of the watershed foliage increased muddy runoff after heavy rains, and in this regard the Vincentian woodsmen "appear to have played in this island the same part as the chena cultivators in Ceylon".[31]

St Vincent authorities attempted, with little real effect, to curb and regulate the local production and sale of charcoal by licensing the activity. The written discussions accompanying the efforts at controlling legally charcoal distribution, furthermore, made it clear that these efforts were bound up with an overriding desire by the planters to restrict labourers' mobility. The stated rationale for licensing, and thereby restricting, charcoal production and sale on St Vincent usually was to preserve the woodlands or ensure adequate rainfall. But planters themselves also denuded forests for fuel and timber and even to make rum. That was a point made by W.G.M. Belton of Liverpool in May 1886, in remarking unofficially about the £5 annual fee assessed charcoal producers in St Vincent. Belton, an erstwhile resident of St Vincent, stated flatly that the law was a piece of "class" legislation, descended from the harsh postemancipation laws framed by planters "for the oppression of the working class . . . [who were treated as] . . . beasts of burden to work their plantations".[32]

Legal deforestation restrictions notwithstanding, officials' actual attempts at controlling highland woodcutters varied in intensity as did the prices of charcoal licences. When deforestation contributed to serious runoff and flooding, as it did in Grenada in the 1890s, officials became serious. Early in 1898, after floods had devastated the towns of Gouyave and Victoria, black rangers were dispatched to the highlands "to arrest without warrants" illegal woodcutters.[33]

From St Lucia the export of logwood (*Haematoxylon cam-pechianum*) to Britain and North America involved an informal gathering of the material by black residents of the island. Used in metropolitan dye industries, Caribbean logwood came mainly from British Honduras and Jamaica, although several tons per year were sent from St Lucia in the mid 1890s. Rural blacks in St Lucia scoured the countryside for logwood, then took it to small village markets and sold it to middlemen. Logwood apparently abounded on the "hill sides not suitable for cane cultivation". And although rural blacks often collected, strictly speaking, on others' plantation lands, a plantation owner was not always inclined to press issues of legality, especially if he was outnumbered: "If you meet a gang of negroes with cutlasses as you are riding home, you do not like very much to interfere with them, and if you take them to a magistrate he will not convict."[34]

Subsistence Agriculture

When D. G. Garraway told the 1897 commissioners in St Lucia that the bounty sugar depression had "forced . . . people to pay greater attention to their holdings", in effect helping "to induce the establishment of a peasant proprietary body", he probably had little appreciation that, in turning inward on their mountain subsistence plots, black St Lucians were indulging in livelihood practices that were, at the very least, one century old.[35] That is because prior to emancipation, slaves in St Lucia and elsewhere in the Windwards, had controlled small agricultural plots on which they often produced enough to feed their families. These highland provision grounds were thereby loci of crop experimentation, plant selection, information transfers and a general adaptation to local environments, altogether providing a reservoir of longstanding local knowledge that was crucial in coming to grips with post-emancipation conditions in the region.

The Barbadian historian Woodville Marshall points out that slaves in the Windwards controlled small agricultural plots well before emancipation. By 1790, according to Marshall, Windward slaves were marketing their own vegetables on their home islands and routinely keeping poultry and small livestock in order to augment imports of fish and grains from mid latitudes.[36] One century later, these activities originating in slavery had been intensified and extended. Windward markets featured a variety of vegetables and fruits that came from mountain gardens. Professor Froude rhapsodized about the hundreds of market women in Dominica, for example, who daily descended on Roseau "with their fish and fowls, fruit and bread, their yams and sweet potatoes, their oranges and limes and plantains".[37] Also, by the 1880s, food crops from Windward provision plots were routinely being shipped to Trinidad, a one-way traffic that, although rarely finding its way into import-export tables, was often reported but apparently under-appreciated by colonial officials. Speaking of Grenada in the mid 1890s, for example, one spokesman left a classic understatement for posterity: "Ground provisions have only a limited value, in so far as they supply local wants and those of the Trinidad market."[38]

The keeping of small animals by individual farmers in the Windwards also provided important sources of trade and export. The residents of the northern extremity of St Vincent hunted down feral goats and sold them to Vincentians along the leeward coast of the island.[39] And few sloops and schooners headed south for Trinidad without a few cattle on board, accord-ing to weekly newspaper reports. Cattle were particularly important in St Lucia, an obvious yet uquantifiable element in local diets. In 1889 an act was passed to reduce the incidence of cattle thieving and illicit butchery in the St Lucian countryside, occurrences of such frequency as to be "excep-tionally discouraging to holders of small stock".[40]

The distinction between kitchen gardens located around dwellings and the more extensive provision grounds in mountain interiors of the Wind-wards also had its origins during slavery.[41] By the 1890s in the highlands of Grenada, the hundreds of small cottages each were surrounded by roosters and hens and their broods of chicks, and occasional pigs, goats and calves. The houses' human inhabitants made occasional attempts to grow flowers, but "these generally give way to Indian corn as the planting season comes on".[42] At a farther remove, were more extensive provision grounds devoted to both subsistence and cash crops. The differences in size, agricultural in-tensity and crop identities between the kitchen or dooryard gardens and the larger provision grounds in the Windwards mountains of the 1880s not only were rooted in an earlier slave history but also help in understanding land fragmentation in the Windwards late in the twentieth century as well.[43]

Marshall's research dealing with Windward slaves' subsistence activities suggests that weekly work in distant provision grounds offered slaves a "par-tial escape" from the plantation. But this activity often required extraordi-nary physical effort to overcome the considerable distances and sloping, rocky terrain.[44] These same constraints also inhibited the cultivation of inte-rior provision grounds of the Windwards in the depression decades of the late 1800s, especially on St Vincent. Unlike in Grenada, where roads and trails seemingly led everywhere, St Vincent's interior was variously described as a roadless succession of knife-edges or backbones of mountains that thwarted pedestrian locomotion by all but the most hardy and adventuresome.

It was not that the interior of St Vincent was considered infertile, but permanent occupation was near impossible and very lonely. The testimony of John Samuel Dick, a carpenter of Dickson's Village on the windward coast of St Vincent, before the 1897 commission clarified these points. Dick purchased 7 acres of interior land in St Vincent in 1888. He planned to cultivate both food and cash crops on the land to keep his family from 'starving'. In 1892 his pregnant wife died at the isolated plot "from want of medical attendance". Four years later the flood of November 1896 sent his provision grounds sliding "in the sea" leaving him only a few breadfruit trees. The time necessarily spent on his highland plot, according to Dick, even prevented him from attending church.[45]

Whereas Dick had purchased his land through instalment payments, others on St Vincent sometimes purchased land for a flat fee. Some in the Windwards rented their subsistence plots. Then there were a variety of land-use arrangements whereby large-scale planters made land available to workers who, in turn, used the land to raise food crops or cash crops or a combination of the two, tenure systems, reminiscent of *metayage* established earlier on St Lucia, that had fallen out of practice in the early 1860s.[46] Land tenure for smallholders of the Windwards in the late nineteenth century, in other words, was the cumulative result of a confusing array of local customs, *ad hoc* practices, planter-worker relationships and rivalries, and layered histories, all adjudicated by a transient assortment of colonial officials. In responding to Governor Moloney's suggestion for a better land registration system in Grenada early in 1898, and in the aftermath of the recent regionwide commission, the British Colonial Office lamented the absence of order in landholding practices which, in an ideal world, "should be, as far as possible, uniform in the West Indian Colonies".[47]

Table 6.1 shows the comparative land holdings by parcel size in St Lucia, St Vincent and Grenada in the late 1890s. It would be misleading to draw any but the roughest conclusions from these data because they were collected by different people, for different reasons, and in different years. Yet these figures correspond with other data collected in the 1890s and together illustrate the contrasts between places. The land hunger of St Vincent, for example, illustrated in Table 6.1 and commented upon by so many, was also shown by the island's 1895 'Land Roll' (from which taxes were derived); the latter enumerated 247 land plots on St Vincent of 3 acres or less, 161 of which were in Kingstown and therefore presumably house lots.[48] The comparative data in Table 6.1 reinforces, most importantly, the sharp contrasts among Grenada as an island of smallholders, St Vincent as monopolized by large-scale planters, and St Lucia, somewhere between the other two extremes.

Within the comparative framework illustrated by Table 6.1, a mosaic of complexity and nuance marked the Windward Islands' land tenure late in the nineteenth century. At the informal end of the land tenure spectrum, squatting was very prevalent, especially in St Vincent's highlands and also throughout St Lucia. On the latter island, as the large central sugar factories struggled for survival at the outset of the sugar depression, the island's Executive Council warmed to the idea of the establishment of a peasantry there. In 1885 new rules were established to facilitate land purchases on St Lucia, although making land available to smallholders, it was warned, should be coupled with a suppression of squatting because "unfortunately squatting has been tolerated for so long in this Colony as to have become almost a system".[49]

Illegal occupation of interior highlands was in part a reaction to cumbersome and inoperable rules and procedures. When St Lucia authorities made some small plots of Crown Land available in 1886, as only one example, they were faced with rival claimants who asserted that the land was already theirs.[50] And even when titles were not disputed, survey expense often diminished the widely held enthusiasm for small land plots. Over and over again, potential smallholders throughout the Windwards lamented the out-of-pocket fees (up to £2/acre) for surveyors to parcel out land plots. Even in Grenada, where all but an interior forest preserve was in private hands, expenses associated with holding land plots were burdensome. Land and house taxes were a principal source of Grenada's colonial revenue, amounting to over £6,000 per year in the late 1890s. But a downturn in cocoa prices reduced smallholders' cash incomes to the point that a "serious problem of backtaxes" arose on the island. The problem was compounded by bailiffs' fees extracted by police magistrates dispatched into the highland villages to collect taxes. The inability of small-scale Grenadian cacao farmers to pay these taxes in 1896 and 1897 threatened their very existence. The only recourse left for some of them was to sell off their properties, a prospect pleasing to some of the island's large landowners—who recognized opportunities to extend their own estates—but inconsistent with those at the

London Colonial Office who saw the region's future in terms of small land-holders.[51]

Yet land in the Windwards, as elsewhere in the Caribbean, represented far more than a commodity to be bought and sold or a vehicle for taxation. The interrelationships between land, especially land used for subsistence cultivation, and human identity had roots that had preceded emancipation in the Windwards. Marshall's research dealing with Grenadian slave society in the late eighteenth century, for example, shows that property among slaves—possibly including provision grounds—was "conveyed from one generation to another".[52] Whatever the particular origins, there is ample evidence from the Windwards in the late 1800s that possessing land had several meanings for highland cultivators. As the Jamaican anthropologist Jean Besson has pointed out, the control of family land as a scarce economic resource in Caribbean societies is often overlain by a simultaneous perception of the same land as having a symbolic, more expansive image.[53]

Family land was particularly important in St Lucia where this widespread Caribbean custom apparently was reinforced by French land law that inspired communal tenure, encouraged parcelling out of lands among heirs, and also predated emancipation.[54] Whatever its origins, the actual occupation of small highland plots in St Lucia in the late 1800s was only dimly understood by local officials. Doubtless the oft-repeated 'squatting' describing St Lucian land holding was a reflection of this ignorance. Surveyor John Quinlan, a native of St Lucia, offered his own assessment of the number and character of small-scale cultivators there to the 1897 commission:

St Lucia contains a population of more than 6,000 peasant proprietors; allowing three men to each property you have 18,000 men . . . They are not lazy; their small properties were purchased with moneys that came to them from their share of sugar as metayers of the old sugar estates, before the depression, and long before the works were opened on the Panama Canal. When the depression came they risked their lives in search of money at Panama. They now risk it with the same object at the Cayenne gold fields.[55]

Note that Quinlan's estimate of the number of peasant proprietors alone on the island in 1897 is roughly twice the number of holdings enumerated in the survey cited in Table 6.1, suggesting a wide range of perceptions or understandings as to just how many people were occupying the land. And his trebling of the number of cultivators "to each property" is en-

Table 6.1 Landholdings in The Windwards

Grenada, 1898

Acres	under 2.5	2.5-5	5-7	7-10
St George	911	262	64	45
St John	548	128	19	22
St Mark	174	64	16	14
St Patrick	871	193	56	27
St Andrew	1,613	280	58	53
St David	772	205	42	30
Carriacou	1,157	60	24	7
Total	6,046	1,192	279	198

St Vincent, 1896

Acres	under 5	5-10	10-20	20-50	50-100	100-200	200-400	500-1000	over 1000
Parcels	270	36	38	40	21	28	56	26	1
Total Acres	505	233	505	1,203	1,453	3,978	17,054	17,522	1,596

Table 6.1 Continued

St Lucia, 1897

Acres	0-2	2-4	6-10	10-20	20-50	50-100	100-500	500-1000	>1000
Castries	147	153	183	141	49	15	17	3	1
Dennery	21	31	77	64	31	8	10	2	1
Gros-Islet	16	54	107	90	54	27	13	3	4
Soufrière	106	154	139	86	44	23	19	2	0
Choiseul	101	159	115	62	24	11	10	3	0
Anse-la-Raye	0	20	48	34	27	11	9	1	1
Vieux Fort	7	33	47	38	11	10	18	4	0
Laborie	37	62	111	55	12	5	6	2	0
Micoud	7	27	51	54	39	19	11	1	4
Total	442	693	878	624	291	129	113	21	11

Sources:

Grenada, 1898: C. O. 884/5/ no. 86, *Correspondence . . . Increase of Peasant Proprietary . . .* (Colonial Office 1900), p 76–77.

St Vincent, 1896: C.O. 884/5 no. 77, *Report on the Condition of St Vincent* (HMSO, 1897), p. 28.

St Lucia, 1897: C.O. 884/5/ no. 82, *Correspondence. . . Royal Commission of 1896-7* (London, 1899), p. 32.

tirely consistent with more recent assessments of St Lucian land tenure where multiple ownership of family land is more the rule than the exception. The island's 1986 agricultural census, for instance, suggested that nearly half the island's holdings were "held jointly by members of an extended family . . . each with a legal and undivided right to cultivate a portion of the land".[56]

Since the occupation of St Lucian land was so poorly understood in the late 1800s, it is obvious that land taxes were not—as they were in Grenada—a feasible means of generating local government revenue. Another reason against St Lucian land taxes was the memory of the violent reaction against them in 1849. So the St Lucia authorities settled on the idea of a 'road tax' of 6 shillings to be paid twice annually by all males from the ages of sixteen to sixty. To say the road tax was only marginally successful would be understatement; authorities and their representatives had great difficulty in collecting these fees. And if those failing to pay were caught, they simply spent their seven days in prison "with great indifference".[57]

The mountainous terrain of St Lucia and its bewildering land tenure patterns often protected black St Lucians from the police constables/road tax collectors. The latter—usually English-speaking Barbadians—received uniformly hostile receptions in the highland villages where residents referred to them as "the queen's dogs".[58] Even if an assiduous tax collector successfully negotiated the winding paths and unhelpful, uncommunicative populace in the St Lucia highlands, he was rarely certain as to the identities of potential taxpayers. Men and boys cultivated different mountain plots, resided in different villages at various times of the year, and used their mobility to befuddle tax collectors. And the many nicknames for men, so typical of the rest of the Caribbean, were all the more confusing because of the local patois: "Here, our peasantry drop their Christian name at the baptismal font, and by the time they develop into [an] adult, are hedged round by numerous sobriquets." The black St Lucians' extra-island mobility also diminished road tax revenues. Those heading for the goldfields of French Guiana in the 1890s were obviously absent when the road tax collectors made their rounds. And the exodus to Panama of several thousand St Lucians in the previous decade had been reflected clearly in annual road tax collection data. The road tax in 1883 was £2,109, a figure dropping in the next few years to £893 in 1885, £1,083 in 1886, £803 in 1887 and £835 in 1888. Then after the French effort in Panama was ended in 1889 and many St Lucians returned to their home island, road tax collections increased. In

1890, over £1,100 in road taxes had been collected in St Lucia from January through September alone.[59]

The character of the agriculture in the scattered mountain plots in St Lucia and elsewhere in the highlands of the Windwards represented, of course, a striking contrast with that of plantations of the region's lowlands. The differences between highlands and lowlands were also contrasts between forested and cleared areas, subsistence and cash crops, and heterogeneity and homogeneity in cultivation. Whereas lowland sugar cane was produced through coordinated, seasonal labour inputs by gangs of workers performing monotonous and repetitive tasks, highland plots were visited informally throughout the year by individuals or family groups who weeded, chased birds away, checked for insect pests, and harvested fruits and vegetables from one weekly visit to the next.

As far as the identify of the subsistence crops themselves are concerned, rigorous species descriptions or inventories from the 1880s and 1890s in the eastern Caribbean were rare. But the many offhand descriptions provide ample evidence that the tropical Antillean subsistence crop core of banana/plantain, maize, beans, peas, squash/pumpkin, sweet potatoes and yams identified by Riva Berleant-Schiller and Lydia Pulsipher were evident in most provision plots at the time. For example, the informal enumeration of the typical ground provisions cultivated in the highlands of Grenada (e.g. "yams, tannias, sweet potatoes, koosh-koosh, manioc, plantains, corn, breadfruit, peas, etc.") late in the 1800s are familiar to field researchers of the region one century later. And Woodville Marshall's rough enumeration of slaves' crop choices in the highlands of the Windwards of the eighteenth century confirm the slavery-era origins of this crop complex.[60]

Variations on this complex occurred from island to island and from one subsistence plot to another. Arrowroot, as discussed earlier, was important on St Vincent. Cacao producers in Grenada and St Lucia almost invariably interspersed low-lying subsistence crops with their trees, and 'catch crops' of corn, beans, peas and root crops yielded important foodstuffs in the first years of a cacao tree's growth. Breadfruit trees shaded provision grounds in the Windwards, especially on St Vincent.

Solitary farmers occasionally worked kitchen gardens and provision grounds in highland plots in the Windwards, but the romanticized notion of highland group effort and reciprocal labour exchanges seems to have had a firm factual basis. In St Lucia, mutual work exchange among men for which no money changed hands was known as *coup de main*, and it was said to exemplify a solidarity and unity among black villagers.[61] Family members often worked together, especially in kitchen gardens around mountain dwellings. Children as young as five or six performed light tasks supervised by grandparents in highland house gardens (unlike the enrolment of children in the harsh 'third-class gangs' in the Barbadian sugar cane plantations). And after this work in their early years in kitchen garden 'training grounds', by age twelve or so they actively cleared and prepared these subsistence plots as they still do today in Windward villages in the highlands.[62]

Important as mutual labour exchanges and group solidarity against outsiders seem to have been, highland subsistence cultivators always were wary of crop thievery when crops became ripe. Estate-produced foodstuffs, especially on Barbados, were always targets for hungry peoples. But highland villagers also stole ripe fruits and vegetables from one another. In St Vincent, small-scale cultivators occasionally grew bitter varieties of cassava, whose roots contained prussic acid that needed removal before cooking, a tedious process that usually inhibited thievery. Yet desperately hungry Vincentians sometimes pilfered even these cassava roots, eating them raw or half-cooked in the depression years, an activity leading to "numerous deaths . . . every year".[63]

Yet Vincentians seem not to have been afflicted by malnutrition as much as Barbadians were, a conclusion drawn from the comparative death rates and infant mortality rates in the depression decades arrayed in Appendix A. And conclusions about comparative malnutrition, death rates and the explanatory importance accorded to the presence of highland subsistence refuges in the Windwards—and their absence in Barbados—must be hedged with uncertainty. The notorious lack of hard data about local food production at the time (not to mention the uncertain relationships between nutrition and death rates) makes that point obvious. But the innumerable qualitative assessments of inter-island well-being, such as the testimony Reverend Payne presented to the royal commissioners in February 1897 concerning the importance of locally produced foodstuffs in the highlands of the Windwards, seem convincing that the Windwards' mountainous interiors and their subsistence potential conferred to those islands' residents distinct survival advantages over the lowland Barbadians.

The 1897 commission hearings regarding highland subsistence production was particularly positive concerning St Lucia. Small-scale producers there were said to be more knowledgeable than elsewhere and, according to E.D.M. Hooper, less destructive to the local forests than in any other nearly islands. According to a local newspaper editor, the key to the well-being of the typical St Lucian resided in the island's physical characteristics: "The able-bodied native peasant does not require to work for wages to live. There is plenty of fertile waste land which he can grow provisions on. There are wild yams in the woods, fish in the streams, game in the forest, crabs in the ravines."[64]

Obviously, this commentary reinforced the idyllic tropical paradise idea, but more sober observers echoed the same points about subsistence sufficiency wherever extensive lands were available for provision planting. When Charles Kingsley visited the back country of Trinidad in about 1870 he described rural livelihood and classified and named the subsistence species planted, noting that local cultivators lacked neither abundance nor variety in available foods as evidenced by the many children who were "eating all day long".[65] Trinidadian subsistence cultivators also depended on their local environment for medicinal weeds and plants. The same was true in St Lucia where in between gardens and in the nooks and crannies around mountain houses, local peoples cultivated and collected medicinal weeds and herbs used in treatment of "colds, fevers, digestive disorders, sores and related skin afflictions, gynecological problems, and obeah".[66]

The December 1888 Castries jailbreak, the one for which Dr Dennehy was reprimanded, led to a rare glimpse of workers' diets and reinforced the importance of subsistence land in local nutrition. Fifteen prisoners, most of them black St Lucians, beat a visiting policeman and burst through the jail doors on 4 December, after the announced reduction in jail rations. Subsequent investigation involved an assessment as to just what the average St Lucian worker ate during the course of a normal day. The consensus was that the residents of Castries had meager diets compared with those from the country. Alexander Lloyd, of the River Doree estate, offered testimony in February 1889. Lloyd pointed out that the typical male labourer often had a small bit of saltfish in his meal along with vegetables, such as root crops or plantains, but that there was a great difference between those with their own subsistence plots and those without. "A well to do negro with provision grounds . . . does not stint himself, but an idle and thriftless man who depends solely on his earnings for his subsistence is content with very little . . ."[67]

Lloyd's observations underline a subtle characteristic of successful livelihood strategies during the depression decades. Success or survival often depended not upon whether an individual had either a wage job or a subsistence plot but upon whether or not he *combined* wages with provision farming. The ill-paid wage labourer of Barbados suffered, obviously, in the depression. The highland subsistence cultivator of St Lucia was better off nutritionally yet lacked sources of cash. Better off than either of them was the typical highland resident of Grenada who had access to a piece of land for subsistence and security and a part-time job as well in order to pay for clothing, school fees or other necessities. The key, ironically, to identifying reliable estate labourers in Grenada in the late 1890s was that they "have land of their own, and [therefore] form a stable and satisfactory class".[68] The data in Appendix A, moreover, suggest that Grenada's relatively low overall death rate in the depression decades may have been a fortuitous result of an overall combination or mix of cash earning and subsistence strategies. And this observation from the late 1800s is consistent with similar findings by many Caribbeanists who acknowledge that livelihood diversification has always been a widespread regional characteristic.

Although official concern in both London and the eastern Caribbean focused on the economics and the botany of sugar cane, subsistence agriculture was not entirely neglected. Daniel Morris' influence in encouraging the establishment and resuscitation of botanic gardens that functioned also as agricultural experiment stations deserves more than passing notice. In St Vincent in particular, the botanic garden's director Henry Powell introduced and planted a wide variety of non-sugar cane plants at the Kingstown gardens during the 1890s, listing these plants in a written memorandum for the 1897 commissioners. More important, Powell provided instructions in pruning, fertilizing and crop care for small-scale farmers and visited all parts of the island after the 1898 hurricane to observe and advise small farmers in the slopes above the coastal estates.[69]

Nor were grassroots agricultural issues always the province of government extension agents. In June 1898 Governor Moloney sent eucalyptus seeds directly to the administrators of St Lucia, St Vincent and Grenada. The seeds, instructed Moloney, were for the directors of the botanic gardens on each of the islands, and their propagation might be best understood by referring to page 229 of the book Moloney himself had written dealing with the forestry of West Africa. His intention was "to have malarial parts of Grenada and Carriacou planted out widely" with eucalyptus trees intended to act "as force pumps to the swampy areas of these Islands". Then during the rest of 1898 over 1,000 small eucalyptus trees were planted in Grenada, the seeds having been sent to the island by the Governor of Australia.[70]

Cacao and Nutmeg

Although the value of cocoa beans exported from Grenada was only half that exported from Trinidad in the depression decades, Grenada was nonetheless considered the region's cacao island, because of that crop's domination of the Grenadian economy. Neither St Vincent—with its porous, ashen soils—nor St Lucia—whose incipient cacao plantations were destroyed in the 1898 hurricane—were thought to be particularly well suited to cacao. Grenada, on the other hand, had ideal physical qualities for it. The island's clayey soils were fertile and water retentive, yet its sloping topography was ideal for drainage. The island's southerly latitude also placed it (in the minds of most authorities) well south of the hurricane tracks. So the perceived absences of non-tropical temperatures and damaging winds, both detrimental to cacao production, enhanced the crop's desirability in Grenada.

Cacao may have been introduced to Grenada as early as 1714 "by trading vessels to the Spanish Main that called at Grenada for water and supplies".[71] Thereafter, most acknowledged, it had thrived in the highlands as a small-scale cash crop during slavery and then beyond emancipation. Cacao's overall acreage and exclusively highland identity had however both changed in Grenada as the island's antiquated sugar industry had succumbed to price reductions and sugar economies of scale in the late 1800s. When the 1897 royal commissioners arrived at St George's in early February, they learned that cacao not only dominated Grenada, especially in the northern and central parts of the island, but that cacao was no longer identified solely with the highlands. According to some, Grenadian cacao on the lowlands "grew and bore better there than on the mountain lands, and cost far less for upkeep".[72]

Usually small-scale Grenadian cultivators, tilling fewer than 5 acres, grew cacao as well as a variety of provisions in the same plot. But into the 1890s estates of more than 100 acres still accounted for far more total acreage on the island than did land legally held by small planters (Table 6.1); some large estates specialized in cacao and some had extensive idle lands, much of these lands in the steep and densely wooded parts of the island. An unspecified number of small cacao producers rented or leased from the larger estates, and a sample of a written cocoa contract appeared in the records of the 1897 commission, specifying, among other things, crop identification, cultivation techniques, building restrictions and possible penalties if the lessee failed to meet specified requirements.[73] Rough islandwide estimates for Grenada in the 1890s put the island's total acreage at about 85,000; of the cultivated land, the 1891 census compilers estimated that 15,545 acres—slightly more than half the cultivated acreage of Grenada— was devoted to cacao. But the compilers pointed out that many smallholdings reported as being in provision crops actually were plots where food crops "were no doubt merely grown as a shelter to the young cocoa." The main cacao parish on the island was St John, in the west central part of Grenada. [74]

Some of cacao's agricultural and economic characteristics helped to explain why it was an ideal crop for smallholders. The land in Grenada considered best for cacao was sloping terrain beneath the 600 foot contour; higher elevations meant steep slopes as well as a surfeit of parasites and mosses that accompanied too much moisture. Ripe cacao pods yielded seeds that farmers planted either in nurseries or directly into cleared fields. The young plants, whether seeds or seedlings, were spaced 8 to 10 feet apart and a banana planted near each to provide 'both stake and shade' and to mark the spot during weeding. With proper care, the young cacao trees grew to about 6 feet in height and began to bear the characteristically brown-purple pods in two and a half to three years, although farmers could not really expect a cacao harvest until the fifth year. During these five years, a typical cacao farmer cultivated and reaped bananas, plantains and root crops from the same land which could repay the cost of clearing and planting and, of course, provide sustenance while the cacao plant matured. Ideally, a cacao tree was in 'full bearing' nine to ten years after its planting and would continue to yield for another twenty, assuming proper care and an absence of disease or insect pest infestation.

Harvesting occurred year round, but the main cacao harvesting seasons were October to January and then April to June. Men harvested the cacao pods with sharpened blades affixed to the ends of poles that were 10 to 12 feet long. As the pods dropped to the ground, women with woven collecting baskets, or sometimes metal tubs, collected them. After picking, the men cut open the pods with cutlasses. The women then extracted the seeds and pulp by hand from inside each pod. Then the seeds were placed inside perforated boxes that were either put into fermentation sheds or shallow pits. Fermented (after five or six days) seeds then dried on wooden trays called 'boucans'. In village areas, this sun-drying of cacao beans often was

9. Cacao estate workers, Grenada, *ca.* 1900
By permission of the Syndics of Cambridge University Library.

accomplished on hides placed alongside the roads where cows, pigs, chickens, dogs and children all wandered about under varying degrees of control. Mechanical bean dryers had been introduced on estates by the 1890s. After drying, cacao beans could be stored for up to three months before they began to deteriorate. Dried cacao beans were exported in 180-pound bags, usually to London, although steamer service to New York for Grenada cacao exporters was available by mid 1893.[75]

Late in the 1890s the Rev. G. W. Branch had owned Good Hope Estate on Grenada for twenty years. Of his 22 acres, 12 were devoted to cacao. Branch considered the soil of Good Hope of only average fertility because of a layer of volcanic tuff just below the surface. He averaged, however, a yield of roughly 1,100 pounds of cacao beans per acre per annum. So, given the rough average price of £3 per hundredweight for Grenada cacao beans between 1881 to 1896, Branch could expect a gross annual cacao income of £33/acre or nearly £400 per year from his 12 cacao acres. The average male field labourer in Grenada in the mid 1890s earned 1s.6d. per day or slightly less than £20 of wages per annum, assuming (inappropriately) that he worked five days were week during every week of the year. These very rough calculations make clear why cacao cultivation—expenses and land rent notwithstanding—was eminently more attractive to Grenadian working peoples than was wage labour.[76]

Not only was Grenadian cacao cultivation financially remunerative, but its socioagricultural dimensions—individualism, freedom from plantation tyranny, and the generally healthy character of its highland identity—all came together to establish cacao as an ideal smallholder crop in the eyes of Archdeacon Gentle and most other observers. Writing in the early 1890s, Hesketh Bell, the Lieutenant-Governor of Dominica, went so far as to suggest that, owing mainly to cacao production, poverty was essentially unknown in Grenada. Shingled, plank houses were replacing mud and thatched-roof huts in the Grenada highlands. Inside these new houses, a growing array of material possessions—manufactured furniture, glass tumblers, newspapers and magazines—were testimonies to economic improvement. Cacao's success had helped erstwhile renters to become freeholders, inspired smallholders to acquire larger land plots, and encouraged squatters to clear "little patches of the forest, and till and cultivate the land free of rent or taxes". Bell's lyrical description of the Grenadian smallholder's prosperity compared him favourably to "many of the European peasantry". As to the assumption that black Grenadian cacao growers' "grandparents" had been "savages . . . in the wilds of Africa", Bell concluded that these advanced Afro-Caribbean smallholders "may furnish the 'coming race' ".[77]

The widespread presence of small quantities of a portable, highly marketable cash crop inspired rampant thievery of cacao beans and even cacao pods in the Grenada highlands. Cacao thieves often worked together, thereby providing a perverse confirmation of the fabled group solidarity among highlanders of the Windwards. In many village communities men without visible means of support or subsistence plots of their own nevertheless lived lives of 'ease and comfort'. And it seemed obvious that they were the ruffians who roamed cacao holdings at night during the harvest seasons in order to pick ripe pods from the trees. The cultivators, in order to thwart such thievery, sometimes picked the pods before they were ripe, thereby diminishing the eventual quality. More common was the thieves' stealing large quantities of beans directly from the boucans or drying sheds.

These were not always simple cases of petty pilfering. In some instances roving gangs of Grenadian thieves overpowered the cacao proprietors before taking their crops. In April 1900, a well-known cocoa thief known as Monsanto or Massanto was found guilty of trespassing on Boulogne Estate in St Andrew parish. Massanto had been armed with a pistol and had fired it at the estate watchmen. Massanto's unsavory reputation, furthermore, included his dabbling in the occult as an obeah man. Similar instances of cocoa thieves taking advantage of the widespread belief in the supernatural in the Grenada highlands were common. Often, teams of thieves impersonated werewolves or 'sham vampires' in order to ward off frightened cacao cultivators while stripping their trees' branches of ripe cacao pods.[78]

Different from the hunger-induced potato raids in Barbados or pilferage of estate crops by impoverished Vincentians, the cacao stealing in the Grenada highlands was unrelated to avoiding starvation. And it usually was the small cacao producer—unable to afford hiring watchmen as the estate owner did—who was the hardest hit. A law in 1889, inspired by a petition signed by 145 cacao smallholders, called for flogging to curtail cacao and nutmeg stealing. Although such punishment was condemned by some as "ancient and barbarous", the popular support for flogging was overwhelming. Between 1891 and 1899, no fewer than 195 Grenadian men were flogged for cacao thievery—most of them more than once—yet the stealing increased. Opinions varied, further, as to whether or not flogging deterred cacao stealing, and several statistical surveys on the subject, such as the one Governor Moloney submitted in October 1900, asserting that flogging prevented cacao stealing,were presented to the Grenada Executive and Legislative Councils in the 1890s.[79]

Licensed cocoa dealers transported dried cacao beans via donkey carts to St George's where the beans eventually were loaded onto ocean-going vessels. The intra-island transport fees increased as a function of distance, and a small army of itinerant cocoa dealers and transporters had emerged on the island by the late 1880s. Their numbers had increased in part because of the low annual cocoa licence fee of one and a half shillings. The widespread exchange of beans and money throughout the island, furthermore, had led to the oft-repeated quip that cocoa 'dealers' and 'stealers' were indistinguishable. And every wooden shack throughout Grenada was said to have a hand-lettered sign outside saying 'licensed cocoa dealer'. The legal response to the dealer proliferation was Ordinance number 14 of 1889 that raised dealers' fees to £10/year. Those disputing the stiff fee warned that it would destroy the grassroots entrepreneurial spirit of both small dealers and female cocoa beverage vendors. In many cases, the £10 fee simply drove the small-scale exchange and transport of dried beans into the hands of "unlicensed itinerant buyers who are constantly breaking the law, but with whom every sympathy is felt" because small producers often were too fatigued to walk the mountain roads and trails themselves to deliver small quantities of dried beans to the dealers in St George's.[80]

As a highland crop, cacao in Grenada shared important ecological characteristics with subsistence agriculture, perhaps the most important being that it often was interspersed with other planted species. But as a cash crop, cacao also shared some of the attributes of lowland sugar cane. As example of this was the role it often assumed as an ecological dominant. By the mid 1880s, according to some, the "mania" inspired by high cacao prices had "driven nearly every other species . . . out of the field", relegating Grenadian provision grounds "to the more remote lands of the mountain districts".[81] More alarming was the conventional wisdom that successful cacao cultivation required fresh soils on newly cleared lands, not acreage that already had been either in cane or old cacao groves. So, according to one observer, the clear-cutting mentality in Grenada animated most cacao estate owners and smallholders alike who, if they considered land ideal for cacao, would "order rows of majestic mountain palms to be ruthlessly cut down without the slightest compunction". These actions, moreover, threatened some of the most beautiful and distinctive forest species in the island so that in a few years vegetational diversity and beauty "will be as rare in Grenada as it is at present in Barbados".[82]

The ruinous runoff, flooding and soil erosion of the 1890s resulting from the deforestation of Grenadian uplands to make way for cacao has been described in chapter 4. And other environmental complications also accompanied the ecological simplification of the island's highland vegetation. In October 1900 the cacao planters on the windward side of Grenada suffered from an infestation caused by a small insect known as 'thrips' (order *Thysanoptera*) that was destroying young trees and inhibiting pod development on mature cacao plants. Daniel Morris, now based in Barbados, recommended fumigation with potassium cyanide. This pesticide strategy was unsuccessful and by late in the year the Grenada Legislative Council had arranged for an entomologist from Kew Gardens to come to study the insect's life cycle and to recommend possible preventive measures.[83] The runoff and slope wash, moreover, not only threatened the lowlands, but Grenada's formerly sparkling highland streams now were often contaminated from refuse that had been carelessly discarded in the cocoa patches. In some of the upland villages, overcrowding, indiscriminate waste disposal, and even the burial of human remains in cacao plots created unsanitary and disease-ridden village environments that rivaled even the dank Barbadian tenantries and Bridgetown slums in unhealthiness.[84]

And similar to sugar cane economically, cacao was subject to price volatility influenced from afar. Despite warnings about overplanting in response to ephemerally high prices, that is precisely what occurred in Grenada in the mid 1880s when a cultivator could count on receiving more than 70 shillings per 100 pounds of dried beans. A decade later, when those trees planted amidst the enthusiasm generated by the high prices of the mid 1880s were coming into full production, the price had dropped to under 50 shillings per hundredweight. The royal commissioners in 1897 thus heard testimony in Grenada suggesting that low prices already were driving erstwhile cacao cultivators out of business. The children of cacao producers, moreover, were not inclined towards agricultural careers. Instead, many of them 'despised' agriculture and looked forward to white-collar jobs. Despite the positive image of the Grenadian smallholder that had become almost an ideal of what the postdepression Caribbean might be, boom-and-bust prices, coupled with the erosional effects of price driven overplanting for cacao, led to growing official concern as the nineteenth century drew to a close.[85]

This concern was modified in part by the increase in nutmeg cultivation into the 1890s. Smallholders and estate owners alike grew nutmeg trees, usually interspersed with cacao, throughout the highlands of Grenada. Nutmegs thrived at somewhat higher elevations than cacao, between 800 and 1,500 feet above sea level. By 1895, 'Spices', mainly nutmeg, accounted for nearly £21,000 in export value from Grenada, the island's second largest export item following cacao (valued at £139,000 for 1895).[86]

Nutmeg trees, like cacao, were planted as seeds, and thereafter the staked seedlings were transplanted from 15 to 30 feet apart. The hardy trees usually established themselves in the highland plots in a year or so but did not reach their full maturity and yielding potential until about fifteen years after planting. Nutmeg trees' thin-shaped leaves were and are a brilliant green, and at maturity the branches bent to the ground producing shade that inhibited weeds and thereby reduced maintenance. Because they could be planted singly or in groves, nutmeg trees were ideal smallholder assets, although the longevity between planting and harvest required a long-term commitment to a particular piece of ground. The salmon-coloured nuts, moreover, ripened throughout the year, providing a year-round source of ready cash. The relatively simple processing involved collecting the ripe seeds when they split open to reveal the lacy, crimson covering of mace around dark brown interior nuts. Then after these brown nuts were dried they were cracked open for the nutmegs that were then packed for export. The simple processing of nutmegs invited thievery, and police notices describing suspected nutmeg thieves abounded in the pages of Grenada's government gazettes in the 1880s and 1890s.[87]

Soufrière's Eruption in 1902

Highland cultivators and all others in the Windwards were accustomed to the tremors and occasional damage created by periodic seismic disturbances far below the earth's surface. A major volcanic eruption in St Vincent in 1812 killed over 100 people, but it had happened so long ago that by the turn of the century it had passed from living memory and was in this regard comparable to the great hurricane of 1831. Yet the periodic jolts and shocks felt by everyone were apparent reminders of potential disaster, and minor earthquakes were occasionally of such severity as to merit mention in colonial correspondence. At 8:49 a.m. on 10 January 1888, an earthquake shook Grenada with sufficient force to crack and damage several of the stone buildings in St George's. Three years later, on 4 July 1891, "a severe earthquake" rattled the residents of St Lucia. Those in St Vincent had felt a series of earthquake shocks in February 1886, and it was said at the time that visitors approaching St Vincent by ship knew the island not by the perfumed scent of spice-laden breezes as in Grenada "but by the sulphurous odor of the Soufrière, which is generally emitting sulphurous fumes".[88]

St Vincent's Mt Soufrière erupted dramatically on 7 May 1902, sending out a thin stream of lava, tons of hot ash, and giant arcs of red-hot rocks and sand. The catastrophe killed 1,327 officially, although unofficial estimates ranged to 1,600 and even higher. The eruption was overshadowed by the explosion of Mt Pelée on Martinique two days earlier that killed 30,000, set ships afire, and sent refugees to neighbouring locales. The geological relationships between the two eruptions was not lost on inhabitants of nearby volcanic islands; residents of St George's, Grenada, for example, noted "the Lagoon" in the harbour bubble ominously in early May as it had thirty-five years earlier prior to the destructive tidal wave, and the bubbling continued into 1903 as St Vincent's volcano emitted minor eruptions. For St Vincent itself, the disaster—less than four years after the 1898 hurricane—was particularly cruel for a place that, according to the Colonial Office, had "within the space of four years been visited by two calamities which it would be difficult, probably impossible, to parallel in the history of a British colony".[89]

Soufrière apparently had lain dormant until becoming an active volcano in about AD 1300. Then it erupted in 1718 and again in 1812.[90] In the first months of 1902 the volcano had rumbled threateningly. The noise and associated tremors reached alarming proportions on 6 May. On that day sounds from Soufrière became "more continuous and louder", and late in the afternoon a vertical column of what appeared to be steam ascended from the crater following "a noise like . . . a cannon". Frightened villagers in the Richmond area, directly southwest of the crater, abandoned their homes and headed down to the police station at Chateaubelair as the volcanic explosions continued through the night. Nor were they the only people in retreat. Governor of the Windwards Sir Robert Llewelyn, who had been visiting St Vincent, took his leave of the island during Soufrière's alarming activity on 6 May, eventually to correspond with London about the subsequent catastrophe from the safety of his office in Grenada.[91]

The major eruption came the next day on the morning of 7 May as "black material was . . . thrown up" during periodic discharges. Then at about 1 p.m. "a huge mushroom-shaped cloud of black smoke, intersected in every direction with electrical flashes, rose many thousand feet". The cloud divided above St Vincent, one part passing over the windward side of the island, the other over the leeward side, a frightening symbol that the island was about to be engulfed by yet another catastrophe. About an hour later, a deafening roar from the volcano preceded the fatal wave of heated gas accompanied by ashes and rocks that altogether destroyed much of the vegetation and killed people and animals throughout the northern third of the island. The undetermined number of Vincentians—apparently several thousand—within the area later described as "devastated", sought refuge in churches, shops and school buildings. And the survivors who later counted the dead found clusters of 20, 30 or 40 bodies huddled together inside buildings, people who apparently had sought safety when, among other things, the thatch roofs of their huts had burst into flame.[92]

One estate worker, forty-year old Charles Alexander, survived the eruption and provided a vivid account of his experience to one of the surgeons treating those who had escaped death. Alexander went to work on the morning of 7 May at Tourama estate despite the sounds and belching ash from Soufrière. At midday, after hearing a huge noise like a "rushing river", he headed home to Overland village. Alexander and about eighty others sought refuge in Victor Sutherland's shop; its metal roof might protect them from the ash and rocks now falling. They shut the doors and windows at about 2 p.m. when they sky darkened. Apparently Alexander passed out from the heat, "choked with the hot stuff going down my belly . . ." When he regained consciousness he found himself lying beneath two corpses. Alexander and only five others in the shop were alive. Alexander watched "the great black cloud . . . full of fire like lightning" through a crack in the window that dropped glowing rocks near the shop. When the eruption ceased at about 4 p.m., Alexander waited until the atmosphere brightened and then, incredibly, walked the 5 miles south along the coastal road to the hospital at Georgetown.[93]

The hardest hit part of the island was the area directly east of Soufrière. Captain F. L. Campbell of the *Indefatigable*, one of the relief ships whose arrivals followed the disaster, described the scene about one week later:

From Owia Bay . . . as far as Georgetown, there is complete destruction of everything, sugar estates, factories, and cattle, if not under lava and mud, under a coating of ashes and stones nearly two feet deep. Nearly everyone in the district was wiped out; all the deaths, 1,400 to 1,500 took place in this neighbourhood, all the 180 wounded are from here, and all the livestock killed . . .[94]

Aftershocks, some of them violent, continued for nearly a year. On 3 September a black cloud from Soufrière was "absolutely vomiting electricity" and led to evacuations from village areas into Kingstown. In the following month, during 15 and 16 October, eruptions from the volcano showered "coarse gritty sand or small stones" as far south as Georgetown. In late March 1903 another outburst spewed sand and scorched trees beyond the area devastated ten months earlier.[95]

The St Vincent eruption of March 1903 sent a towering black cloud 90 miles east to Barbados. The cloud reached Bridgetown at 9 a.m. on 22 March, observers in Barbados later calculating that the dust had been travelling at the speed of 40 miles per hour in the upper atmosphere. As the cloud enveloped Barbados, it created midday darkness so that "it was impossible to read even large type". Ash from the cloud fell in Barbados from about 11:15 a.m. until 1:30 p.m. when it began to diminish, and all was clear by 5 p.m. as the cloud headed farther east. Roughly 3 tons of volcanic ash per acre were estimated to have fallen in Barbados on that day, the heavier amounts in the vicinity of Bridgetown. Barbadian planters reported enhanced fertility on their estates thereafter owing to the Vincentian ash, perhaps the only good that came to the region from Soufrière's eruption.[96]

The St Vincent eruption was of less overall severity than was the catastrophe in Martinique, and it is important that the descriptions and outcomes of both explosions were reported together in official British Colonial Office records. The British paid far more attention to the events in their own colony, although they could hardly ignore the stream of refugees from the Mt Pelée eruption who fled to nearby British islands. A message to London from Dominica on 12 May 1902, described scenes of Martinique brought by those who had come to Dominica after the eruption. Rivers were overflowing on Martinique, new craters opening up, and nearly a week of smoky "total darkness" had enveloped the French colony. An unspecified number of unfortunate St Lucians had been visiting family and friends on Martinique when Pelée exploded so that they "shared the fate of the inhabitants of St Pierre". And a month after Pelée, survivors from Martinique still were coming to St Lucia, receiving shelter from St Lucian relatives and small doles provided by both the St Lucian and French governments.[97]

The stark physical geographical changes in the northern part of St Vincent wrought by Soufrière's eruption began to be reclaimed by the tropical environment almost as soon as the noise stopped. A month after the May 1902 eruption, runoff from heavy rains had cut rivulets through the ash in the northeastern part of the island. The tireless botanic garden curator, Henry Powell, ascended Soufrière's slopes two weeks after the secondary eruption in October. Powell, accompanied by the botanic station curators of Lagos and Sierra Leone, spent one and a half hours at the summit observing Soufrière's boiling interior; then they returned by sliding down the knife-edge dunes of ash that had been created by running water. Daniel Morris came from Barbados to conduct an inspection tour of all of St Vincent in the last week of 1902. Although noting the malaise produced by years of economic depression, compounded by the twin disasters of hurricane and eruption, Morris also reported seeing crops growing up through layers of ash, concluding that the newly ejected material eventually would enhance the island's overall fertility.[98]

The efforts to restore normality for the island's human populace began immediately after the eruption on 7 May. The coasting steamer from St Lucia arrived with food and water even before an accurate body count was available. Doctors came from Barbados, Grenada, and the British army detachments of the Eastern Caribbean. Nearly 200 persons were admitted to local hospitals, many who had walked miles after suffering severe burns. The need to evacuate themselves and also having to wait before seeing doctors meant that a surprisingly small number of the Vincentian survivors displayed symptoms of shock. The absence of shock, which was "an invariable sequel of intense burns in Europeans", was interpreted by one British army doctor on the scene as a reflection of poss "the lower nervous organization of the coloured race"![99]

Food, blankets, medical supplies and clothing from nearby islands and also from British and American ships arrived in St Vincent within a week. Vincentian authorities established distribution points for food and blankets at five points around the island in order to accommodate those remaining in their own villages as well as those refugees, now mainly in the Kingstown area, from the northern parts of the island where ashes and charred stumps were all that was left. The underground cable between St Vincent and St Lucia was severed during the eruption, so first-hand reports and requests had to travel by ship from St Vincent to either Grenada or St Lucia before being cabled elsewhere. London assured Vincentian authorities that they

10. Looking west from Orange Hill Estate, St Vincent, after the 1902 eruption
Collection: Foreign and Commonwealth Office Library, London.

could draw £1,000 if necessary, from Crown Agents at once, but it soon became obvious that far more was needed. Within a month Governor Llewelyn estimated that 500 workers' houses would have to be rebuilt. He had by then ordered £5,000 worth of timber from the United States and Canada and estimated that £50,000 would be necessary for rebuilding and for maintaining the homeless on St Vincent until the end of 1902. Most important, the future of the island was of immediate concern.[100]

It was not as if planning the future of St Vincent—or the other small islands of the Eastern Caribbean, for that matter—had been ignored. Indeed, much of the correspondence between London and the Caribbean colonies in the 1890s had dealt precisely with land issues, development and the future. The 1897 royal commission report, brimming with data and suggestions for future land use, was still fresh in many minds. And Governor Moloney's actions in pushing through legislation to purchase moribund Vincentian estates for eventual resale in small plots to black cultivators had been a positive development emerging from the wreckage left by the 1898 hurricane.

Yet the post-eruption relief and resettlement on St Vincent was clumsy and ill-conceived, and it generated animosity from, it seems, all concerned. One month after the May 1902 eruption Governor Llewelyn reported to London that he was attempting to relocate the 500 families uprooted by the disaster. Two estates, Campden Park and Rutland Vale, eventually were purchased for resettlement purposes. But London's immediate response to Llewelyn was vague, loaded with provisos, and marked by distrust of the large-scale Vincentian planters who they did want to compensate with relief funds. And for all the plans and schemes for possible resettlements and smallholder developments, the Colonial Office's main suggestion to Llewelyn was to send the eruption refugees elsewhere. By late June 1902 the Secretary of State informed him that emigration really was the best solution and that the governors of both Jamaica and British Honduras had been contacted and were "receptive" to the idea of receiving homeless Vincentians.[101]

Llewelyn became a target from all sides for the damage and discontent that had rained down from Soufrière and which had been amplified by mismanagement from as far away as London. His departure during the original eruption had never been forgiven by Vincentian planters and clergy, two of whom penned a damning letter to London in July 1902, speaking of unprecedented "widespread dissatisfaction" with his rule. They continued on to elaborate his lack of tact, his tendency to concentrate power in himself rather than with local councils, a possibly inappropriate concession to Grenadian lumber dealers who profited from the disaster, and his overall policies seemingly designed "to weaken the industrial spirit which is so necessary . . . among the labouring classes".[102]

In October 1902 the Colonial Office, apparently dissatisfied with Llewelyn's handling of the relief work, appointed Captain Arthur Young, the Chief Secretary of Cyprus, as a special officer in charge of the effort. By that time St Vincent had received nearly £65,000 in relief funds, over £52,000 of it from the Lord Mayor of London's Mansion House Fund. Some of the money was disbursed directly in small cash doles distributed weekly at several locations around the island; over 6,000 persons still were receiving the money payments in mid November. Another 1,450 men and boys were repairing and improving roads and being paid from what was now called the "eruption fund". Some £5,000 was spent for lumber in 1902. Captain Young had reduced the dole and road work by January 1903, and £35,000 remained in the fund. Roughly £3,000 of the money later went to agricultural development projects in St Vincent. Eventually £25,000 became a "permanent investment" in England, interest from the sum to be used for poor relief in St Vincent.[103]

The dole reduction in St Vincent had been accomplished by a London-imposed 'labour test' in November 1902, designed to reduce payments to those eligible to work. Further, old persons living with able-bodied family members were denied relief payments. And the idea that mothers capable of work should merit money payments because of the need to care for their children was dismissed in London. Secretary Chamberlain himself noted that subsidized child care by mothers was inadmissible: "As it is possible, and I believe usual in St Vincent, for such children to be left under the charge of their older brothers and sisters."[104]

These hard measures were part of London's continuing insistence that the best remedy for St Vincent's beleaguered population was substantial emigration, a plan that failed because of the Vincentians' unwillingness to leave. Throughout the relief crisis in the eruption's aftermath, Llewelyn had attempted to push London's emigration proposal, and he had thereby earned the enmity of those below him. Llewelyn, prodded by the Colonial Office, had published a decree in late September that relief was no longer available to those not taking advantage of emigration opportunities. A public meeting at the Kingstown public library in mid October assailed Llewelyn in particular and emigration as a solution. Spokesmen asserted that food brought to St Vincent now was "rotting" in local warehouses so that misery-induced migration might be accomplished. Reports of the meeting suggested a consensus among "all classes", including the planters who were unwilling to lose labourers to other islands and their workers who wanted to stay on their home island.[105]

The Vincentians' unwillingness to emigrate reinforced the same collective attitude that had prevailed after the 1898 hurricane. The few Vincentians who had headed for Trinidad then had been dissatisfied, and most of them already had returned. The Colonial Office had difficulty understanding why West Indian subjects who had been so ravaged by disaster in the past four years would not respond to an invitation to emigrate. The Vincentians doubtless had little appreciation for grand colonial designs when it was they who were being encouraged to head for far-off places from which they may never return to family and friends. Besides, land settlement schemes on St Vincent had been discussed and rumoured for years, and after the hurricane some of these long-awaited land settlements already had been set in motion, however tentatively. With their own lands, black Vincentians could produce their own food, as well as something to sell. And with their own land, weather and earthquake hazards not withstanding, they might be immune to the decrees, whims and plans of planters and colonial officers. Among those spokesmen against Llewelyn's and the Colonial Office's emigration scheme was the Wesleyan minister James H. Darrell who reported to a local newspaper in late 1902 what he had been preaching to the local population. Darrell pointed out that the government should acquire for the people of St Vincent "good and suitable lands on our eastern and southern coasts on which to settle" and predicted with a biblical parable what black Vincentians, and those on nearby islands, apparently had desired all along: "Trust in the Lord, and do good; dwell in the land and verily thou shalt be fed."[106]

Soufrières' eruption in 1902, among its many other effects, underlined the immediacy among Colonial Office planners in London that decisions were necessary about the West Indies. The officials could no longer procrastinate by requesting more background information. In the 1897 Royal Commission report, they already had hundreds of pages of recent, first-hand information gathered from several points of view. The truly valuable parts of that report had been gleaned in particular places from knowledgeable observers, and it was information that usually was applicable to the island at hand, not to the region as a whole. The same was true for the erup-

11. Wallibu Estate, St Vincent after the 1902 eruption
Collection: Foreign and Commonwealth Office Library, London.

tion of 1902. The explosion really was confined to St Vincent within the British Caribbean, and nowhere else. The singularity that the St Vincent eruption presented, moreover, was symptomatic of a larger sociopolitical complexity; the British Caribbean was never smaller or greater than the sum of its insular parts because the parts only rarely fit together. The assumption that they did and the anxieties this assumption created is the subject of the concluding chapter.

Chapter Seven
The Eastern Caribbean in 1900: Region, Insularity and Change

The final report of the 1897 royal commission probably was as important as a descriptive benchmark for the fin-de-siècle British Caribbean as it was a document pointing in new directions for regional land use. The report's summary findings—submitted to the Colonial Office in London in September 1897—spoke of a tired Caribbean sugar cane industry that dominated the region's cultivable land but which was of declining value to the local populace, a situation that existed nearly everywhere except on Grenada where sugar was no longer exported. And nearly every other generalization the commissioners attempted for the region was hedged with similar provisos because of the striking intraregional variety from one place to the next. To be sure, the depression's intensity was felt everywhere but with varying effects because "conditions and prospects . . . vary very materially in the different Colonies".[1]

Early on the report emphasized the potential for the local labourers to create more strife and trouble owing to the depression conditions; the typical Afro-Caribbean resident of the region was "excitable and difficult to manage, especially in large numbers, when his temper is aroused". This emphasis reinforces the suggestion that local riots and disturbances were the real catalysts helping to precipitate the commission's formation. Yet the report's summary also reflected an apparently genuine feeling of responsibility for colonial subjects and even strands of a benign humanitarianism that the commissioners had encouraged and developed in their several months of research; working-class Britons, according to the commissioners, had enjoyed cheap sugar at the expense of the depressed West Indian islands. In a broader sense, the empire was ultimately responsible for the creation of the British Caribbean itself: "We have placed the labouring population where it is, and created for it the conditions . . . under which it exists . . ."[2]

The commission report and its findings, in other words, were not only lengthy, but also multifaceted and ambivalent, typical of the attitude of the Colonial Office bureaucracy at the time where conversations ". . . voiced the strident clichés of social Darwinism . . . [and] also contained the familiar rhetoric of nineteenth-century humanitarianism".[3] And disregarding the equivocal character of the report and its findings seems analytically unhelpful. Probably few would accept entirely C.Y. Shephard's enthusiastic 'Magna Charta' pronouncement about the commission report fifty years after its publication. Nor does Michael Craton's recent categorization of the commission's recommendations as a case of divide and rule between rural and urban workers and "merely one more hegemonic tactic" help to clarify understanding of the report's significance.[4]

Although the most important of the commission's unanimous final recommendations indeed called for the settlement of labourers "on small plots of land as peasant proprietors", they also achieved unanimity on four others: the improvement of minor agricultural industries and cultivation systems in general, especially for "small proprietors"; better inter-island communications; the establishment of a trade in fresh tropical fruit with New York and eventually with London; and the "grant of a loan from the Imperial Exchequer for the establishment of Central Factories in Barbados". The region's geographical variation precluded the recommendation of political federation that had been advocated by C. S. Salmon and others: "We are . . . unable to recommend such federation . . . [as] . . . the Colonies, as we have said, are widely scattered, and differ very much in their conditions . . ."[5]

Nor was the three-man commission able to achieve unanimity on perhaps the single most important practical issue facing them, that of whether to propose countervailing tariffs to protect the British Caribbean sugar industry from bounty-supported beet sugar from the Continent. Although Barbour and Grey declined to recommend such tariffs, the commission's chairman, Henry Norman, urged that for sugar imported by the United Kingdom "duties . . . be levied . . . to an amount equal to the bounty that has been paid on it by any foreign Government". Failing to adopt these measures, according to Norman, would ruin West Indian planters, distress the British Caribbean labouring and artisan classes, perhaps render the islands ungovernable, and lead the region to "serious disaster".[6] So after three months' travel in the Caribbean followed by a stop in New York combined with preliminary and concluding hearings in London, all of which resulted in thousands of pages of testimony, the commission fell short of making a single unanimous practical decision about the underlying macroeconomic cause of the depression.

The fundamental cause of this disagreement probably had been embodied in the nature of the charge given originally to the commissioners, to survey the nature and conditions of the sugar industry in the British Caribbean colonies as a whole. Such a regional survey constituted, of course, the study of an abstraction that could be readily visualized, graphed, discussed and compared as if it were real at the London Colonial Office. But British Caribbean cultivators made decisions about crop combinations, fertilizer ratios, irrigation systems and marketing strategies on the basis of local insular geographical variables, not the British Caribbean region. Even more so, the working peoples of the region lived their lives on particular islands characterized by local topographies, vegetation, soil types and climatic conditions. Planning and observation could be done at the regional level. Yet any implementation whatever of these plans would invariably have to be done in particular places. Hence, the very obvious yet always vexing distinction between region and place dogged the commissioners at every turn, causing them continuously to comment on differences and variety within the British Caribbean. And local geographies, which provided the material bases for subsistence activities, had taken on even more importance in the wake of depressed sugar prices.

The unanimous commission recommendations had of course acknowledged the region-place distinction in recommending central sugar factories for Barbados. And within the relatively small four-island area of Barbados and the Windwards, differences in both geography and commission recommendations represented a microcosm of the variety found within the British Caribbean. For Barbados the commissioners saw the continuation and improvement of the local sugar industry as "the only hope of supporting . . . the present population". In direct contrast, Grenada, the prototypical peasant island always extolled by the commissioners, was encouraged to extend its already successful smallholder emphasis. The commissioners saw in St Vincent, as expected, the dire need for transformation from a planter dominated island to one of peasant producers with land expropriation a suggested means of achieving this desired change. St Lucia occupied something of a middle ground; the central factories were disappointing, coaling and military operations seen to be important, and "the most important measure to be taken . . . the settlement of the people on the land".[7]

The ultimate importance of insularity in understanding and possibly implementing the commission's proposed changes was not the same as parochialism. Quite the opposite, many in the islands were becoming more aware than ever before of global issues that influenced their local sugar cane industries. At an anti-bounty meeting in Bridgetown in mid December

1897, held in response to receiving first copies of the commission's final report, the Barbadian master-in-chancery, W. K. Chandler, spoke of a recent shipboard conversation he had with a German merchant. The German doubted that his country ever would voluntarily rescind the bounty system for sugar beets. One reason was the balance of political power held by German agrarian interests between the imperialists and socialists. Another was that high beet prices reduced German emigration to the United States, keeping a ready supply of potential soldiers at home.[8]

Despite the wide-ranging influences on the British Caribbean sugar industry, the report of the royal commission was read first and foremost when it came to any of the islands for the recommendations and observations it made for that particular place. And different recommendations obviously led to different responses. Although reinforcing Barbados' sugar monoculture, it had an almost revolutionary effect, for example, in St Vincent. As early as October 1897 groups of labourers around the island—following the newspaper accounts of the report's recommendations—endorsed the breakup of local estates and anticipated resistance by the island's 'monopolists' who could be counted on to 'pooh-pooh' the findings. But the situation on St Vincent had become so severe that there was no turning back from the planning, discussions and land surveys that had gone on for years. On 14 March 1898 the British Parliament voted a sum of £15,000 to settle smallholders on the island. Almost immediately Governor Moloney drafted a land acquisition bill, and his administrator compiled a list of twenty-nine 'abandoned' sugar cane estates on St Vincent suitable for 'expropriation'. In introducing the proposal for smallholder funds to Parliament, Colonial Secretary Joseph Chamberlain had appealed to both Caribbean conditions and European precedent; he explained that the commission's description of the presence on St Vincent of abandoned lands and underemployed working peoples was analogous to the situation in Ireland where people and land recently had been brought together only after land expropriation schemes were accomplished with government funds.[9]

Imperial Ambivalence

The successful sponsorship of a parliamentary grant-in-aid for St Vincent smallholders was however a stance only recently adopted by Chamberlain so that he could push more general yet still selective land reform in the British

Caribbean. When he first received the report of the royal commission in the autumn of 1897 he favoured active support of the sugar plantocracy throughout the islands, even if it meant imposing countervailing duties on European beet sugar as Henry Norman had advocated in his dissent at the conclusion of the report. In general, the commissioners' report disappointed Chamberlain. Certainly they had emphasized the terrible plight of the British Caribbean—something everyone had known for a decade—but their equivocal position as to a possible remedy left the overall responsibility for decisions to the Colonial Office in London. On 8 November 1897, Chamberlain circulated a memorandum to fellow cabinet members that advocated attacking the European sugar bounties by "placing a considerable duty on all bounty-fed sugar". The decision, he affirmed, was his because "the Royal Commission have not given much assistance to the solution of the problem". Chamberlain asserted that taking this bold yet responsible step would clarify once and for all if the British Caribbean sugar industries were really viable. Further, it finally would "put an end to the grumble that the West Indies would gain more by joining the United States than by remaining British islands".[10]

Chamberlain's suggested tariff reform was rejected by the cabinet, in particular by Treasury Secretary Sir Edward Hamilton, and Chancellor of the Exchequer Michael Hicks Beach. The latter asserted that the placing of sugar duties on bounty-fed beet sugar would simply be too costly to British consumers and therefore very dangerous politically. Chamberlain then countered that the only way to save the West Indies from ruin was by government intervention of a different kind, a series of financial grants for local economic transformations, the solution that the commissioners originally had recommended in concluding their report; he further pointed out that the estimated cost of £580,000 to implement the proposed changes in the islands was "totally inadequate" and that more funds would be necessary. Neither Hicks Beach nor Chamberlain was completely pleased with any direct imperial intervention on behalf of the West Indies because it went against the grain of prevailing *laissez-faire* attitudes and had only limited precedent.[11]

So the policy evolving for the West Indies involved a combination of government and private initiatives; although Chamberlain had initially favoured saving the West Indian sugar industry through tariff reform after seeing the commissioners' report, he had even earlier supported smallholders as active commercial producers within the broader British realm. It was, in Thomas Holt's words, a "colonial policy [that] folded this new found commitment to peasant proprietorship into the older doctrine of imperial consolidation and expansion".[12]

On 26 July 1898, Chamberlain, emboldened by parliament's approval of the St Vincent grant, issued a circular letter to West Indian governors advocating the formation of small-scale settlements elsewhere in the region as had been suggested in the recent commission report. Such settlements, according to Chamberlain, should be "carefully chosen" as well as "within comparatively easy reach of a market" and of a "permanent character" rather than temporary squatter settlements which were well known as detrimental to local soil fertility, timber and water supplies. These new settlements, cautioned Chamberlain further, should not be sited so as to compete with plantations for labour.[13]

In the southeastern Caribbean the governors' replies were predictable. Governor Moloney of the Windwards, already planning specific changes for St Vincent, not only endorsed the idea of smallholders but also emphasized freehold land tenure because tenants could not be counted on for "the permanent improvement of . . . property". Governor Hay of Barbados took the letter to his executive committee where it was "unanimously considered as inapplicable to Barbados under existing conditions".[14]

The problems facing Chamberlain and the Colonial Office were, again, both regionwide and insular, and overall solutions involved simultaneous attempts to coordinate disparate intraregional landholding systems that were diverging at an accelerating rate. Although small settler schemes were obviously necessary in some places, the large wage-earning populations on the sugar islands could, according to most, be supported only by estate labour. Yet maintaining the sugar islands meant more than simply extending the status quo in a few selected places. The growing American presence in the region meant that, in the eyes of one British observer in 1899, Cuba and Puerto Rico were on the verge of dramatic agricultural transformations: "Should the British possessions lying at their very doors continue to jog along in the same antiquated fashion as heretofore, the contrast will be painfully striking . . ."[15]

The commissioners knew from their recent observations that diverging land-use systems created special difficulties when they existed in close proximity with one another, a point underlined in Chamberlain's circular letter when he highlighted possible competition for labour between small plots and estates. The commission report, in acknowledging this point, had noted "that it is *not impossible* for the two systems, of large estates and peasant holdings, to exist side by side with mutual advantage" (emphasis added).[16]

Yet reassurance about what was and was not within the realm of theoretical possibility provided little direction in guiding practical land-use decisions. The advice from Governors Moloney and Hay—men who represented an elite point of view but, more important, men on the spot—represented more practical guidelines. Among the small islands of the Caribbean, particular uses of land would be more successful as islandwide systems rather than varying internally between peasant plots and plantation estates. At the end of the nineteenth century in the southeastern Caribbean, these were then the divergent courses the small British islands were taking. Barbados remained devoted to sugar cane. The others were to become—or already had become in Grenada's case—islands of smallholders. These were the principal contrasts reflected by the London Colonial Office's inability to choose between two inherently different uses of land for the region as a whole. The region's insularity and environmental variation had thereby allowed the British to choose both uses of land at the same time, thereby reinforcing inter-island contrasts.

Land-Use Changes in the Windwards

Chamberlain's letter recommending the active consideration of the establishment of local peasantries to all of the West Indian governors was dated exactly one and a half months before the giant hurricane of September 1898 hit Barbados and then continued westward to devastate St Vincent. And observers at that time as well as modern historians have suggested that the hurricane was, at the very least, a catalyst for subsequent local land use changes. One Colonial Office spokesman in 1900 asserted that "In St Vincent the taking over of private lands was an extreme measure . . . to avoid starvation after the hurricane . . ."[17] A century later, Chamberlain's biographer Peter Marsh points out that in the midst of the cabinet discussions in 1897 and 1898 over the level of funding necessary to implement recommended economic changes in the Caribbean "[a] devastating hurricane . . . helped Chamberlain to ensure that the package was well funded".[18]

Yet a catalyst is not a cause. Although the beginnings of land-use changes described in this book at the ends of chapters three and six followed in the wakes of the 1898 hurricane and then the volcanic eruption in St

Vincent four years later, these kinds of changes had been discussed actively for more than a decade. Recall that Governor Sendall considered the storm of August 1886 a fine opportunity to initiate St Vincent land-use changes, a full decade before the British parliament voted to pay for the establishment of village settlements there. And Joseph Chamberlain's entertaining the idea of a central sugar mill for St Vincent after the 1898 hurricane suggests that even that disaster had not convinced him entirely of the inevitability of the break up of the island's sugar cane estates.

The smallholder ideal also had been actively discussed and implemented for some time well beyond the Eastern Caribbean. Government officials in Barbados, the Windwards and elsewhere in the fin-de-siècle British Caribbean made numerous references to Irish land devolution. Extending that point, Thomas Holt's recent scholarship shows how British officials throughout the empire in the late 1800s were influenced by similar events in several parts of the world. The pan-Caribbean applicability of these kinds of ideas, moreover, had been personified throughout the 1897 royal commission proceedings by the agriculturalist Daniel Morris. In composing Appendix A of the commissioners' final report, Morris pointed out that both sugar cane and other tropical crops in the West Indies could be adequately cultivated in the region by smallholders; he also reminded readers that he had been advocating for years how smallholders actually could expand cultivated West Indian lands that, in his estimation, were badly underutilized.[19]

Yet recommended change for parts of the Caribbean region that foresaw the conversion of large estates to small-scale plots was not to be equated with freedom from interference or outside control. The Colonial Office planners recommended strict supervision of farm activities. It was an extension of the contemporary agricultural development wisdom put forward by thinkers like Benjamin Kidd who advocated tropical development by "natives" only if they were provided European guidance. The geographer Janet Momsen uses the term "imposed schemes" to capture the character of this supposedly grassroots British Caribbean land-use planning introduced from the top down; she suggests further that the perception and eventual use of these schemes and land settlements by the villagers themselves were far different from the planners' original intents.[20]

This insistence by government officials for supervision and direction of small-scale growers had been incorporated into local planning discussions for years. Early in 1890 Governor Hely-Hutchinson led an overnight camping party into the upper Richmond Valley in the interior of St Vincent, an experience that inspired his glowing report of the area's potential for the establishment of a local peasantry. The governor predicted that small-scale cultivators could be brought into "civilization" under watchful government supervision. He reckoned that such a settlement there could be every bit as successful as in Grenada, where prosperity had flowered because Grenadian smallholders and planters there had worked "side by side", the latter group providing valuable and exemplary behavior and advice.[21]

The issue of official control and direction of future small-scale Caribbean cultivators became intertwined with implementation plans that followed the recommendations of the 1897 commission. In April 1898, the director of Kew Gardens, Dr Thiselton-Dyer, proclaimed the sugar industry in the Lesser Antilles a lost cause and saw the region's hopes for the future bound up with an experiment which, according to him, would go the same way as the region's dying sugar cane industry "unless it is controlled by competent technical supervision".[22]

Control and supervision were to extend beyond proclamations about people directing people and included specifying the kinds of geographical characteristics necessary to ensure agricultural success. The royal commissioners were convinced that the inaccessibility of the remote island interiors guaranteed failure. Chamberlain's circular letter in July 1898 had therefore highlighted accessibility and proximity to markets via adequate roads as necessary conditions for small-scale agricultural success. The point was already appreciated in the Caribbean itself. The previous October, for instance, a St Vincent newspaper pointed out that it was "idle to expect that a peasant proprietary body can be established . . . [in areas] . . . practically inaccessible for want of roads ... a great distance from any shipping Bay".[23]

But accessibility and road quality represented only two characteristics among many that might help agricultural schemes prosper. Early in 1899 Governor Moloney enumerated other ingredients for success among smallholders. Besides accessibility, he thought the ideal plot size should be between 5 and 15 acres; anything smaller would lack commercial incentive and represent merely a 'yam-piece'. In the first years of smallholder establishment, proximity to an alternate wage source probably would be important. A spirit of community would be crucial; Moloney thought that Grenadian success was exemplified among the small-scale farmers there by "the cheerful readiness with which they cooperate in helping one another". He did not favour an extension of the *metayer* system whereby a labourer was given subsistence privileges in exchange for clearing another's future cacao plot because the two systems worked at cross-purposes.[24]

The colonial authorities, while insisting that Caribbean peoples needed their expert and civilizing guidance, could not always agree upon the direction this guidance was to take. In autumn 1898, Moloney's draft bill sought authorization for land acquisition on St Vincent for small cultivators and specified the way in which land units and dwellings thereon were to be arranged. He wanted a cottage built on each land parcel, explaining that this settlement arrangement helped underpin Grenada's agricultural success. London officials, including Sidney Olivier, disagreed, suggesting that a spread out population was inconvenient "for the provision of services".[25]

Settlements spread throughout the hills and mountains of the Windwards also were inconsistent with central control and thereby represented danger of a regionwide relapse into 'African' livelihood patterns, the overall concern that dominated official questions about control and direction. It was of course a fear that was decades old, reinforced by contemporary discussions of releasing the region's black labour force from its subservient plantation existence and also given credibility by Professor Froude's rantings about "Hayti" during his quasi official travels late in the 1880s. The problems of retrogressive 'African' customs and behaviour, further, had been a staple of the testimony gathered by the royal commissioners, particularly in relation to remote highland island interiors.

The fear that 'African' behaviour would naturally arise in unsupervised settlement areas had accompanied the early planning discussions in the 1880s. When Governor Hely-Hutchinson camped in the Richmond Valley in 1890 and then recommended it as a settlement zone, he elaborated on why supervision was vital. In remote rural areas throughout the Windwards he had observed near-naked women, a sure sign of immorality and decadence. And even in Grenada, where the success of Afro-Caribbean cultivators was explained in part by their proximity to white planters, belief in obeah and jumbies still was widespread.[26]

Hely-Hutchinson's ideas were echoed throughout the late 1890s as small settlements gained footholds, fears apparently as widespread in London as among officials in the islands. Colonial Office commentary about fine-tuning land settlement laws in St Vincent early in 1902 pointed out why the cultivation, handling and marketing of settlers' subsistence crops had to be scrutinized by the officers of the Imperial Agricultural Department of the West Indies: "The great danger is that the peasants may relapse into African methods of producing yams, etc., and go backward instead of forward . . ."[27]

The agriculture department in question had been established officially in September 1899. At that time the various colonial governors were notified that an imperial grant would pay for such an institution for the next ten years, provided that local governments raised revenues to augment those funds. The department itself (and the ten-year grant) had been a recommendation of the 1897 royal commission which noted approvingly that several islands already had botanic gardens.[28] Although the department was established formally in 1899, Daniel Morris was named director a year earlier. The department sponsored annual agriculture conferences in Barbados from 1899 to 1902 and in Trinidad in 1905, quarantine problems (smallpox in Barbados, yellow fever in St Lucia) preventing conferences in the intervening years. More important, Morris proved an active and eager coordinator of inter-island agricultural activities. In mid 1900 he prescribed chemical pesticides for use in the Windwards, sprays proven effective in both Ceylon and South Africa. And the descriptions and diagrams he provided following the geophysical disasters in St Vincent in 1898 and 1902—reports he prepared in his capacity as the director of the regional agriculture department—are among the most reliable records available for those events.[29]

The establishment of the agriculture department, recommended by the 1897 commission in the spirit of its smallholder emphasis, was consistent with calls for supervision and control over black smallholders. And it is understandable that rural blacks suspected the agricultural officials of having less than benign interests in their activities; visits by extension officers into rural Jamaican farm plots at the time to advise about appropriate pruning and planting techniques often were suspected official ploys to tax banana crops. Yet the regional agriculture department intended to coordinate extension services throughout the British Caribbean was, more directly, an outgrowth of the tradition of the region's botanic gardens that had always been overshadowed by sugar cane. The spirit of these gardens was extended further into the twentieth century with the establishment of the Imperial College of Tropical Agriculture east of Port of Spain, Trinidad in 1922 on the grounds of St Augustine estate, originally purchased by the local government in 1900 for experimental agricultural work.[30]

St Vincent became the British Caribbean island changed most by the implementation of the 1897 commission's recommendations. Its transformation, considered a possibility for years, received real momentum from the commission. Yet even after the March 1898 smallholder grant, change was hesitant, slow and complicated in a social atmosphere charged with old animosities. Late in 1898, Morris and visiting land surveyors from Jamaica and Grenada evaluated several of the 'abandoned' St Vincent estates. The Crown then purchased three of the plantations for smallholders in January and February 1899, for £2,605, a negotiated price lower than that requested by the owners but higher than surveyors' estimates. The labourers were no less suspicious of these proceedings adjudicated and implemented by white "land monopolists or the relatives or solicitors of the monopolists". Villagers' interpretations of imperial intent, furthermore, included, in the words of some planters, widespread "silly ideas" that they were to receive money or land as gifts from the Crown, largesse now being withheld by local planters.[31]

Despite the complications, Vincentian land gradually came under the control of black labourers. The final approval in London of Moloney's land law in January 1899, was the legal basis for the initial government purchase of three plantations. By the end of the year ten estates totalling 3,000 acres were purchased and two others (1,500 total acres) approved for sale. By late 1901 the St Vincent government purchased fourteen states that together totalled slightly more than 5,000 acres. After the 1902 eruption, two more (nearly 1,800 additional acres) were bought for families whose crops were destroyed by Soufrière. By March 1904 some £14,000 had been disbursed to buy Vincentian estates totalling 7,000 acres, and in June of that year a committee approved the use of another £10,000 to acquire land for small settlers, money that had come to the island "for the relief of sufferers by the eruption".[32]

Whereas the St Vincent land-use changes may be traced through records kept by colonial authorities who emphasized their own benign acts toward the island's black workers, the latter group's resistance to post-disaster expediencies was telling. The post-hurricane and post-eruption emigration schemes pushed hard by London and its local representatives—and possibly intensified by the widely alleged withholding of lumber and food intended for local peoples—were total failures because the blacks would not leave. The enumeration of expended funds and acreages released to black smallholders thereby represents more a grudging capitulation of a beleaguered plantocracy to black resistance than it does a 'giving' of land to small-scale cultivators.

Nor was the resistance to emigration the only thwarting of European sponsored plans for the island through black non-compliance. Captain Young's report of the post-eruption relief for St Vincent in January 1903 suggested that Alexander Porter's estates in the Carib country in the north be purchased and allotted among smallholding cane farmers, a grandiose scheme tributary to a central factory run "upon co-operative principles". Porter died the following month—perhaps symbolizing the literal passing away of the island's old regime—and the severe volcanic aftershocks in March 1903 decreased blacks' enthusiasm for any such scheme near Soufrière. In any case, the plan was shelved by authorities who doubted the success of a cooperative sugar scheme dependent upon "a population notoriously improvident".[33]

These same improvident cultivators were however eager to respond to government suggestions about their own small-scale production of cotton. Early in 1904 the Imperial Agriculture Department used £2,000 from eruption relief funds to establish a central cotton gin on St Vincent and also to distribute seed and establish experimental cotton plots. From these beginnings, cotton and arrowroot—both crops identified with Vincentian smallholders—had far outpaced sugar cane on the island by the 1920s. The resistance to some official plans or suggestions and acceptance of others by black smallholders, moreover, suggests that their balking exemplified as much practical self-interest as it did dogmatic reaction; while interviewing older small-scale farmers in the 1940s, C.Y. Shephard found that a consensus recalled local government officials as active and helpful toward the new settlers when Vincentian estates were being parcelled out in the first years of the twentieth century.[34]

Next to St Vincent, Carriacou was the Windward island most directly influenced by the commission's recommendations. The commissioners had stopped for only two days in Grenada and had visited Carriacou only briefly. Yet the testimony they received about its damaging system of absentee land tenure and short-term rental contracts made Carriacou a prime target for land reform in their final report: "In Carriacou, as in St Vincent, we do not hesitate to recommend expropriation . . . after payment of reasonable compensation, in the case of the owner of any estate which has . . . ceased to be cultivated . . . if [it] . . . should be suitable for settlement in small lots . . ."[35]

In autumn 1897, the curator of the Grenada botanic garden, W.E. Broadway, visited Carriacou, interviewed some of the inhabitants there, and reported his findings to Governor Moloney. Broadway had observed the island's denuded landscape, "strange and ruinous system" of wandering live-stock, and the relative absence of young men who were working in Trinidad and Venezuela. These negative features were related to widespread absentee ownership, a tenure arrangement that—according to those Broadway inter-viewed—provided no incentives for growing coffee or cocoa as on Grenada. Nine months later 230 renters on Carriacou petitioned Moloney to buy Carriacou's Beausejour estate that surrounded the main town of Hillsborough so that subsequent smallholders could plant corn there "for the support of life". The response in London was favourable.[36]

In January 1899, Moloney requested imperial funds to buy "non-resi-dential" estates in Carriacou for smallholders. Subsequent correspondence with London provided Colonial Office perspectives on Carriacou which was seen as "about midway in the scale of West Indian disintegration be-tween Antigua or St Vincent and the Virgin Islands . . . [an island that] still retains . . . an inferior and cheap cotton which survived here when sugar ex-pelled it elsewhere". London further hoped that the availability of land plots would dissuade the island's men from their annual wage-earning sojourns.[37]

During 1901 government representatives opened discussion with ab-sentee owners of three estates on Carriacou. Actual surveying of Beausejour began in October 1902, eight months before the government purchased the estate for £2,667. As soon as Beausejour land was available, applications for parcels "poured in", and, as had happened in St Vincent, the prescriptions put forward by government planners were modified by the insistence of lo-cal demands. Original plans had specified 5-acre plots each, lest smaller par-cels became the "yam pieces" Moloney deplored. Yet the crush of applicants effectively reduced the sizes of plots, a concession made by government offi-cials to avoid "bitter disappointment and possible failure of the scheme". The officials then parcelled out the 480 acres of Beausejour into 160 lots, 146 of which were sold by August 1903. A similar crush of applicants occu-pied Harvey Vale, in the southwest of the island, two months earlier where there was an "inrush of tenants" taking over land plots even before it was formally purchased from the owner.

The government also tried its hand at reorienting the means by which cotton was processed for export. Until 1903 the owner at Beausejour also owned Carriacou's only cotton gin; small-scale producers had to wait until his carters came for their crops, and they were also assessed carting and gin-ning fees. In 1903 the British Cotton Growing Association presented a cotton gin and seed press to the Grenada government for use on Carriacou. Daniel Morris, from his vantage point in Barbados, sympathized with the developments on Carriacou, and he directed the laying out of experimental corn and cotton plots there in 1903 by representatives of the regional agriculture department.[38]

Carriacou's parent island of Grenada was the model the commissioners were attempting to replicate elsewhere. They had "no ground for any special apprehension regarding the future" of Grenada and recommended further "settlement of the Creole population on the land as small proprietors". The only warning about continued settlement in Grenada cautioned against clearing the forested Crown lands at the summits in the wake of the disastrous flooding and erosion in the late 1890s. In 1900, for the first time, more than 8,000 (a total of 8,176) small land plots were registered on Grenada, an indication that Grenada's material prosperity was being extended.[39] The lowered prices for cocoa in 1896 and 1897 caused concern, but prices rebounded after 1900 so that Grenadian small holders continued to concentrate on cacao. It was not until the damaging (and, given Grenada's southerly latitude, very surprising) hurricane of September 1921 that Grenadian cacao production declined. That weather event, combined with crop disease and competition owing to widespread cacao cultivation in West Africa, led Grenada small growers eventually to turn from cacao to nutmeg and other spices.[40]

A major recommendation by the 1897 commission for St Lucia called for educational reform so that the island's populace could be "weaned" from its dependence on *patois* and subsequent reforms more easily carried out. But the linguistic divide continued to underpin problems in St Lucia, small-scale (*patois* speaking) cane growers taking little interest in any central factory operated by anglophone engineers. These divisions flared dramatically in 1907 when a protest among the Castries coal carriers spread to the countryside, leading to incendiarism and several shooting deaths. For a tense two days the few white residents of St Lucia feared a "disastrous massacre", and order was preserved by the hastily requested presence of the Dutch man-of-war *Gelderland* and its contingent of marines who stayed at Castries until tempers cooled. British and Dutch political (and their own linguistic) differences were thereby overcome when more fundamental Caribbean divisions—those involving race and class—had threatened to explode into an islandwide conflagration.[41]

Although the commission recommended an extension of smallholding for St Lucia, it called for no formal estate sales or smallholder schemes as on St Vincent and Carriacou. St Lucia's incomprehensible land tenure situation did not lend itself to the formal parcelling out of land plots. Rather, the St Lucians seemed to be working things out on their own: "When the sugar industry began to go down in 1884, the people turned . . . to the cultivation of small plots . . . on their own account . . . some on land for which they pay rent or which they cultivate on the metayer system. A good many are believed to be squatters . . ." These informal attitudes toward the land also seemed to guarantee St Lucia's eventual identity as a smallholder island into the twentieth century, leading, in one economist's view, to "excessive fragmentation and multiple ownership" of land, characteristics that "discouraged permanent forms of occupancy" on St Lucia. The island's sugar cane acreage continued its withdrawal into ever-smaller peri-factory enclaves. The St Lucian sugar industry was perhaps not the 'sinking ship' as it has been described in the 1890s, but by the 1920s sugar already accounted for less than half of the island's exports.[42]

Sugar Cane's Continuity in Barbados

Although the commission's recommendations in favour of smallholders claimed the attention of most contemporary observers, as well as those who have since commented on the report, these suggested changes—as the commissioners had emphasized—were never intended to be applied regionwide. The individual character of each island prevented it. Whereas land settlement schemes were inaugurated on Carriacou, where sugar cane had been abandoned for decades, and on St Vincent, where it was disappearing fast, such action could hardly be taken where sugar cane continued to support entire islands. That would, very obviously, lead to "serious consequences" according to J.W. Root writing in London in 1899. "People who glibly advise the West Indies to abandon sugar", offered Root, "do not realize what they are talking about, and might just as well recommend Lancashire to relinquish cotton-spinning, or the West Riding of Yorkshire to retire from the woollen trade."[43]

Root, and others with similar points, had Barbados in mind as an example. Yet Barbados was so fundamentally dependent on sugar cane that it really could not be characterized as exemplary or prototypical. Quite the opposite, the royal commission's summary comments about the island's uniqueness clarified why central sugar cane milling for Barbados was among the report's major regional recommendations: "The condition of Barbados is markedly different from that of any other Colony in the West Indies . . . There are no Crown lands, no forests, no uncultivated areas, and the population has probably reached the maximum which the island can even under favourable circumstances support."[44]

Sugar cane, it was obvious to everyone, had to remain Barbados' economic staple. More than that, the issue on Barbados was never really sugar cane versus subsistence cropping; it was about the proposed changes within the industry itself. Official correspondence between Barbados and London as well as the commission's discussion focused on the island's working peoples and how much they needed the industry's wages. Further, any projected economic scenarios that disregarded Barbados' thorough domination by sugar cane were mere abstractions. Job identities, lines of credit, insurance arrangements, status aspirations, local land courts and everything else on Barbados were based on the island's traditional means of cultivating cane and producing raw sugar. So in May 1898, when Barbadian officials and others in the British Caribbean were pondering the commission's recommendations, the Barbados *Advocate* warned against lumping all of the region's islands together for planning purposes: "The idea which seems to prevail in certain quarters in England that the West India Islands are mere tropical farms to be leased out by the Colonial Office without reference to the inhabitants is, we have on more than one occasion had to point out, a very mistaken one as far as Barbados . . . is concerned . . ."[45]

The 'inhabitants' the *Advocate* had in mind went unspecified, but those on Barbados standing to gain from the status quo or lack of interference from the Colonial Office were the white planters, merchants and estate managers, whose positions and authority were intertwined with Barbados' antique sugar cane industry. Projected modernization in Barbadian sugar cane, on the other hand, could create dramatic socioeconomic reorganization. The central milling prescribed by the 1897 commission would sweep away the small-scale estates, decrepit wind-powered factories and aging boiling houses and replace them with steam-powered factories. 'Outside capitalists' soon became the term and slogan used by the Barbadian planters to identify those feared external entrepreneurs who soon would descend on Barbados; these outsiders, if one were to believe the wailing, would simply take advantage of the commission's recommendations to bring in their modern equipment with which to reorient the island's landscape and then suck it dry.

Yet the other 90 percent of Barbados' inhabitants were increasingly restive, probably expecting more than promises or rhetoric from the commission's recommended changes that had, presumably, been suggested for everyone. In the summer of 1898 a drought (though not nearly as severe as 1894–95) reduced local subsistence crops, and the outbreak of war between the United States and Spain increased the price of bread in Bridgetown by 20 percent. In early July, hundreds of hungry black Barbadians invaded Bowmanston plantation in St John parish on a 'potato raid', a disturbance punished by beatings and several arrests by the contingent of police dispatched from Bridgetown. Yet the Bowmanston incident was localized, unlike the islandwide alarm created by the shooting death of Archibald Pile three weeks later. An unknown assailant shot Pile—the speaker of the House of Assembly and one of Barbados' leading planters—in the back while he was driving his buggy home from Bridgetown. The doctor's initial assessment was that the wound was "not in a vital spot". But Pile died on 2 September, and tension heightened throughout the island.[46]

One week later the hurricane washed away all concerns except those of immediate survival. In the next several months both Barbadian officials and those in the Colonial Office sought some sort of long-term relief for the island's sugar industry beyond the money and supplies coming for immediate use. Committees composed of Barbadian legislators explored the possibility of trade reciprocity with the United States, American foodstuffs for Barbadian sugar and molasses. But the Americans sought reduced duties in exports to Barbados that would possibly wipe out any gains realized from the Barbadian end.[47]

Joseph Chamberlain himself attempted to resuscitate the Barbadian sugar cane industry by proposing to turn much of it over to Thomas Lipton—the self-made millionaire who already had purchased tea plantations in Ceylon—through negotiations that began in August 1898 and lasted into 1900. Chamberlain's ideal of a grand business/government partnership in improving colonial economies would have perhaps become reality in the British Caribbean had he successfully persuaded Lipton in the arrangement; but the possibility never came about. Lipton initially proposed to invest up to £600,000 in central sugar factories in St Kitts, Antigua and Barbados. He eventually withdrew his offer in fear of continuing European beet sugar bounties and what he considered inadequate government guarantees for his investments. The Barbadian plantation owners were also reluctant. Fearing their financial eclipse by Lipton, the ultimate "outside capitalist", most of them banded together to thwart a proposed system whereby they would deliver their canes to a central sugar factory that he owned.[48]

Not wishing to be castigated as obstructionists, several leading Barbadian planters met at the Bridgetown Club in July 1900 and formed a "central factory movement", pledging to become shareholders in a movement toward centralization that was under local control. The Colonial Office nodded its approval and praised local initiative, probably anticipating (correctly) that nothing would come of it. Twenty months later Barbadian governor Frederic Hodgson informed London, once again, of urgency and crisis owing to depression in the sugar industry; C.P. Lucas, Joseph Chamberlain's principal Caribbean desk officer, passed Hodgson's memorandum on to the colonial secretary, identifying it as an "important dispatch".[49]

Hodgson's memo enumerated the same urgent conditions that London had been hearing for two decades. More than one-third of the island's sugar estates were staying afloat by borrowing on the current crop; more than 10 percent were in receivership; workers were noticeably emaciated and susceptible to disease. But the difference this time was a circular issued by the leading Bridgetown merchants on 20 February 1902, of no more advances to local estates unless the industry improved. The following month a private dispatch to the Colonial Office included a typewritten extract from *The Barbados Agricultural Reporter* of 1 March 1902:

The events of the fortnight are historical. The Merchants' Circular is the death warrant of our Sugar Cane Industry—of the only industry possible in this island. The ultimatum of the Merchants is really the ultimatum of the Colonial Bank— the last word of English financiers who thereby acknowledge that their Government has robbed our Industry of the last vestige of its credit. The Bankers and Merchants—like wise men—are endeavouring to save themselves and while there is yet time, to leave the scuttled ship.[50]

Although the dispatches from Barbados early in 1902 cannot be regarded definitive causes, significant tangible improvements came about in that year. On 2 March, despite division in the British cabinet on how to achieve it, Joseph Chamberlain successfully pushed through a treaty abolishing European sugar bounties at the Brussels Convention. The five-year treaty, achieved via Chamberlain's implied threat of countervailing tariffs, came into force the following year. More directly, later in 1902 the imperial Parliament, finally acting on the overall recommendations of the 1897 commission, made an £80,000 free grant to the Barbados sugar industry, as part of an overall grant of £250,000 to eight different colonies in the British Caribbean "dispersed on the basis of islands that needed it most".[51]

The £80,000 grant became an immediate bone of contention among all elements (other than the workforce) of Barbados' sugar producing society. Few individuals among the merchants, estate owners, bankers and insurance agents lacked opinions as to the deployment of the money. It subsequently was all deposited as the capital underpinning the establishment of the Barbados Sugar Industry Agricultural Bank, the money to be loaned out to individual sugar cane estates. By 1904 more than one-quarter of the island's estates were borrowing from the fund, thereby keeping their particular operations—and much of the island's sugar cane industry—alive. The changes in sugar prices after the rescinding of European bounties were neither dramatic nor instantaneous. From 7 shillings per hundredweight on the London market in 1902, sugar's price rose to 11 in 1910. In the second decade of the twentieth century sugar's price then surged (to 30 shillings per 100 pounds) in World War I and even higher before a slide early in the 1920s.

The Barbados sugar industry changed in the first two decades of the century. Although the direction was toward greater centralization as the 1897 royal commission had recommended, there were no sweeping transformations such as those that would have accompanied a takeover by Thomas Lipton. Rather, the changes were more subtle responses to external events. First, the rush to Panama by thousands of the most able Barbadian labourers to work for the Americans from 1904 to 1914 reduced the island's labour supply. So Barbadian planters could no longer substitute an oversupply of labour for needed modernizations. Second, the combination of increased sugar prices and the lessened labour supply helped to intensify local cane cultivation and improve the island's sugar processing equipment. In 1911 the Barbadian legislature passed a bill mandating central milling "along cooperative lines". Sugar cane acreage on the island increased in the following decade owing to increased prices, although the number of sugar factories fell from 329 to 263. Most important, there were nineteen central sugar factories on Barbados by 1921, their increased milling capacities attracting canes from nearby estates whose crops had only recently been processed by now defunct wind-powered grinding mills. These changes led to different expectations and roles within the island's labour force. Barbados had thus maintained its identity and continuity as a sugar cane island by undergoing internal transformations, a process that might be called changing in order to remain the same.[52]

Regional Control, Insular Responses

The British decision to reduce greatly a permanent military presence in the Caribbean region after the turn of the century may be interpreted in different ways. The growing American domination left little room for competition in the region. From a British viewpoint, preoccupation with South Africa and southern Asia combined with a series of uprisings in tropical Africa meant that their own military forces might be deployed more profitably elsewhere. However one reads the British military withdrawal, it marked a major historical and geopolitical watershed in the Caribbean region.[53]

Early in 1905 the Colonial Office notified the several British Caribbean governors that "a fortified base in the Windward Islands is not a strategical necessity to the British Navy" and "that all white infantry shall, as soon as possible, be withdrawn from the West Indies". Nearly all troops were then withdrawn, save for half a battalion of the local West India Regiment that was transferred from Barbados to Jamaica. The predictable responses from local governors raised questions about how outnumbered white residents now would defend themselves. Governor Carter arranged for the HMS *Diamond* to be in port when the soldiers left Barbados in November because "some of the rougher element of both sexes" in Bridgetown had been overheard plotting about making trouble upon the troops' departure. Governor Llewelyn made similar arrangements for St Lucia during the next month, fearing that some members of the local West India Regiment might attempt to "pay off old scores" before they shipped out for West Africa.[54]

So seven decades after slave emancipation, most of them witnessing regional economic decline, the British Caribbean islands had inherited (1) overpopulation, (2) a relic infrastructure and (3) a colonial bureaucracy possessed of fiscal and political authority representing a mother country that was now, at best, indifferent toward but still in control of the region. The terrible depression decades at the end of the nineteenth century had magnified the regional malaise, and local outbursts had inspired the formation of the royal commission and its work. The commission really had followed, in the broadest sense, the overall strategy that Britain had pursued since emancipation in the Caribbean. In the words of the historian William Green, the

British followed a policy that would "preserve traditional property rights and utilize existing human and material resources in the colonies without imposing excessive restraints on freedmen".[55] Where the 1897 commission had departed from the past and, literally, broken new ground was in strongly advocating the extension of property rights to the freedmen themselves, at least in some of the islands. Such a strategy was consistent with enlightened economic thinking at the time. Further, it gave freedmen a greater economic stake in their own islands while leaving them under British political control. According to Thomas Holt "Some leeway for black independent economic activity could be tolerated—was even necessary perhaps—but power must remain firmly in British hands."[56] This leeway, which might defuse local restlessness, doubtless was part of the geopolitical calculus that helped reduce the British military commitment to the region.

The commission's recommendations were regional recommendations. Late in the nineteenth century the conception and delineation of the British West Indies as a geographical region sustained careers and influenced policies at the London Colonial Office. At the staff building located on Downing Street in 1895, most officials and clerks were assigned to particular departments organized to deal with "geographically defined areas of the empire", one of which was the West Indies.[57] And the West Indies as a diagnostic region already had a decades-long pedigree at the Colonial Office. Michel-Rolph Trouillot points out that at about the time of emancipation the "Caribbean desk in particular had fallen under the increasing power of permanent clerks. From then on and for many decades, bureaucrats and intellectuals of liberal or reformist persuasion, rather than elected or nominated politicians, designed and oversaw the implementation of colonial policy."[58]

This regional mind-set or map as reality represented more than simply a commonsensical way to organize spheres of imperial influence on the world map posted at Downing Street; it also influenced the people residing in the British Caribbean. The sugar bounty depression affected most places there, so it was obviously acknowledged as a regional problem. Labourers' outbursts in individual Caribbean localities, when combined with rumoured threats from most of the other places, also became—in the minds of the men at the Colonial Office—regional in nature. And the conduct of the royal commission which was given a regional mandate and focus but whose findings had to be implemented island by island is important to keep in mind. Because of this regional mentality, one could argue, the timing and extent of the land-use changes on St Vincent and Carriacou were really pre-cipitated by the labour riots of the sugar workers in St Kitts and Guyana, though these latter groups were themselves to remain, owing to their par-ticular geographical circumstances, members of sugar proletariats rather than landed peasantries. The cause-and-effect plausibility of this argument can be understood only by acknowledging the regional attitude maintained in London. As the geographers Piers Blaikie and Harold Brookfield note in discussing the research concept they call "regional political ecology": "The adjective 'regional' is important because it is necessary to take account of environmental variability . . . [and] . . . 'regional' also implies the incorpora-tion of environmental considerations into theories of regional growth and decline."[59]

The geographical variation from island to island was certainly no mys-tery to the officials in the Caribbean nor to those in London who read their reports. And the royal commissioners' proviso about the islands' great vari-ety occurs routinely—and almost apologetically—throughout their final re-port. Yet the maddening tendency for each island to go its own way, tenden-cies based on their geographical differences, was simply inconsistent with the imperial regional designs shaped during the discussions beside the wall map in the London Colonial Office.

The exasperation felt in London was extended to all segments of the Caribbean populations. Volatile workers, recalcitrant planters, plodding of-ficials and divided committees all seemed to whine and object. And dealing with unending and varying Caribbean complaints and issues taxed the most patient London officials. Joseph Chamberlain, frustrated in his dealings with the Port of Spain municipal council during the city's water riots in 1903, queried in writing whether it was even worth convincing local au-thorities to adopt the material benefits of modern life that Britain could be-stow upon them: "I have an idea that we press sanitation and civilization too strongly on some of these backward communities. If they like bad water or insufficient water it might be well to let them find out the results for themselves."[60]

But relaxation of central control, most directly through slave emancipa-tion and less directly by the overall decline in the Caribbean sugar industry, had allowed a drift toward differentiation among the British islands by the latter half of the nineteenth century. In the era of sugar and slaves, the social geography of the region was more homogeneous. To be sure, conditions of slavery varied from island to island, but its sociolegal core—the white ownership of black people—did not. The ubiquity of sugar cane, moreover, which is "a highly versatile plant . . . [that] . . . can be grown successfully under a wide range of conditions" lent a superficial similarity to the geographically varied islands of the region.[61] Then an inevitable geographical drift—marked by first subtle then growing differences in how people, crops and land were combined—took place in the following decades. This drift or differentiation, although based in part on the physical characteristics of each place, was not influenced by physical features in a facile, deterministic sense. Mountainous islands, witness St Vincent until 1900 and St Kitts throughout the twentieth century, were not inevitably taken over by small-scale cultivators.

An even more fundamental explanatory geographical characteristic that helps in understanding the unfolding differences among the islands of the nineteenth-century British Caribbean is what everyone knows and has always said about the region, namely that it is a realm characterized by fragmented insularity. Each island was a discrete entity, its boundaries drawn by nature. Inhabitants of each island made daily decisions and thereby lived their lives entangled in a web of laws and economic arrangements influenced from afar but also according to local topography, soils, water availability and climatic conditions which—for most islands residents—were the tangible elements of the only world they knew. As the geographer David Lowenthal noted years ago with a remark that is far from belabouring the obvious, "To my mind, the most apposite realm for societies in the West Indies is the island."[62]

Whereas the island-region distinction was a source of endless frustration for distant British planners and officials, it was certainly less mysterious to the inhabitants of the islands. And it was probably during this period, certainly more than in the past, when insular identities were formulated and reinforced among the islanders themselves, identities based precisely on the places from which individuals came. The hard-driving, aggressive Barbadians, whose characteristics some British officials attributed to landlessness, were also seen as domineering and condescending by J. J. Thomas and other West Indians. St Lucians—enigmatic, strange sounding, and possessed of special fishing skills possibly based on supernatural connections—were associated with the volcanic beauty of their home island. The multicultural setting of the Trinidadians helped to explain their zest for life. Guianese became mudlanders; and every one of the smaller islands, such as prosperous Grenada and threadbare St Vincent, became associated with specific cultural stereotypes. Also, mutual antipathies between neighbouring islanders, centred on these stereotypical identities unknown or laughable to outsiders, must have been formed or at least strongly reinforced during this period. And these competing insular identities, well known today to anyone even vaguely associated with the English-speaking Caribbean, have frustrated nearly all attempts toward political or economic coalescence in the twentieth century.

The physical geographical elements that made up particular island realms of the eastern Caribbean in the late 1800s were dynamic, rather than passive, backdrops, a woeful understatement given what happened then. The passage of the 1898 hurricane and the volcanic eruptions four years later must have convinced the British Colonial Office, sick of the fractious particularism, that the region's problems bordered on hopeless. Writing elsewhere about the effects of the twin disasters on St Vincent, I have suggested that they helped set in motion the land-use changes there that already were contemplated and even underway because they discouraged local planter resistance to these proposed changes.[63] More recently the historian Stuart Schwartz has pointed out that a disastrous hurricane that devastated much of Puerto Rico in August 1899 might have had similar long-term influences there. Schwartz explains that United States-supported relief efforts in Puerto Rico after the hurricane at the turn of the century "did not cause the political decision to place Puerto Rico in a dependent status, but it did create a context that made that decision easier".[64]

The hurricanes at either end of the Caribbean at the turn of the century were indeed crucial 'contexts' in which trends and directions may have been set in motion. Yet recognizing their contextual influences is no more important than acknowledging the overall physical geographical bases for the long-term unfolding of Caribbean history. At the opening of the twentieth century the small islands of the British Caribbean were pawns within larger geopolitical events. Demands and influences from North America and Europe were filtered through an aging colonial bureaucracy, itself being challenged from below by increasingly restive working peoples. Understanding these events is clarified with a fuller appreciation of the region's physical geographical characteristics with insularity at the base. An underlying reason that "the Caribbean . . . goes its own way" and is "the despair of classifiers, area studies programmes" and others in Sidney Mintz's well-known provocation is not only because of differences in language, culture and human variation from one place to another; it also is because the islands' physical realities—often the ultimate basis by which West Indians identify themselves and one another—continue to be under-appreciated by those attempting to impose their own externally derived meanings upon the individual localities that make up the Caribbean region.[65]

Early in the 1930s—more than three decades after the 1897 commission—the American geographer R. H. Whitbeck visited the eastern Caribbean and then published a brief article about the islands he had toured. In discussing the region's "past and present", Whitbeck contrasted its former status as a "source of astounding wealth" with what had since become a region of "distressing loss and bitter complaint". He attributed the region's problems to an "exaggerated sense of individualism obviously arising from insularity" and extended the discussion to include island life elsewhere in the world. "It is a case of insular psychology gone mad," explained the author about the islands of the British Caribbean. "When any proposal to unite these subunits or units is made, it meets with determined opposition".[66] Whitbeck did not identify the larger whole of which these "subunits" were a part, but it was doubtless the same mental regional construct that was maintained by and so troubling to the men of the Colonial Office, to the members of the 1897 royal commission, and which continues to frustrate academics, planners and politicians alike one century later.

Appendix

This appendix arrays the reported demographic data for Barbados and the Windwards from 1882 to 1902 as reported in the relevant census reports and annual official gazettes. Where data wree not available, "n/a" is indicated.

Barbados

	Total Population	Live Births	Total Deaths	Infant Deaths	Still-Births
1882	172,905	6909	4135	n/a	n/a
1883	173,950	7710	4379	n/a	n/a
1884	174,995	7674	4088	n/a	n/a
1885	176,040	7887	4886	n/a	n/a
1886	177,085	7339	4550	n/a	n/a
1887	178,310	7402	4182	n/a	n/a
1888	179,175	7725	3814	n/a	n/a
1889	180,220	7399	6261	n/a	n/a
1890	181,265	7419	5000	n/a	n/a
1891	182,306	7769	6794	n/a	n/a
1892	182,306	6993	3729	n/a	n/a
1893	182,306	7896	4956	n/a	n/a
1894	182,306	7281	6367	n/a	n/a
1895	182,306	7395	4588	1638	n/a
1896	182,306	7036	4937	1767	266
1897	182,306	7396	4963	1860	445
1898	182,306	7107	7415	2610	712
1899	182,306	6947	4968	2038	n/a
1900	182,306	7127	4663	1932	469
1901	182,306	7221	5762	2511	477
1902	182,306	6566	5532	2376	455

Grenada

	Total Population	Live Births	Total Deaths	Infant Deaths	Still-Births
1882	43,830	1835	866	251	79
1883	44,872	1835	863	218	78
1884	45,914	1852	971	273	n/a
1885	46,956	1877	1120	291	88
1886	47,998	1875	935	232	98
1887	49,040	2014	1032	287	114
1888	50,082	2099	1014	272	131
1889	51,124	2164	1108	297	134
1890	52,166	2206	1172	293	115
1891	53,209	2350	1065	290	107
1892	54,317	2328	1057	295	137
1893	55,425	2353	1273	319	122
1894	56,533	2348	1069	288	123
1895	57,641	2505	1096	289	119
1896	58,749	2319	1053	253	131
1897	59,857	2208	1276	280	110
1898	60,965	2519	1196	330	98
1899	62,073	2495	1019	274	135
1900	63,181	2533	1108	278	123
1901	64,288	2650	1316	n/a	129
1902	64,534	2549	1210	n/a	128

St Lucia

	Total Population	Live Births	Total Deaths	Infant Deaths	Still-Births
1882	38,918	1692	827	190	106
1883	39,285	1653	1180	291	98
1884	39,652	1461	1312	276	95
1885	40,019	1651	951	214	110
1886	40,386	1496	1086	209	115
1887	40,753	1448	938	203	97
1888	41,120	1437	907	219	117
1889	41,487	1572	952	275	101
1890	41,854	1574	1013	219	130
1891	42,220	1771	1037	273	158
1892	42,986	1604	1002	252	156
1893	43,752	1960	1070	312	201
1894	44,518	1817	922	260	163
1895	45,284	1822	1011	231	177
1896	46,054	1763	998	278	174
1897	46,816	1665	1004	288	159
1898	47,582	1691	1047	279	167
1899	48,348	1700	1026	307	165
1900	49,114	1850	942	222	145
1901	49,883	1781	1102	271	177
1902	49,815	1676	1096	264	139

St Vincent

	Total Population	Live Births	Total Deaths	Infant Deaths	Still-Births
1882	40,599	1859	932	218	90
1883	40,650	1919	1011	263	83
1884	40,701	1937	1098	231	105
1885	40,752	1903	953	232	118
1886	40,803	1881	963	266	107
1887	40,854	1853	932	241	108
1888	40,905	1905	790	213	86
1889	40,956	1899	1025	272	107
1890	41,007	1761	1357	261	110
1891	41,054	1351	n/a	n/a	n/a
1892	41,905	1908	n/a	n/a	n/a
1893	41,136	1929	1031	n/a	97
1894	41,177	1983	732	204	120
1895	41,228	1955	860	217	122
1896	41,269	1971	930	352	107
1897	41,310	1751	n/a	n/a	n/a
1898	41,351	1818	1236	319	120
1899	41,392	1600	819	244	148
1900	41,433	1708	660	189	140
1901	41,474	1751	672	185	127
1902	41,515	1551	2192	228	119

Notes

Notes to Chapter 1

1. *Report of the West India Royal Commission* (London: HMSO, 1897), Appendix C, Part III, "Barbados", 169. References to the 1897 report are hereafter cited as RC (1897).

2. Philip D. Curtin, *The Rise and Fall of the Plantation Complex* (Cambridge: Cambridge University Press, 1990), 73–77.

3. Jack P. Greene, *The Intellectual Construction of America: Exceptionalism and Identity from 1492 to 1800* (Chapel Hill: University of North Carolina Press, 1993), 30.

4. See Eric Williams, *From Columbus to Castro: The History of the Caribbean, 1492–1969* (London: André Deutsch, 1970), 226, for a description of externally caused famine in Jamaica and the British Leewards during the American War of Independence.

5. Sidney W. Mintz, "Foreword" to Ramiro Guerra y Sánchez, *Sugar and Society in the Caribbean: An Economic History of Cuban Agriculture* (New Haven: Yale University Press, 1964), xvi–xvii.

6. British government officials who drafted the 1833 emancipation act were not unaware of the importance of the variety of environments in which West Indian emancipation would occur. See William A. Green, *British Slave Emancipation: The Sugar Colonies and the Great Experiment, 1830–1965* (Oxford: Clarendon Press, 1976), 116–18.

7. Sidney W. Mintz, *Caribbean Transformations* (Chicago: Aldine, 1974), 234–36; Bonham C. Richardson, "Slavery to freedom in the British Caribbean: ecological considerations", *Caribbean Geography* 1 (1984): 164–75.

8. Thomas C. Holt, *The Problem of Freedom: Race, Labor, and Politics in Jamaica and Britain, 1832–1938* (Baltimore: Johns Hopkins University Press, 1992), 322–32.

9. RC (1897), Appendix C, Part VII, "St Lucia", 53.

10. R.W. Beachey, *The British West Indies Sugar Industry in the Late 19th Century* (1957; reprint, Westport, CT: Greenwood Press, 1978), 146–47. See Luis Martínez-Fernández, *Torn Between Empires: Economy, Society, and Patterns of Political Thought in the Hispanic Caribbean, 1840–1878* (Athens: University of Georgia Press, 1994) for a valuable perspective on longstanding United States interests in the Greater Antilles.

11. Williams, *From Columbus to Castro*, 536–37.

12. RC (1897), Appendix C, Part VIII, "St Vincent", 119–20.

13. Holt, *The Problem of Freedom*, 332–35.

14. Daniel Morris, "Botanical federation in the West Indies", *Nature* 35 (13 January 1887): 249.

15.   RC (1897), 70.

16.   Holt, *The Problem of Freedom*, 335.

17.   C.Y. Shephard, "Peasant agriculture in the Leeward and Windward islands", *Tropical Agriculture* 24 (1947): 63.

18.   Gordon K. Lewis, *Main Currents in Caribbean Thought: The Historical Evolution of Caribbean Society in Its Ideological Aspects, 1492–1900* (Baltimore: Johns Hopkins University Press, 1983), 3.

19.   Samuel Eliot Morison, *Admiral of the Ocean Sea: A Life of Christopher Columbus* (Boston: Little, Brown and Co., 1942), 400–11.

20.   Michael T. Ryan, "Assimilating new worlds in the sixteenth and seventeenth centuries", *Comparative Studies in Society and History* 23 (1981), 536.

21.   Richard S. Dunn, *Sugar and Slaves: The Rise of the Planter Class in the English West Indies, 1624–1713* (Chapel Hill: University of North Carolina Press, 1972), 33. My suggestion that Caribbean environments were taken for granted by many European authorities and planters did not prevent wonderful efforts by nature writers and others in describing the region. Sloane is only one of many such writers excerpted in *The Islands and the Sea: Five Centuries of Nature Writing from the Caribbean*, edited by John A Murray (New York: Oxford University Press, 1991).

22.   Robert Dirks, *The Black Saturnalia: Conflict and its Ritual Expression on British West Indian Slave Plantations* (Gainesville: University of Florida Press, 1987), 9–10.

23.   William Cronon, *Changes in the Land: Indians, Colonists, and the Ecology of New England* (New York: Hill and Wang, 1983); Carolyn Merchant, *Ecological Revolutions: Nature, Gender, and Science in New England* (Chapel Hill: University of North Carolina Press, 1989).

24.   Carl O. Sauer, *The Early Spanish Main* (Berkeley: University of California Press, 1966).

25.   Otis P. Starkey, *The Economic Geography of Barbados: A Study of the Relationships between Environmental Variations and Economic Development* (New York: Columbia University Press, 1939).

26.   Riva Berleant-Schiller and Lydia M. Pulsipher, "Subsistence cultivation in the Caribbean", *Nieuwe West-Indische Gids* 60 (1986): 1–40.

27.   David Watts, *The West Indies: Patterns of Development, Culture and Environmental Change since 1492* (Cambridge: Cambridge University Press, 1987).

28.   *Caribbean Geography* is a joint geography/education journal at the University of the West Indies in Jamaica. Also, and in this same vein, environmental knowledge and education in the Caribbean may have passed a milestone with the publication of *Environment and Development in the Caribbean: Geographical Perspectives*, edited by David Barker and Duncan F.M. McGregor (Kingston, Jamaica: The Press University of the West Indies, 1995).

29.   Michael Craton, *Testing the Chains: Resistance to Slavery in the British West Indies* (Ithaca: Cornell University Press, 1982), 67–80.

30.   Walter Rodney, *A History of the Guyanese Working People, 1881–1905* (Baltimore: Johns Hopkins University Press, 1981), 3.

31.   David Barry Gaspar, *Bondmen and Rebels: A Study of Master-Slave Relations in*

Antigua (Baltimore: Johns Hopkins University Press, 1985), 256–58.

32. Sidney W. Mintz, "The Caribbean region", *Daedalus* 103, no. 2 (Spring 1974): 61.

33. David Lowenthal, "Caribbean views of Caribbean land", *Canadian Geographer* 5 (1961): 1–9.

34. Jean Besson and Janet Momsen, eds, *Land and Development in the Caribbean* (London: Macmillan Caribbean, 1987).

35. B.W. Higman, "Ecological determinism in Caribbean history", Elsa Goveia Memorial Lecture given at the University of the West Indies, Cave Hill, Barbados, 1986. (This lecture is published in *Inside Slavery: Process and Legacy in the Caribbean Experience*, edited by Hilary Beckles, 51-77 [Kingston, Jamaica: Canoe Press University of the West Indies, 1996].)

36. RC (1897), Appendix C, Part VII, "St Lucia", 78.

37. Bonham C. Richardson, "Detrimental determinists: applied environmentalism as bureaucratic self-interest in the fin-de-siècle British Caribbean", *Annals of the Association of American Geographers* 86, no. 2 (June 1996): 213–34.

38. Sauer, *The Early Spanish Main*, 206–7.

39. RC (1897), Appendix C, Part III, "Barbados", 169.

40. "Eruption of la Soufrière, 1902", *Sojourn* (St Vincent) 1, no. 1 (July–August 1983): 2.

41. Stuart B. Schwartz, "The hurricane of San Ciriaco: disaster, politics, and society in Puerto Rico, 1899–1901", *Hispanic-American Historical Review* 72, no. 3 (1992): 303.

42. Bonham C. Richardson, "Catastrophes and change on St Vincent", *National Geographic Research* 5, no. 1 (Winter 1989): 111–25.

Notes to Chapter 2

1. E.J. Hobsbawm, *The Age of Empire, 1875–1914* (New York: Vintage Books, 1989), 59.

2. Robert Gilpin, *War and Change in World Politics* (Cambridge: Cambridge University Press, 1981), 194–97.

3. Richard H. Collins, *Theodore Roosevelt's Caribbean: The Panama Canal, the Monroe Doctrine, and the Latin American Context* (Baton Rouge: Louisiana State University Press, 1990).

4. Michael Craton, "The transition from slavery to free wage labour in the Caribbean, 1780–1890: a survey with particular reference to recent scholarship", *Slavery and Abolition*, 13, no. 2 (August 1992): 37–67; see also Craton's "Reshuffling the pack: the transition from slavery to other forms of labor in the British Caribbean, ca. 1790–1890", *Nieuwe West-Indische Gids* 68 (1994): 23–75; William A. Green, *British Slave Emancipation: The Sugar Colonies and the Great Experiment, 1839–1865* (Oxford: Clarendon Press, 1976); Barbara L. Solow and Stanley L. Engerman, eds, *British Capitalism and Caribbean Slavery: The Legacy of Eric Williams* (Cambridge: Cambridge University Press, 1987).

5. Eric Williams, *From Columbus to Castro: The History of the Caribbean, 1492–1969* (London: André Deutsch, 1970), 366–67.

6. Manuel Moreno Fraginals, "Plantations in the Caribbean: Cuba, Puerto Rico, and the Dominican Republic in the late nineteenth century", in *Between Slavery and Free Labor: The Spanish-Speaking Caribbean in the Nineteenth Century*, edited by Manuel Moreno Fraginals, Frank Moya Pons, and Stanley L. Engerman (Baltimore: Johns Hopkins University Press, 1985), 3–21.

7. Noel Deerr, *The History of Sugar*, Volume 2 (London: Chapman and Hall, 1950), 561.

8. Donald Wood, *Trinidad in Transition: The Years after Slavery* (London: Oxford University Press, 1968), 295–97.

9. Alan H. Adamson, *Sugar without Slaves: The Political Economy of British Guiana, 1838–1904* (New Haven: Yale University Press, 1972), 41–46.

10. Eric R. Wolf, *Europe and the People without History* (Berkeley: University of California Press, 1982), 311–13.

11. Dale Tomich, *Slavery in the Circuit of Sugar: Martinique and the World Economy, 1830–1848* (Baltimore: Johns Hopkins University Press, 1990), 69.

12. J.H. Galloway, *The Sugar Cane Industry: An Historical Geography from its Origins to 1914* (Cambridge: Cambridge University Press, 1989), 132.

13. See the testimony of A.E. Bateman, deputy controller-general, Commercial and Statistical Department of the Board of Trade, London, in the *Report of the West India Royal Commission* (London: HMSO, 1897), 139–49. References to the 1897 report are hereafter cited as RC (1897).

14. Deerr, *The History of Sugar*, vol. 2, 531.

15. RC (1897), 15, 123–24, 130.

16. Sidney W. Mintz, *Sweetness and Power: The Place of Sugar in Modern History* (New York: Viking, 1985), 143.

17. RC (1897), 129.

18. RC (1897), 153.

19. George Carrington, *Our West Indian Colonies* (London: The Anti-Bounty League, 1898), 20–21.

20. London Trades' Council, *Conference of Delegates from the Organised Trades of the United Kingdom in Favour of Free Trade and Condemnatory of Foreign State Bounties* (London: Co-operative Printing Society, 1888).

21. RC (1897), 24.

22. P.P. 1888/LXXII/794, Annual report for St Vincent for 1887.

23. Green, *British Slave Emancipation*, 353. For the Morant Bay episode see Gad Heuman, *'The Killing Time': The Morant Bay Rebellion in Jamaica* (Knoxville: University of Tennessee Press, 1994) as well as Thomas C. Holt, *The Problem of Freedom: Race, Labor, and Politics in Jamaica and Britain, 1832–1938* (Baltimore: Johns Hopkins University Press, 1992), chapter 8.

24. H. A. Will, *Constitutional Change in the British West Indies, 1880–1903: With Special Reference to Jamaica, British Guiana, and Trinidad* (Oxford: Clarendon Press, 1970), 11.

25. Michel-Rolph Trouillot, "Discourses of rule and the acknowledgement of the peasantry in Dominica, WI, 1838–1928", *American Ethnologist*, 16, no. 4 (No-

vember 1989): 708–709. Also see Bonham C. Richardson, "Detrimental determinists: applied environmentalism as bureaucratic self-interest in the fin-de-siècle British Caribbean", *Annals of the Association of American Geographers* 86, no. 2 (June 1996).

26. Benjamin Kidd, *The Control of the Tropics* (New York: Macmillan, 1898); D.P. Crook, *Benjamin Kidd: Portrait of a Social Darwinist* (Cambridge: Cambridge University Press, 1994).

27. Holt, *The Problem of Freedom*, 324–26.

28. Sydney Olivier, *White Capital and Coloured Labour* (1929; reprint, New York: Russell and Russell, 1971), 56.

29. James H. Stark, *Stark's History and Guide to Barbados and the Caribbee Islands* (Boston: Photo-Electrotype Co., 1893), 195.

30. James Anthony Froude, *The English in the West Indies* (London: Longmans, 1888), 5–6, 258.

31. J.J. Thomas, *Froudacity: West Indian Fables by James Anthony Froude* (1889; reprint, London: New Beacon Books, 1969).

32. C.S. Salmon, *The Caribbean Confederation: A Plan for the Union of the Fifteen British West Indian Colonies* (London: Cassell and Co., 1888). See also two other relevant monographs Salmon wrote during the same decade: *Capital and Labour in the West Indies* (London: Civil Service Printing and Publishing Co., 1883); and *Depression in the West Indies: Free Trade the Only Remedy* (London: Cassell and Co., 1884).

33. Will, *Constitutional Change*, 232. See also P.T. Marsh, *Joseph Chamberlain: Entrepreneur in Politics* (New Haven: Yale University Press, 1994), 305.

34. Colonial Office to the Treasury, 9 November 1896, *Correspondence Relating to the Sugar Industry in the West Indies* (London: HMSO, 1897), 100–102.

35. William P. Dillon, N. Terence Edgar, Kathryn M. Scanlon, and Kim D. Klitgord, "Geology of the Caribbean", *Oceanus* 30, no. 4 (1987): 42–52.

36. Charles Kingsley, *At Last: A Christmas in the West Indies* (London: Macmillan, 1871), 47.

37. *The Grenada Handbook, Directory and Almanac* (London: Wyman and Sons, 1910), 57–67; *The West Indies: General Information for Intending Settlers* (London: HMSO, 1904), 47–54, 78–99.

38. This section on Barbados draws on material in Bonham C. Richardson, *Panama Money in Barbados, 1900–1920* (Knoxville: University of Tennessee Press, 1985), 13–104.

39. C.O. 321/74, "Depressed condition of the sugar industry", 26 July 1884.

40. C.O. 28/229/no. 142, "Vaccination, contagious diseases, registration of deaths", 14 August 1891.

41. RC (1897), 167.

42. RC (1897), 168.

43. C.O. 321/160/no. 84, "Central sugar factory", 12 July 1895.

44. C.O. 321/159/ "Sugar factories", 11 January 1895; C.O. 884/7/no. 116, *Memorandum Respecting the Saint Lucia Central Sugar Factory*, August 1902, 1–9.

45. C.O. 321/123/ "Land Tax", 25 October 1890, 8–13.

46.   *Memorandum . . . Saint Lucia Central Sugar Factory*, August 1902, 9.
47.   RC (1897), Appendix C, Part VII, "St Lucia", 81.
48.   F.O. 288/34, Sendall to Knutsford, 264.
49.   RC (1897), Appendix C, Part VII, "St Lucia", 62.
50.   RC (1897), Appendix C, part VII, "St Lucia", 69–70.
51.   Sydney Olivier, *The Economics of Coloured Labour* (London: Alexander and Shepheard, 1906), 4.
52.   C.O. 884/8/no. 126, *Further Correspondence Relating to the Volcanic Eruptions in St Vincent in 1902 and 1903* (May 1903), 49–53.
53.   C.O. 321/102/no. 6, "Cramacou lands", 8 January 1887.
54.   C.O. 321/173/no. 32, "Administrator to governor", 7 June 1897.
55.   C.O. 321/85/no. 90, Enclosure of 9 May 1885, "Falling off of revenue", 2–3.
56.   C.O. 321/85/nos. 102 and 103, "General survey of the colony" 16 September 1885.
57.   RC (1897), Appendix C, Part VIII, "St Vincent", 95.
58.   RC (1897), Appendix C, Part VI, "Grenada", 15.
59.   C.O. 321/173/no. 32, "Administrator to governor", 3.
60.   C.O. 321/129/no. 125, "Census, 1891", 23 September 1891, 12.
61.   RC (1897), Appendix C, Part VI, "Grenada", 25.
62.   C.O. 105/10, *The Grenada Government Gazette for 1895*, 333.
63.   C.O. 321/105/no. 95, "Purchase of cocoa and nutmegs".
64.   C.O. 105/9, *The Grenada Government Gazette for 1892*, 530.
65.   C.O. 321/111/no. 100, "Purchase of cocoa ordinance", 14 September 1889.
66.   C.O. 321/196/no. 229, "Flogging for praedial larceny", 21 October 1900.
67.   C.O. 105/14/ "Reports of district medical officers 1903", 2 April 1904.
68.   C.O. 321/129, "Federation of the Windwards", 2 December 1891.
69.   C.O. 321/129/no. 125, "Census, 1891", 11–12.
70.   C.O. 321/129/no. 125, "Census, 1891", cover letter by Governor Hely-Hutchinson.
71.   George Brizan, *Grenada, Island of Conflict: From Amerindians to People's Revolution, 1498–1979* (London: Zed Books, 1984), 214.
72.   C.O. 321/196/no. 215, "Carriacou estates", 10 October 1900.
73.   P.P. 1901/XXXIX, Army medical report for 1899, 361–64.
74.   C.O. 321/130/no. 136, "Disturbance between soldiers and police", 20 August 1891.
75.   Thomas, *Froudacity*, 95–97; David Vincent Trotman, *Crime in Trinidad: Conflict and Control in a Plantation Society, 1838–1900* (Knoxville: University of Tennessee Press, 1986), 97.
76.   C.O. 321/101/no. 68, "Memorial of J.E. Quinlan and 2 Others", 22 July 1887.
77.   C.O. 321/96, "Legislative Council", 19 July 1886.
78.   C.O. 321/97, "Legislative Council", 9 September 1886.
79.   RC (1897), Appendix C, part I, "London", 86.
80.   C.O. 321/86/no. 27, "Suspension of Mr. Risk", 1 March 1885.
81.   C.O. 321/146/no. 104, "W. G. Donovan", 16 August 1893.
82.   *Who Was Who, 1897–1915* (London: Adam and Charles Black, 1966), 5th ed.
83.   Richard A. Howard, "A history of the botanic garden of St Vincent, British

West Indies", *The Geographical Review*, 44, no. 3 (July 1954): 389–92.

84. C.O. 28/233, "Harbour improvements", 29 April 1893.

85. Hilary McD. Beckles, *A History of Barbados: From Amerindian Settlement to Nation-State* (Cambridge: Cambridge University Press, 1990), 126–27.

86. Olivier, *White Capital and Coloured Labour*, 29.

87. Richardson, *Panama Money in Barbados*, 72–80.

88. RC (1897), Appendix C, Part VIII, "St Vincent", 111.

89. C.O. 321/85/no. 132, "Excise Ordinance 1885", 8 December 1885.

90. C.O. 321/188/no. 174, "Land taxation", 12 August 1899.

91. C.O. 321/167/no. 57, "Addl. income and land tax ordce.", 7 July 1896.

92. C.O. 321/170/no. 178, "Condition of islands", 21 September 1897.

93. RC (1897), Appendix C, Part III, "Barbados", 213.

94. C.O. 32/16, *Barbados Official Gazette*, 14 November 1895, 1504–5.

95. C.O. 32/17, *Barbados Official Gazette*, 9 January 1896, 54.

96. RC (1897), Appendix C, Part VIII, "St Vincent", 117.

97. RC (1897), Appendix A, "Grenada", 111.

98. RC (1897), Appendix C, Part VII, "St Lucia", 78.

99. P.P. 1884/LV, *Report on the West Indian Incumbered Estates Court*, 845.

100. RC (1897), Appendix A, "Barbados", 97, and Appendix C, Part I, "London", 101.

101. P.P. 1893–94/LX, St Vincent report for 1892, 251.

102. P.P. 1896/LVII, Annual report for Barbados for 1895, 24.

103. Claude Levy, *Emancipation, Sugar, and Federalism: Barbados and the West Indies, 1833–1876* (Gainesville: University Presses of Florida, 1980), 154.

104. Kelvin Singh, *Bloodstained Tombs: The Muharram Massacre 1884* (London: Macmillan, 1988).

105. Rosalie Schwartz, *Lawless Liberators: Political Banditry and Cuban Independence* (Durham: Duke University Press, 1989), 239–42.

106. Craton, "The transition from slavery to free wage labour", 45.

107. C.O. 321/123, "Land tax", 25 October 1890; for a description of events leading to the 1849 St Lucia riots see chapter three in Michael Louis, " 'An equal right to the soil': the rise of a peasantry in St Lucia", PhD diss., Johns Hopkins University (1982).

108. For a fuller description and analysis of the Grenada riots see Bonham C. Richardson, "A 'respectable' riot: Guy Fawkes night in St George's, Grenada, 1885", *Journal of Caribbean History* 27, no. 1 (1993): 21–35.

109. The description of the disturbances in St Vincent are compiled from C.O. 321/133/no. 87, "Expected disturbances at Kingstown", 19 November 1891, no. 88, "Disturbances at Kingstown", 20 November, and no. 90, "Chief justice's ordinance", 28 November.

110. RC (1897), Appendix C, Part VIII, "St Vincent", 97.

111. C.O. 884/9/no. 147, "Notes on West Indian riots, 1881–1903", 5.

112. Glen Richards, "Collective violence in plantation societies: the case of the St Kitts labour protests of 1896 and 1935", mimeo, Institute of Commonwealth Studies, University of London, October 1987, 14 pp.

113. C.O. 28/220, "Act 20 of 1886–87, To Enable Sugar Plantations to be Culti-

vated and Managed for a Limited Period", 9 August 1886.

114. C.O. 28/241, "Negro rising", 10 July 1896.

115. C.O. 28/240/no. 129, "Defence", 31 July 1896.

116. Walter Rodney, *A History of the Guyanese Working People, 1881–1905* (Baltimore: Johns Hopkins University Press, 1981), 158.

117. C.O. 884/9/no. 147, "Notes on West Indian riots, 1881–1903."

118. Bonham C. Richardson, "Depression riots and the calling of the 1897 West India Royal Commission", *Nieuwe West-Indische Gids* 66, nos. 3 and 4, 169–91.

119. Holt, *The Problem of Freedom*, 332.

120. RC (1897), Appendix C, Part I, "London", 25.

Notes to Chapter 3

1. Lafcadio Hearn, *Two Years in the French West Indies* (1890; reprint, New York: Harper and Brothers, 1923), 60.

2. James Anthony Froude, *The English in the West Indies* (London: Longmans, 1888), 53–54.

3. C.O. 321/113/no. 63, "Report of the police commission", 14 March 1889, 8–9.

4. K.C. Vernon and D.M. Carroll, *Soil and Land-Use Surveys, No. 18: Barbados* (Trinidad: Imperial College of Tropical Agriculture, 1965), 4.

5. C.O. 28/257/no. 107, "St Vincent disaster", 17 May 1902, 253. The volcanic ash from St Vincent apparently reached Barbados via what are now known as upper tropospheric westerlies. Although these winds are not completely understood, it is obvious that surface wind trajectories are not always similar to those aloft. See Roger G. Barry and Richard J. Chorley, *Atmosphere, Weather, and Climate* (London: Routledge, 1992), 6th ed., 110–20.

6. Project report to the government of St Vincent, *UNESCO Man and the Biosphere Project* (Barbados: Institute of Social and Economic Research, 1982), 8.

7. C.O. 28/220/no. 5, "Concentration of troops at Castries", 9 January 1886, 11–12.

8. Stephen Jay Gould, *The Mismeasure of Man* (New York: Norton, 1981) is perhaps the best known source in the broad area of exposing how 'science' was used to foster and reinforce social differences at the time, but the literature about environmental and cultural differences and their influences upon generations of European encounters with the tropics is by now vast and nuanced. See, as only one recent example, Richard H. Grove, *Green Imperialism: Colonial Expansion, Tropical Island Edens, and the Origins of Environmentalism, 1600–1860* (Cambridge: Cambridge University Press, 1995) which includes a worthwhile chapter about St Vincent.

9. C.O. 321/81/ "House of Lords", 20 May 1884.

10. David N. Livingstone, "Climate's moral economy: science, race, and place in post-Darwinian British and American geography", paper presented at a confer-

ence on "Geography and Empire", Queen's University, Kingston, Ontario, 18–20 April 1991, 10–11.

11. David N. Livingstone, "The moral discourse of climate: historical considerations on race, place, and virtue", *Journal of Historical Geography* 17 (1991): 421.

12. Benjamin Kidd, *The Control of the Tropics* (New York: Macmillan, 1898), 54. Kidd, although a climatic determinist, actually had quite benevolent sentiments toward the oppressed, and his writings were more more nuanced than most scholars have realized. See D.P. Crook, *Benjamin Kidd: Portrait of a Social Darwinist* (Cambridge: Cambridge University Press, 1994).

13. *The West Indies: General Information for Intending Settlers* (London: HMSO, 1904), 79–81, 89.

14. L.W. Sambon, "Acclimatization of Europeans in tropical lands", *Geographical Journal* 12, no. 6 (1898): 594.

15. Sydney Olivier, *White Capital and Coloured Labour* (1929; reprint, New York: Russell and Russell, 1971), 110.

16. Philip D. Curtin, ed., *Imperialism* (New York: Walker and Company, 1971), 139. This excerpt is from Carlyle's vitriolic "Occasional discourse on the nigger question" published originally in 1849.

17. C.O. 321/107, "Charges against Dr Dennehy", 23 February 1889.

18. C.O. 321/119, "Poor relief", 6 June 1890.

19. C.S. Salmon *Depression in the West Indies: Free Trade the Only Remedy* (London: Cassell and Co., 1884), 4–5.

20. C.O. 884/7/no. 117, *Further Correspondence . . . Volcanic Eruptions in St Vincent and Martinique in 1902*, 70.

21. C.O. 884/8/no. 126, *Further Correspondence Relating to the Volcanic Eruptions in St Vincent in 1902 and 1903*, 11–12.

22. C.O. 321/196/no. 206, "Diseases of plants", 7 October 1900.

23. Philip D. Curtin, *Death by Migration: Europe's Encounter with the Tropical World in the Nineteenth Century* (Cambridge: Cambridge University Press, 1989), 133.

24. Sambon, "Acclimitization of Europeans in tropical lands", 602.

25. See Bonham C. Richardson, *Panama Money in Barbados, 1900–1920* (Knoxville: University of Tennessee Press, 1985), 27–30, for a discussion of the smallpox outbreak of 1902–1903 and the resultant quarantine imposed on Barbados.

26. C.O. 321/94/no. 66, "Effect of climate of St Lucia on European troops", 23 July 1886.

27. C.O. 28/229/no. 137, "Defence of the colony; transfer of troops to St Lucia", 5 August 1891.

28. Curtin, *Death by Migration*, 137–39.

29. *Report of the West India Royal Commission* (London: HMSO, 1897), Appendix C, Part III, "Barbados", 183–84. References to the 1897 report are hereafter cited as RC (1897).

30. *The West Indies: General Information for Intending Settlers*, 48, 80.

31. C.O. 32/23, C. Hutson, "Report . . . July–December, 1899", *Barbados Official Gazette* (21 May 1900), 979.

32. C.O. 321/168/no. 89, "Floods", 11 December 1896.

33. C.O. 321/154/no. 138, "Heavy gale", 30 October 1894.

34. P.P. 1895/LXIX, Windward Islands, Reports for 1894, 650; *The Grenada Handbook, Directory and Almanac* (London: Wyman and Sons, 1910), 67–68; C.O. 321/188/no. 207, "Rainfall", 16 October 1899; C.O. 321/188/no. 211, "Corn crop of Carriacou", 24 October 1899.

35. P.P. 1898/LIX, Report for Barbados for 1897, 300.

36. RC (1897), 55.

37. C.O. 32/18, *Barbados Official Gazette*, "Report on the police force 1897", 5.

38. C.O. 32/16, *Barbados Official Gazette*, "Report of the poor law inspector, July–December 1894", 689.

39. C.O. 28/235/no. 102, "Sugar cane disease and indigo planting", 26 July 1894; C.O. 28/250/no. 200, "Forestry report", 13 September 1899.

40. P.P. 1886/XLV, Report for St Vincent for 1885, 515.

41. C.O. 28/239/no. 53, "Emigration commission", 588–92.

42. C.O. 321/177/no. 131, "Land taxation in Carriacou", 2 August 1898; C.O. 321/196/no. 215, "Carriacou estates, report of G.W. Smith", 10 October 1900; C.O. 321/210/no. 162, "Purchase of Beausejour Estate", 1 December 1902.

43. Information about the 1886 St Vincent hurricane is compiled from records from the Wesleyan Methodist Missionary Society, West Indies, Box no. 232, no. 3032 and no. 3038; C.O. 264/15, St Vincent *Official Gazettes* of 4 September 1886, 291–94, and 4 November 1886, 355–57; and C.O. 321/97/no. 99, "Damage done by cyclone", 3–4.

44. "The hurricane of August 1831", *Journal of the Barbados Museum and Historical Society* 31 (May 1966): 180–88.

45. C.O. 32/15, *Barbados Official Gazette*, 18 October 1894.

46. P.P. 1895/LXIX, Report for Barbados for 1894, 56–57.

47. "Hurricane 'Janet' at Barbados", *Journal of the Barbados Museum and Historical Society* 23 (August 1956): 162–63.

48. Personal interview.

49. *Correspondence Relating to the Hurricane on 10th–12th September 1898, and the Relief of Distress Caused Thereby* (London: HMSO, 1899), 20–22.

50. Sir Ralph Williams, *How I Became a Governor* (London: John Murray, 1913), 240, 242.

51. C.O. 264/21, St Vincent *Official Gazette*, 22 September 1898.

52. C.O. 884/6/no. 92, *The West Indies and Imperial Aid*, 1905, 38.

53. *Correspondence . . . the Hurricane on 10th–12th September 1898*, 27–28, 34.

54. C.O. 32/21, *Barbados Official Gazette*, January–June 1899, 371, 1747–49.

55. *Correspondence . . . the Hurricane on 10th–12th September 1898*, 59–60.

56. *Correspondence . . . the Hurricane on 10th–12th September 1898*, 104; C.O. 321/193, no. 232, "Condition of labouring classes", 7 July 1899; C.O. 264/22, *St Vincent Official Gazette for 1900*, 182.

57. C.O. 321/181, "Increase of police force", 8 November 1898; C.O. 884/6/no. 92, *The West Indies and Imperial Aid*, 1905, 41.

58. *Correspondence . . . the Hurricane on 10th–12th September 1898*, 117–21.

59. C.O. 884/6/no. 91, *Grant in Aid of Land Settlement in St Vincent*, 1.

60. *Correspondence . . . the Hurricane on 10th–12th September 1898*, 54; C.O. 321/191/no. 72, "Visit of Sir C. Quilter", 3 March 1899.

61. C.O. 321/180/no. 154, 157 and 159, each titled "Peasant proprietary" and dated 13, 14 and 21 October 1898.

62. C.O. 321/181/no. 171, "Peasant proprietary", 28 October 1898; *Correspondence . . . the Hurricane on 10th–12th September 1898*, 7. See Bonham C. Richardson, "Catastrophes and change on St Vincent", *National Geographic Research* 5, no. 1 (Winter 1989), for a fuller discussion of St Vincent's transformation after the hurricane and subsequent volcanic eruption in 1902.

Notes to Chapter 4

1. C.O. 321/108, "Arrival of JaJa", 9 June 1888; also see *The Sentinel* newspaper (Kingstown, St Vincent) of 15 June 1888. Edward L. Cox, "Rekindling the ancestral memory: King JaJa of Opobo's exile on Barbados and St Vincent, 1888–1891." Elsa Goveia Memorial Lecture. Unpublished typescript (Cave Hill, Barbados: University of the West Indies, October 1966), 50.

2. Michael Crowder, *A Short History of Nigeria* (New York: Praeger, 1966), 196–200.

3. C.O. 321/105, "Deportation of JaJa", 27 April 1888.

4. C.O. 321/151/no. 64, "Tour to the Grenadines", 17 May 1894.

5. *Report of the West India Royal Commission* (London: HMSO, 1897), Appendix C, Part III, "Barbados", 223. References to the 1897 report are hereafter cited as RC (1897).

6. *The Sentinel* (St Vincent), 8 April 1887, emphasis in original.

7. C.O. 321/108, "JaJa", 21 July 1888.

8. C.O. 321/108/no. 93, "JaJa", 15 September 1888; C.O. 321/117/no. 96, "JaJa", 26 August 1889; C.O. 28/229/no. 79, "Return of JaJa to Opobo", 5 May 1891.

9. K.C. Vernon and D.M. Carroll, *Soil and Land-use Surveys, No. 18: Barbados* (Trinidad: Imperial College of Tropical Agriculture, 1965), 11.

10. C.O. 321/157, no. 18, "Damage done by storm", 6 February 1895; for a good description of runoff processes in the Windwards see *St Lucia: Country Environmental Profile* (Barbados: The Caribbean Conservation Association, 1991), 31–32.

11. *Report of the Royal Commission Appointed in December 1882, to Inquire into the Public Revenues . . .* Part II. *Grenada, St Vincent, Tobago, and St Lucia* (London: Eyre and Spottiswoode, 1884), 136, hereafter cited as RC (1882); P.P. 1897/LIX, Annual report for the Windward Islands, 1895, 554–55; C.O. 321/171/no. 221, "Carriacou", 20 November 1897.

12. C.O. 321/176/no. 4, "River floods", 6 January 1898.

13. *The Sentry* newspaper (St Vincent), 3 December 1897.

14. P.P. 1898/LIX, Annual report for St Vincent, 1896, 776–77.

15. J.V. DeGraff, "Determining the significance of landslide activity: examples from the Eastern Caribbean", *Caribbean Geography* 3 (March 1991): 29–42.

16. P.P. 1899/LXII, Annual report for St Lucia, 1898, 455; *Grenada: Country Environmental Profile* (Barbados: The Caribbean Conservation Association, 1991).

17. P.P. 1902/LXIV, Report for Barbados, 1901–1902, 52–53.

18. P.P. 1884/LIV, Annual report for St Vincent, 1883, 485; *The St Vincent Witness*, 19 November 1885; *The Sentry* (St Vincent), 17 September 1897.

19. RC (1897), Appendix C, Part I, "London", 89; C.O. 321/161, "Report by Professor J.B. Harrison . . .", 11 April 1895.

20. C.O. 321/96, no. 28, "Kingstown water supply", 3 April 1886; C.O. 321/97, no. 127, "Kingstown water supply", 3 October 1886.

21. W.H.E. Garrod, "Our water supply", *Journal of the Barbados Museum and Historical Society* 19 (1952): 108–9; C.O. 321/148/no. 99 and no. 122, each entitled "Castries water supply", of 27 July and 22 September 1893.

22. "The situation", *The Barbados Agricultural Reporter*, 5 October 1894; C. Hutson, "Report of the poor law inspector, January–June, 1894", *Barbados Official Gazette* (6 December 1894), 1439; "The half-yearly report of the poor law inspector, July–December, 1897", *Barbados Official Gazette* (12 May 1898), 842–43.

23. "Sanitary commissioners' report on Bridgetown and suburbs", *Barbados Official Gazette* (17 November 1884).

24. Sir Rupert W. Boyce, *Health Progress and Administration in the West Indies* (London: John Murray, 1910), 156–57; Peter Jordan, *Schistosomiasis: The St Lucia Project* (Cambridge: Cambridge University Press, 1985), 35–37; C.O. 105/14, "Reports of district medical officers 1903", *The Grenada Government Gazette for 1904* (2 April 1904).

25. C.O. 321/206/no. 186, "Yellow fever at garrison", 6 December 1901; C.O. 321/211/no. 41, "Yellow fever", 26 March 1902.

26. C.O. 321/211/no. 55, "Dr Low's report on yellow fever", 23 April 1902; C.O. 321/211, "Yellow fever: health of Castries", 1 May 1902.

27. C.O. 321/80, *St Lucia Gazette*, 18 February 1884, 79.

28. C.O. 318/280, "Defence of W. Indies", 30 July 1890; C.O. 321/99, Admiralty to Colonial Office, 11 June 1886.

29. C.O. 321/80, *St Lucia Gazette*, 18 February 1884.

30. James Anthony Froude, *The English in the West Indies* (London: Longmans, 1888), 134–35; P.P. 1887/LVII, Annual report for St Lucia for 1886, 192.

31. C.O. 321/130/no. 159, "Castries harbour", 8 October 1891; C.O. 321/144, "Insanitary conditions of Castries harbour", 23 March 1892; C.O. 321/150, "Sewage of Castries", 25 July 1893.

32. C.O. 321/154/no. 98, "Crime", 8 August 1894.

33. RC (1897), Appendix C, Part VII, "St Lucia", 58; A.H. Verrill, *The Book of the West Indies* (New York: E.P. Dutton, 1917), 91–92.

34. Frank C. Hutson, "The Bridgetown dry dock", *Journal of the Barbados Museum and Historical Society* 34 (March 1973): 104–7; RC (1897), Appendix C, Part III, "Barbados", 221.

35. *The West Indies: General Information for Intending Settlers*, p. 88; *The Grenada*

Handbook . . . 1910, pp. 66, 69, 72.

36. C.O. 105/10, *Grenada Gazette,* 10 October 1894, 427.

37. "Passenger traffic", *The Sentinel* (St Vincent), 29 June 1888.

38. C.O. 884/5/no. 77, *Report on the condition of St Vincent,* (London: HMSO, 1897), 10; C.O. 321/183/no. 80, "Overloading of small craft", 12 May 1898.

39. C.O. 321/173/no. 61, "Cyclone", 8 July 1897; *St Lucia: Country Environmental Profile* (Barbados: The Caribbean Conservation Association, 1991), 3–5.

40. Douglas C. Pyle, *Clean Sweet Wind: Sailing Craft of the Lesser Antilles* (Preston, MD: Easy Reach Press, 1981). C.O. 321/204/no. 142, "Coasting trade conditions", 8 October 1901; Froude, *The English in the West Indies,* 156; F.A. Fenger, *Alone in the Caribbean* (New York: George H. Doran Company, 1917), 55.

41. Horace Beck, "The bubble trade", *Natural History* 85, no. 10 (December 1976): 38–47; Jane C. Beck, "West Indian Sea Magic", *Folklore* 88 (1977): 194–202.

42. *The Grenada Handbook, Directory and Almanac* (London: Wyman and Sons, 1910), 59.

43. RC (1882), 49.

44. C.O. 321/177/no. 129, "Communication between Grenada and St Vincent Grenadines", 2 August 1898.

45. C.O. 321/163/no. 3, "Legislative Councils", 8 January 1896; C.O. 321/102/ no. 115, "Seizure of smuggled rum", 11 November 1887.

46. C.O. 321/102/no. 125, "Act of piracy in Grenadines", 3 December 1887.

47. C.O. 257/12, *St Lucia Gazette,* 29 March 1888, 131; C.O. 321/152/no. 82, "Visit to St Vincent and St Lucia", 9 July 1894.

48. Froude, *The English in the West Indies,* 176. See also Bonham C. Richardson, "Human mobility in the windward Caribbean, 1884–1902", *Plantation Society* 2, no. 3 (May 1989): 301–19.

49. RC (1897), Appendix C, Part VII, "St Lucia", 52–53.

50. Bonham C. Richardson, *Panama Money in Barbados, 1900–1920* (Knoxville: University of Tennessee Press, 1985), 107–8.

51. J.E. Duerden, "The marine resources of the British West Indies", *West Indian Bulletin* (Imperial Department of Agriculture for the West Indies, Barbados) 2 (1901): 121–63; C.O. 28/257/no. 97, "Fishing industry", 8 May 1902.

52. *The Sentry* (St Vincent), 21 January 1898.

53. RC (1897), Appendix C, Part III, "Barbados", 233.

54. See the *Country Environmental Profiles* published by the Caribbean Conservation Association in Barbados in 1991 for *Grenada,* 113; *St Lucia,* 131; and *St Vincent and the Grenadines,* 101. Froude, *The English in the Caribbean,* 149 describes canoes in Dominica.

55. RC (1897), Appendix C, Part III, "Barbados", 233.

56. *Grenada: Country Environmental Profile,* 113.

57. Jane C. Beck, "West Indian sea magic", 194; W.F. Rathjen and J.R. Sullivan "West Indies whaling", *Sea Frontiers* 16, no. 3 (May–June 1970): 130–37.

58. See Fenger, *Alone in the Caribbean,* 42–69, for a spirited account of folk whaling in the Grenadines. This brief section on whaling also relies on two articles by John E. Adams, "Historical geography of whaling in Bequia island, West Indies", *Caribbean Studies* 11, no. 3 (October 1971): 55–74; and "Shore whal-

ing in St Vincent island, West Indies", *Caribbean Quarterly* 19 (1973): 42–50. Also see Adams' more recent article about the "Last of the Caribbean whalemen", *Natural History* 103, no. 11 (November 1994): 64–72.

59.   C.O. 321/149/no. 9, "Grenadines", 17 March 1893.
60.   *The Sentry* (St Vincent), 19 March 1897.
61.   Fenger, *Alone in the Caribbean*, 43.
62.   C.O. 28/236/no. 162, "Gale", 20 October 1894.
63.   C.O. 28/236/no. 166, "Heavy gale", 29 October 1894, 226–27.

Notes to Chapter 5

1.   *Report of the Royal Commission Appointed in December 1882, to Inquire into the Public Revenues . . . Part II. Grenada, St Vincent, Tobago, and St Lucia* (London: Eyre and Spottiswoode, 1884), 19. Hereafter cited as RC (1882).
2.   C.O. 321/125, Confidential, "Ill feeling between planters and labourers", 13 January 1890.
3.   C.O. 321/171/no. 221, "Carriacou", 20 November 1897.
4.   C.O. 32/17, "The report of the Barbados emigration committee", *Barbados Official Gazette* (13 January 1896), 94–97.
5.   *The Grenada Handbook, Directory and Almanac* (London: Wyman and Sons, 1910), 51.
6.   *Report of the West India Royal Commission* (London: HMSO, 1897), Appendix C, Part VIII, "St Vincent", 91. References to the 1897 report are hereafter cited as RC (1897).
7.   C.O. 321/173, no. 32, "Administrator to governor", 7 June 1897, 2–3.
8.   C.O. 321/121, no. 79, "Land tax", 21 June 1890.
9.   D. Morris, *Report on the Economic Resources of the West Indies* (London: HMSO, 1898), 67–68.
10.   A.H. Verrill, *The Book of the West Indies* (New York: E.P. Dutton, 1917), 107–8.
11.   C.O. 321/183, no. 34, "Roads", 4 March 1898; C.O. 321/197, no. 30, "Goldsworthy Track: Castries-Dennery Road", 10 February 1900; C.O. 321/197, no. 73, "Recruitment of labourers for Cayenne", 9 April 1900.
12.   C.O. 32/17, "Report of Barbados emigration committee", 74.
13.   C.O. 884/5/no. 82, *Correspondence Relating to the Report of the West India Royal Commission of 1896–97*, 54–55; RC (1897), Appendix C, Part VIII, "St Vincent", 94.
14.   The academic literature on the multiple meanings of Caribbean land is now substantial. The classic article is David Lowenthal, "Caribbean views of Caribbean land", *Canadian Geographer* 5 (1961): 1–9.
15.   B.W. Higman, *Jamaica Surveyed: Plantation Maps and Plans of the Eighteenth and Nineteenth Centuries* (Kingston: Institute of Jamaica Publications, 1988), 291.
16.   C.O. 321/195, no. 44, "Report of parochial boards commissioners", 14 March 1900; and no. 151, "Land and house tax", 2 August 1900.

17.   C.O. 321/139, no. 103, "Jacquin Lands", 1 August 1892.
18.   C.O. 257/22, "Report of the Commission . . . Survey and Crown Lands De-
       partments", *St Lucia Official Gazette*, 28 August 1903, 22.
19.   C.O. 700/ St Vincent 3.
20.   The 'Three Chains' boundary was employed elsewhere in the Windwards at the
       time. See Michel-Rolph Trouillot, *Peasants and Capital: Dominica in the World
       Economy* (Baltimore: Johns Hopkins University Press, 1988), 90.
21.   C.O. 321/102, no. 6, "Cramacou lands", 8 January 1887.
22.   C.O. 321/85, nos. 102 and 103, "General survey of the colony", 16 September
       1885.
23.   See chapter 9, "Political economy and race: peasants in the age of empire", in
       Thomas C. Holt, *The Problem of Freedom: Race, Labor, and Politics in Jamaica
       and Britain, 1832–1938* (Baltimore: Johns Hopkins University Press, 1992).
24.   C.O. 321/85, no. 129, "Proposed survey of Crown Lands", 26 November 1885;
       C.O. 321/96, no. 60, "Proposed survey of colony", 9 June 1886; C.O. 321/
       102, no. 5 of 1887, "An ordinance to ascertain . . . boundaries between lands . .
       ."
25.   C.O. 321/102, no. 78, "Crown Lands boundaries" and no. 126, "Right of way
       to Crown Lands", 5 December 1887.
26.   C.O. 321/125, no. 42, "Crown Lands boundary survey", 5 May 1890.
27.   C.O. 321/155, no. 33, "Crown Lands Dept.", 17 April 1894.
28.   C.O. 321/207, no. 81, "Ownership of land near Camden Park Estate", 14 June
       1901.
29.   C.O. 321/96, no. 59, "Sale of Cramacou lands", 9 June 1886.
30.   C.O. 321/192, no. 150, "Peasant proprietary", 8 May 1899.
31.   C.O. 321/133, Confidential, "Agitation in St Vincent", 3 December 1891.
32.   *The Sentry* (St Vincent), 21 January 1898.
33.   C.O. 321/125, Confidential, "Peasant proprietary", 10 May 1890.
34.   C.O. 321/108, no. 11, "Survey and disposal of Crown Lands", 24 January
       1888, 2.
35.   RC (1897), Appendix C, Part VII, "St Lucia", 80.
36.   RC (1897), Appendix C, Part III, "Barbados", 160.
37.   James Anthony Froude, *The English in the West Indies* (London: Longmans,
       1888), 101.
38.   J.H. Sutton Moxly, *An Account of a West Indian Sanatorium and a Guide to Bar-
       bados* (London: Sampson Low, Marston, Searle, and Rivington, 1886), 187.
39.   J.W. Root, *The British West Indies and the Sugar Industry* (Liverpool: J.W. Root,
       1899), 73.
40.   Sidney W. Mintz, *Sweetness and Power: The Place of Sugar in Modern History*
       (New York: Viking, 1985), 50.
41.   RC (1897), Appendix C, Part VIII, "St Vincent", 100.
42.   C.S. Salmon, *Capital and Labour in the West Indies* (London: Civil Service
       Printing and Publishing Co., 1883), 25, 56.
43.   RC (1897), Appendix A, 96–97.
44.   Personal interview with Sir Frank C. Hutson, Bridgetown, Barbados, 6 May
       1982.

45. RC (1897), Appendix C, Part I, "London", 107–8.

46. C.O. 321/161, "Report by Professor J.B. Harrison . . .", 11 April 1895.

47. Noel Deerr, *The History of Sugar*, Volume 1 (London: Chapman and Hall, 1950), 200–1; RC (1897), Appendix A, 116–17.

48. F.C. Hutson, "Sugar manufacture *c.*1900", *Journal of the Barbados Museum and Historical Society* 34 (1974): 214; C.O. 28/245, Confidential, "Central factories", 1 April 1898; RC (1897), Appendix A, 97, and Appendix C, Part III, "Barbados", 231–32.

49. RC (1897), Appendix A, 98. J.H. Galloway, Botany in the service of empire: the Barbados cane-breeding program and the revival of the Caribbean sugar industry, 1880s–1930s, *Annals, Association of American Geographers* 86, no. 4 (December 1996): 682–706.

50. G.C. Stevenson, "Sugar cane varieties in Barbados: an historical review", *Journal of the Barbados Museum and Historical Society* 26 (1959): 67–93.

51. R. Howard, "A history of the botanic garden of St Vincent, British West Indies", *The Geographical Review* 44, no. 3 (July 1954): 381–93.

52. Daniel Morris, "Botanical federation in the West Indies", *Nature* 35 (13 January 1887): 249.

53. Charles Kingsley, *At Last: A Christmas in the West Indies* (London: Macmillan, 1871), 384–85.

54. C.O. 28/236, no. 171, "Sugar cane disease", 14 November 1894; C.O. 28/237, Confidential, "Sugar cane diseases", 10 April 1895.

55. Deerr, *The History of Sugar*, vol. 1, 194; C.O. 28/237, Confidential, "Labouring population", 13 February 1895.

56. C.O. 321/161, "Report by Professor J.B. Harrison . . .", 11 April 1895; C.O. 264/19, *St Vincent Official Gazette* (May 10, 1894), 170.

57. C.O. 28/254, no. 89, "Cane fires", 21 May 1901, 410–11.

58. C.O. 28/255, no. 222, "Cane fires prevention", 2 December 1901. Also see Bonham C. Richardson, *Panama Money in Barbados, 1900–1920* (Knoxville: University of Tennessee Press, 1985), 97–98 and 150–51, for black Barbadians' unwillingness to identify incendiaries in the early twentieth century.

59. Letter from "Diogenes", *The Sentry* (St Vincent), December 3, 1897.

60. C.O. 321/206, no. 80, "Cotton industry at Choiseul", 12 June 1901.

61. RC (1897), Appendix C, Part III, "Barbados", 164.

62. E.D.M. Hooper, "Report upon the forests of Saint Vincent", *The Sentinel* (St Vincent) 6 May 1887. There are no accounts among the reports from the turn of the century of so-called terracing for which St Vincent is well known late in the twentieth century. According to Lawrence S. Grossman (personal communication) what usually is called terracing on St Vincent is better termed the 'ridge and furrow' system that probably was introduced into the island in the 1930s.

63. Letter from "S.F.B.", *The Sentinel* (St Vincent), May 4, 1888; RC (1897), Appendix C, Part VIII, "St Vincent", 113; J.S. Handler, "The history of arrowroot and the origin of peasantries in the British West Indies", *Journal of Caribbean History* 2 (1971): 46–93.

64. P.P. 1898/LIX, Report for Barbados for 1897, 303.

65. No official Barbadian census was taken in 1901. Instead, the registrar arrived at

an estimate of 195,588, based upon the 1891 census (182,306) and then taking into account birth, burial and known emigration data for each year of the following decade. C.O. 28/254, no. 114, "Census", 20 June 1901.

66.   David Lowenthal, "The population of Barbados", *Social and Economic Studies* 6 (1957): 448–49; RC (1897), Appendix C, Part III, "Barbados", 218–19.

67.   C.S. Salmon, *The Caribbean Confederation: A Plan for the Union of the Fifteen British West Indian Colonies* (London: Cassell and Co., 1888), 75, and his *Depression in the West Indies: Free Trade the Only Remedy* (London: Cassell and Co., 1884), 28–29. For a most worthwhile exchange regarding postemancipation population densities see W.A. Green, "The perils of comparative history: Belize and the British sugar colonies after slavery", *Comparative Studies in Society and History* 26, no. 1 (January 1984): 112–19, followed by O.N. Bolland's reply, 120–25.

68.   C.O. 32/17, "The report of the Barbados emigration committee", *Barbados Official Gazette* (13 January 1896), 101.

69.   Froude, *The English in the West Indies*, 114.

70.   C.O. 32/16, *Barbados Official Gazette* (14 November 1895).

71.   C.O. 32/16, C. Hutson, "Report of the poor law inspector, July–December, 1894", *Barbados Official Gazette* (10 June 1895), 689.

72.   Verrill, The Book of the West Indies, 100–1.

73.   C.O. 321/146, Confidential, "Emigration from Barbados", 15 June 1893.

74.   H. de R. Walker, *The West Indies and the Empire: Study and Travel in the Winter of 1900–1901* (London: T. Fisher Unwin, 1901), 133.

75.   C.O. 321/125, Confidential, "Peasant proprietary", 10 May 1890.

76.   L.W. Sambon, "Acclimatization of Europeans in tropical lands", *Geographical Journal* 12, no. 6 (1898): 589.

77.   C.O. 32/13, J. Elliott, "Report on the police force for the year 1891", *Barbados Official Gazette* (28 March 1892), 346.

78.   RC (1897), Appendix C, Part III, "Barbados", 172.

79.   C.O. 884/5/no. 77, *Report on the Condition of St Vincent* (London: HMSO, 1897), 6.

80.   RC (1897), Appendix C, Part VIII, "St Vincent", 98.

81.   P.P. 1884 /LIV, Annual report for St Lucia, 1893, 496.

82.   C.O. 28/239, no. 53 "Emigration commission", 27 March 1896.

83.   South Place Institute, *British America* (London: Kegan Paul, Trench, Trübner and Co., 1900), 439.

84.   C.O. 32/17, "The report of the Barbados emigration committee", *Barbados Official Gazette* (13 January 1896), 72.

85.   C.O. 28/225, no. 116, Act 49 of 1887–1888, "To amend Reformatory and Industrial Schools Act '83". C.O. 28/248, "Immigration of reformatory boys to Trinidad", 20 July 1898.

86.   RC (1897), Appendix C, Part III, "Barbados", 177, 218.

87.   RC (1897), Appendix C, Part VIII, "St Vincent", 98.

88.   C.O. 28/256, no. 19, "Return of floggings", 22 January 1902, and no. 47, "Praedial larceny", 28 February 1902, 415.

89.   Salmon, *Depression in the West Indies*, 13.

90. RC (1897), Appendix C, Part III, "Barbados", 213.
91. RC (1897), Appendix C, Part VIII, "St Vincent", 97.
92. C.O. 32/13, C. Hutson, "Report of the poor law inspector July–December 1892", *Barbados Official Gazette* (21 April 1892), 465.
93. P.P. 1895/LXIX/38–40, Annual report for Barbados for 1894.
94. Philip D. Curtin, *Death by Migration: Europe's Encounter with the Tropical World in the Nineteenth Century* (Cambridge: Cambridge University Press, 1989), 49–50, 131.
95. C.O. 257/8, R.P. Cropper, "The second annual report of the protector of immigrants", September 2, 1880.
96. RC (1897), Appendix C, Part VI, "Grenada", 29.

Notes to Chapter 6

1. C.O. 321/142, no. 71, "Administrator's visit to Chateaubelair and Soufriere road", 6 August 1892, and /149, no. 45, "Tour through island", 24 August 1893.
2. J.S. Brierley, "Land fragmentation and land-use patterns in Grenada", in *Land and Development in the Caribbean*, edited by J. Besson and J. Momsen (London: Macmillan Caribbean, 1987), 197.
3. C.O. 321/187, no. 100, "Peasant proprietary", 8 May 1899.
4. *Report of the Royal Commission Appointed in December 1882, to Inquire into the Public Revenues . . . Part II. Grenada, St Vincent, Tobago, and St Lucia* (London: Eyre and Spottiswoode, 1884), 57–58, hereafter cited as RC (1882).
5. *Report of the West India Royal Commission* (London: HMSO, 1897), Appendix C, Part I, "London", 45. References to the 1897 report are hereafter cited as RC (1897).
6. J.S. Udal, "Obeah in the West Indies", *Folklore* 26 (1915): 263.
7. H.J. Bell, *Obeah: Witchcraft in the West Indies* (London: Sampson Low, Marston and Co., 1893), 148–49, 166–67.
8. C.O. 321/80, no. 2, "Civil status report", 6 June 1883, 8–9.
9. Udal, "Obeah in the West Indies", 286.
10. Daniel Morris, "Botanical federation in the West Indies", *Nature* 35 (13 January 1887): 250.
11. C.O. 32/22, *Barbados Official Gazette*, 16 October 1899, 3027; RC (1897), Appendix C, Part VII, "St Lucia", 35; C.O. 321/163, no. 56, "Denudation of forest lands", 13 May 1896.
12. Lafcadio Hearn, *Two Years in the French West Indies* (1890; reprint, New York: Harper and Brothers, 1923), 48.
13. James Anthony Froude, *The English in the West Indies* (London: Longmans, 1888), 159.
14. P.P. 1895/LXIX, Windward Islands. Reports for 1894, 655.
15. RC (1882), 95.
16. RC (1897), Appendix C, Part VII, "St Lucia", 82.

17. South Place Institute, *British America* (London: Kegan Paul, Trench, Trübner and Co., 1900), 341. Also see Michael Louis, " 'An equal right to the soil': the rise of a peasantry in St Lucia", PhD diss., Johns Hopkins University (1982), 49–50, 225–26 for generalizations about the importance of land in St Lucia and how it helped black smallholders cope with colonial oppression.

18. *Grenada: Country Environmental Profile* (Barbados: The Caribbean Conservation Association, 1991), 91.

19. Hearn, *Two Years in the French West Indies*, 45–46.

20. C.O. 321/104, "Mr Hooper's forest report", 5 August 1887.

21. RC (1897), 37.

22. Richard Grove, "St Vincent, the birthplace of modern conservation: the eighteenth century context of the Kings Hill Forest legislation", International Conference on the History of Environmental Institutions, St Vincent, 2–5 April 1991, 10. See also Grove, "Origins of Western environmentalism", *Scientific American* 267 (July 1992): 42–47, as well as his *Green Imperialism: Colonial Expansion, Tropical Island Edens, and the Origins of Environmentalism, 1600–1860* (Cambridge: Cambridge University Press, 1995).

23. R. Howard and J. Howard, eds, *Alexander Anderson's Geography and History of St Vincent* (Cambridge, MA, 1983), 37–38.

24. C.O. 321/75, no. 8, "Draft forest preservation ordinance", January 24, 1884, 39–79.

25. C.O. 28/250, no. 200, "Forestry Report", 13 September 1899, 361.

26. C.O. 321/171, no. 221, "Carriacou", 20 November 1897.

27. F.A. Fenger, *Alone in the Caribbean* (New York: George H. Doran Company, 1917), 38.

28. C.O. 321/184, no. 118, "Gov's tour of inspection", 6 July 1898, 21.

29. C.O. 321/75, no. 8, "Draft forest preservation ordinance", 24 January 1884, 104–5.

30. RC (1882), 19, 125–26.

31. C. Lucas, *A Historical Geography of the British Colonies* (Oxford: Clarendon Press, 1890), 219–20; E.D.M. Hooper, "Report upon the forests of Saint Vincent", *The Sentinel* (Kingstown), 22 April 1887.

32. C.O. 321/99, "Grievances of the working classes", 7 May 1886.

33. C.O. 321/176, no. 63, "Forest conservancy", 29 April 1898.

34. RC (1897), Appendix C, Part I, "London", 98.

35. RC (1897), Appendix C, Part VII, "St Lucia", 53.

36. W.K. Marshall, "Provision ground and plantation labour in four Windward islands: competition for resources during slavery", *Slavery and Abolition* 12 (1991): 51, 56.

37. Froude, *The English in the West Indies*, 154.

38. RC (1897), Appendix C, part VI, "Grenada", 31.

39. C.O. 884/8/no. 126, *Further Correspondence Relating to the Volcanic Eruptions. . . *(May 1903), 66–67.

40. C.O. 321/114/no. 105, "Ordinance to prevent cattle stealing", 18 June 1889.

41. Marshall, "Provision ground and plantation labour", 51.

42. Bell, *Obeah*, 126–27.

43. J.S. Brierley, "Kitchen gardens in the Caribbean, past and present: their role in small-farm development", *Caribbean Geography* 3 (1991): 16.

44. Marshall, "Provision ground and plantation labour", 52, 60.

45. RC (1897), Appendix C, Part VIII, "St Vincent", 103–4.

46. William A. Green, *British Slave Emancipation: The Sugar Colonies and the Great Experiment, 1839–1865* (Oxford: Clarendon Press, 1976), 254–55.

47. C.O. 321/176, no. 25, "Registration of titles", 17 February 1898.

48. C.O. 264/19, "Land roll, 1895", *St Vincent Official Gazette*, 6 June 1895, 253–63.

49. C.O. 321/91, Confidential, "Amended regulations for the sale of Crown Lands", 1 September 1885.

50. C.O. 321/94, no. 84, "Sale of small lots of Crown Lands", 1 September 1886.

51. C.O. 321/164, "House and land tax", 22 December 1896; C.O. 321/170, no. 175, "House and land tax", 18 September 1897.

52. Marshall, "Provision ground and plantation labour", 58.

53. Jean Besson, "A paradox in caribbean attitudes to land", in *Land and Development in the Caribbean*, edited by J. Besson and J. Momsen (London: Macmillan, 1987), 13–45.

54. Christine Barrow, *Family Land and Development in St Lucia* (Barbados: Institute of Social and Economic Research, 1992), 16–19. See also Michaeline A. Crichlow, "An alternative approach to family land tenure in the anglophone Caribbean: the case of St Lucia", *Nieuwe West-Indische Gids* 68, nos. 1 and 2 (1994): 77–99.

55. RC (1897), Appendix C, Part VII, "St Lucia", 80.

56. *St Lucia: Country Environmental Profile* (Barbados: The Caribbean Conservation Association, 1991), 203. See also Acosta and Casimir, "Social origins of the counter-plantation system", in *Rural Development in the Caribbean*, edited by P.I. Gomes (New York: St Martin's Press), 40.

57. C.O. 321/121, no. 79, "Land tax", 21 June 1890.

58. RC (1897), Appendix C, Part VII, "St Lucia", 68.

59. C.O. 321/123, Confidential, "Land tax", 25 October 1890.

60. Riva Berleant-Schiller and Lydia M. Pulsipher, "Subsistence cultivation in the Caribbean", *Nieuwe West-Indische Gids* 60 (1986): 1–40; *The Grenada Handbook, Directory and Almanac* (London: Wyman and Sons, 1910), 80; Marshall, "Provision ground and plantation labour", 55.

61. RC (1897), Appendix C, Part VII, "St Lucia", 73.

62. Brierley, "Kitchen gardens in the Caribbean", 24.

63. C.O. 264/23, "Hints and information in regard to cassava poisoning", *St Vincent Official Gazette* (14 May 1903), 114–15.

64. RC (1897), Appendix C, Part VII, "St Lucia", 58. For Hooper's comments about St Lucia agriculture see Appendix A, 118.

65. Charles Kingsley, *At Last: A Christmas in the West Indies* (London: Macmillan, 1871), 378.

66. Barbara E. Fredrich, "Dooryard medicinal plants of St Lucia", *Yearbook of the Association of Pacific Coast Geographers* 40 (1978): 71. Barbadians also commonly used local plants for medicinal purposes. See Iris Bayley, "The bush-teas

of Barbados", *Journal of the Barbados Museum and Historical Society* 16 (May 1949): 103–12.

67. C.O. 321/112, Confidential, "Charges against Dr Dennehy", 23 February 1889.

68. RC (1897), Appendix C, Part VI, "Grenada", 22.

69. RC (1897), Appendix C, Part VIII, "St Vincent, " 102–3; C.O. 321/178, no. 63, "Botanic gardens", 20 April 1898.

70. P.P. 1900/LIV/Report on Grenada for 1898, 384–85; C.O. 321/176, no. 95, "Malarial districts", 6 June 1898.

71. Harley Milstead, "Cacao industry of Grenada", *Economic Geography* 16 (1940): 195.

72. RC (1897), Appendix C, Part VI, "Grenada", 31.

73. RC (1897), Appendix C, Part VI, "Grenada", 23.

74. C.O. 321/129, no. 125, "Census 1891", 23 September 1891, 12.

75. The discussion about cacao cultivation and technology was compiled from *The Grenada Handbook . . . 1910*, 78–79; A.H. Verrill, *The Book of the West Indies* (New York: E.P. Dutton, 1917), 141–43; G.A.R. Wood and R.A. Lass, *Cocoa* (New York: Longmans)4th ed., 262, 448–49, and 496; and information from the RC (1897) section about Grenada. See also C.O. 321/145, no. 26, "Direct steam service to New York", 1893.

76. RC (1897), Appendix C, Part VI, "Grenada", 19, 22; Harold Hamel-Smith, *Some Notes on Cocoa-planting in the West Indies* (London: 1901), 16–17.

77. Bell, *Obeah*, 129–31.

78. C.O. 321/128, no. 70, "Larceny-cocoa and nutmeg plantations", 17 June 1891; C.O. 321/196, no. 230, "Praedial Larceny", 21 October 1900; Bell, *Obeah*, 169.

79. C.O. 321/188, no. 222, "Working of cocoa and nutmegs ordinance", 9 November 1899; C.O. 321/196, no. 229, "Flogging for praedial larceny", 21 October 1900.

80. C.O. 321/110, no. 95, "Purchase of cocoa and nutmegs", 31 August 1889; C.O. 321/111, no. 100, "Purchase of cocoa ordinance", 14 September 1889; C.O. 105/9, "Report of the commission. . .Sale of cocoa and nutmegs", *Grenada Government Gazette*, 13 December 1893, 528–30.

81. *The Equilibrium* (Grenada), 14 May 1885.

82. Bell, *Obeah*, 126; RC (1897), Appendix C, Part IV, "Trinidad", 317.

83. C.O. 321/196, no. 206, "Diseases of plants", 7 October 1900 and no. 262, "Cocoa disease", 22 November 1900.

84. C.O. 105/14, "Reports of district medical officers 1903", *Grenada Government Gazette for 1904*.

85. RC (1897), Appendix C, Part VI, "Grenada", 19, 23–24, 27.

86. RC (1897), Appendix A, 112, and Appendix C, Part VI, "Grenada", 15.

87. *The Grenada Handbook . . . 1910*, 79–80; Verrill, *The Book of the West Indies*, 140–41.

88. *The Grenada Handbook . . . 1910*, 59; P.P. 1893–94/LX/218, St Lucia Report for 1891; *The St Vincent Witness* (newspaper), 18 February 1886.

89. C.O. 321/212, "Volcanic eruption", 13 May 1902.

90.   H. Sigurdsson, "In the volcano", *Natural History* 91, no. 3 (March 1982): 60–66, 68.

91.   The best description of Soufrière's eruption is found in C.O. 884/7, no. 117, *Further Correspondence.. . . Volcanic Eruptions in St Vincent and Martinique in 1902* (Colonial Office, December 1902), xii + 93 pp. The material cited here is from pages 14–15 and 34–35.

92.   W.A. Garesche, *The Complete Story of the Martinique and St Vincent Horrors* (New York: L.G. Stahl, 1902), 159–60.

93.   C.O. 884/7, no. 117, *Further Correspondence . . .*, 14–15.

94.   P.P. 1902/LXVI, *Correspondence . . . Volcanic Eruptions in St Vincent and Martinique. . .* (London: HMSO, 1902), 1167–69.

95.   Bonham C. Richardson, "Catastrophes and change on St Vincent", *National Geographic Research* 5, no. 1 (Winter 1989): 120.

96.   C.O. 884/7/no. 119, *Further Correspondence . . .*, 105.

97.   P.P. 1902/LXVI/1102, Bell to Chamberlain, 12 May 1902; C.O. 321/211, nos. 75 of 22 May 1902 and 513 of 6 June 1902, each entitled "Refugees from Martinique."

98.   C.O. 884/7/119, *Further Correspondence. . .* (1903), 90–91, 105; *The Sentry* (St Vincent), 31 October 1902..

99.   C.O. 884/7/119, *. . . Volcanic Eruptions in St Vincent . . .* (1902), 14–15.

100.   P.P. 1902/LXVI/1117, *Correspondence . . . St Vincent and Martinique . . .* (1902).

101.   P.P. 1904/LX/566–70, *Further Correspondence. . . St Vincent and Martinique . . .* (1903); C.O. 884/6/no. 92, *The West Indies and Imperial Aid* (1905), 45.

102.   C.O. 884/7/no. 117, *Further Correspondence . . .* (1902), 34–35.

103.   P.P. 1904/LX/615, 639, *Further Correspondence . . . St Vincent and Martinique . . .* (1903); C.O. 884/6/no. 92, *The West Indies and Imperial Aid* (1905), 47–49.

104.   P.P. 1904/LX/643, *Further Correspondence. . .* (1903).

105.   P.P. 1904/LX/632–35, *Further Correspondence . . .* (1903).

106.   C.O. 884/7/119, *Further Correspondence . . . Volcanic Eruptions in St Vincent . . .* (1903), 77–79.

Notes to Chapter 7

1.   *Report of the West India Royal Commission* (London: HMSO, 1897), 2. References to the 1897 report are hereafter cited as RC (1897).

2.   RC (1897), 7, 64.

3.   R.V. Kubicek, *The Administration of Imperialism: Joseph Chamberlain at the Colonial Office* (Durham, NC: Duke University Press, 1969), 34.

4.   Michael Craton, "Reshuffling the pack: the transition from slavery to other forms of labor in the British Caribbean, ca. 1790–1890", *Nieuwe West-Indische Gids* 68 (1994): 63.

5.   RC (1897), 23, 70.

6.   RC (1897), 72–74.

7.   RC (1897), 29–34, 41–50.

8.   C.O. 28/244, no. 255, "Report of the R. Commission", 23 December 1897.

9.   *The Sentry* (St Vincent), 8 October 1897; C.O. 321/179, Confidential, "Peasant proprietary", 12 May 1898; C.O. 884/6/ no. 91, *Grant in Aid of Land Settlement in St Vincent* (1899), 1–3.

10. I.M. Cumpston, ed., *The Growth of the British Commonwealth, 1880–1932* (London: Edward Arnold, 1973), 103–6; see also Peter T. Marsh, *Joseph Chamberlain: Entrepreneur in Politics* (New Haven: Yale University Press, 1994), 410–13.

11. Kubicek, *The Administration of Imperialism*, 76–78.

12. Thomas C. Holt, *The Problem of Freedom: Race, Labor, and Politics in Jamaica and Britain, 1832–1938* (Baltimore: Johns Hopkins University Press, 1992), 332.

13. C.O. 884/5/no. 86, *Correspondence Respecting Measures for the Increase of Peasant Proprietary . . .* (March 1900), 1; Holt, *The Problem of Freedom*, 335.

14. C.O. 884/5/no. 86, *Correspondence Respecting Measures . . .* , 2–3.

15. Root, *The British West Indies and the Sugar Industry*, ix–x.

16. RC (1897), 18.

17. C.O. 321/196/no. 218, "Public Lands Acquisition (Small Holdings) Ordinance 1900", 10 October 1900.

18. Marsh, *Joseph Chamberlain*, 411.

19. Holt, *The Problem of Freedom*, 322–32; Daniel Morris, RC (1897), Appendix A, p. 82.

20. Janet Momsen, "Land settlement as an imposed solution",*Land and Development in the Caribbean*, edited by J. Besson and J. Momsen (London: Macmillan Caribbean, 1987), 46–69; historian Jack P. Greene, *The Intellectual Construction of America: Exceptionalism and Identity from 1492 to 1800* (Chapel Hill: University of North Carolina Press, 1993), 47, points out that a rage for 'projects' and 'schemes' applied by Europeans to American lands dates to the sixteenth century.

21. C.O. 321/125/no. 44, "Upper Richmond Valley", 7 May 1890 and Confidential, "Peasant proprietary" 10 May 1890.

22. C.O. 321/186/ Kew Gardens, "Land for peasant proprietary",

23. *The Sentry* (St Vincent), 15 October 1897.

24. C.O. 321/187/no. 100, "Peasant proprietary", 8 May 1899.

25. C.O. 321/181/no. 171, "Peasant proprietary", 28 October 1898.

26. C.O. 321/125, Confidential, "Peasant proprietary", 10 May 1890.

27. C.O. 321/212/no. 5, "Regulations under land settlement ordinance", 14 January 1902.

28. C.O. 884/5/no. 88, *Agricultural Department in the West Indies* (1899), 1–5; RC (1897), 66–68.

29. C.O. 884/6/no. 92, *The West Indies and Imperial Aid* (1905), 16–20; C.O. 321/196/no. 206, "Diseases of plants", 7 October 1900.

30. Sydney Olivier, *White Capital and Coloured Labour* (1929; reprint, New York: Russell and Russell, 1971), 306; Gertrude Carmichael, *The History of the West*

Indian Islands of Trinidad and Tobago, 1498–1900 (London: Alvin Redman, 1961), 288–89; Carl C. Campbell, *Colony and Nation: A Short History of Education in Trinidad & Tobago, 1834–1896* (Jamaica: Ian Randle Publishers, 1992), 31–32.

31. C.O. 321/179, Confidential, "Peasant proprietary", 12 May 1898; C.O. 884/6/ no. 91, *Grant in Aid of Land Settlement in St Vincent* (1899), 1–3.
32. C.O. 321/191/no. 21, "Land Settlement Ordinance, 1899", 19 January 1899; C.O. 884/6/no. 92, *The West Indies and Imperial Aid* (1905), 15.
33. C.O. 884/6/no.92, *The West Indies and Imperial Aid* (1905), 47; C.O. 884/8/ no. 126, *Further Correspondence Relating to the Volcanic Eruptions . . .* (1903), 66–67.
34. C.O. 884/6/no. 92, *The West Indies and Imperial Aid* (1905), 47–48; C.Y. Shepherd, "Peasant agriculture in the Leeward and Windward islands", *Tropical Agriculture* 24 (1947): 71; G. Wright, "Economic Conditions in St Vincent, BWI", *Economic Geography* 5, no. 3 (July 1929): 236–59.
35. RC (1897), 44.
36. C.O. 321/170/no. 176, "Carriacou", 18 September 1897; C.O. 321/176/no. 103, "Peasant proprietary in Carriacou", 18 June 1898.
37. C.O. 321/187/no. 28, "Carriacou: peasant proprietary", 29 January 1899; C.O. 321/196/no. 218, "Public Lands Acquisition (Small Holdings) Ordinance 1900", 10 October 1900; C.O. 321/203/no. 71, "Peasant proprietary in Carriacou", 1 June 1901.
38. P.P. 1904/LIX, *Report on Land Settlement in Carriacou* (HMSO, 1903), 517–23.
39. RC (1897), 42–43; C.O. 106/94, *Grenada Blue Book, 1900* (London: HMSO, 1901), 22–23.
40. *The Grenada Handbook, Directory and Almanac* (London: Wyman and Sons, 1910), 203; Harley Milstead, "Cacao industry of Grenada", *Economic Geography* 16 (1940): 195.
41. RC (1897), 47; C.O. 884/7/no. 116, *Memorandum Respecting the Saint Lucia Central Sugar Factory* (1902), 9; Ralph Williams, *How I Became a Governor* (London: John Murray, 1913), 379–91.
42. RC (1897), 44–45; Carleen O'Loughlin, *Economic and Political Change in the Leeward and Windward Islands* (New Haven: Yale University Press, 1968), 42; Eric Williams, *From Columbus to Castro: The History of the Caribbean, 1492–1969* (London: André Deutsch, 1970), 440.
43. J.W. Root, *The British West Indies and the Sugar Industry* (Liverpool: J.W. Root, 1899), 73.
44. RC (1897), 29.
45. C.O. 28/245, Confidential, 17, "Central sugar factories", 28 May 1898.
46. C.O. 28/246, Confidential, 24, "Conditions of colony", 20 July 1898; no. 136, "Shooting of Mr A. Pile", 23 July 1898, 130; Bonham C. Richardson, *Panama Money in Barbados, 1900–1920* (Knoxville: University of Tennessee Press, 1985), 65–66.
47. C.O. 28/247, Confidential, "Reciprocity with USA", 12 October 1898.
48. Kubicek, *The Administration of Imperialism*, 126–27; H.A. Will, "Colonial

policy and economic development in the British West Indies, 1895–1903", *The Economic History Review* 23 (1970): 138–39.

49. C.O. 28/256, Confidential, "Sugar industry", 8 March 1902.
50. C.O. 28/259/ Wilkinson & Gaviller to Colonial Office, 24 March 1902.
51. C.O. 884/6/no. 92, *The West Indies and Imperial Aid*, 80–83; R.W. Beachey, *The British West Indies Sugar Industry in the Late 19th Century* (1957; reprint, Westport, CT: Greenwood Press, 1978), 166–68.
52. Richardson, *Panama Money in Barbados*, 40–41, 176–80.
53. For the American geopolitical presence in the Caribbean see, among many other sources, Richard H. Collins, *Theodore Roosevelt's Caribbean: The Panama Canal, the Monroe Doctrine, and the Latin American Context* (Baton Rouge: Louisiana State University Press, 1990). For competing British geopolitical commitments see R. Hyam, *Britain's Imperial Century, 1815–1914: A Study of Empire and Expansion* (New York: Barnes and Noble, 1976), 96–97.
54. C.0. 884/8/no. 142, *Correspondence Relating to the Garrisons in the West Indies* (London: 1906), 4, 6, 49, 62.
55. W.A. Green, "The perils of comparative history: Belize and the British sugar colonies after slavery", *Comparative Studies in Society and History* 26, no. 1 (January 1984): 117.
56. Holt, *The Problem of Freedom*, 316.
57. Kubicek, *The Administration of Imperialism*, 15.
58. Trouillot, "Discourses of rule", 708.
59. Piers Blaikie and Harold Brookfield, *Land Degradation and Society* (London: Methuen, 1987), 17.
60. Will, "Colonial policy and economic development", 143.
61. Frank Blackburn, *Sugar-cane* (London: Longman, 1984), 43.
62. David Lowenthal, "The range and variation of Caribbean societies", *Annals of the New York Academy of Sciences* 83 (1960): 787.
63. Bonham C. Richardson, "Catastrophes and change on St Vincent", *National Geographic Research* 5, no. 1 (Winter 1989).
64. Stuart B. Schwartz, "The hurricane of San Ciriaco: disaster, politics, and society in Puerto Rico, 1899–1901", *Hispanic-American Historical Review* 72, no. 3 (1992): 334.
65. Sidney W. Mintz, "The Caribbean region", *Daedalus* 103, no. 2 (Spring 1974): 45.
66. R.H. Whitbeck, "The Lesser Antilles — past and present", *Annals of the Association of American Geographers* 23 (1933): 23–25.

Bibliography

Most of the sources of primary evidence used in this book are found in London-area archives. The original Colonial Office (C.O.) documents are housed at the Public Record Office on Ruskin Avenue at Kew. Some of the more important regionwide and confidential Colonial Office records from the late nineteenth century are also on microfiche at the Institute of Commonwealth Studies, Russell Square, at the University of London. The Institute also maintains a splendid library with a number of books about the Eastern Caribbean from the time period of the study, several cited in the bibliography that follows. The newspaper citations in the chapter notes refer almost entirely to original copies and microfilmed newspapers located at the Colindale branch of the British Library. A few newspaper citations and also two references to personal interviews come from research in Barbados in 1981–1982.

More accessible primary information for researchers who are based outside Britain are the British Sessional Papers or Parliamentary Papers (P.P.) found on microcards in many North American university libraries. The official report of the 1897 Royal Commission may be found on the microcards, and it is also available in a more manageable 'hard copy' form in Volumes 7 and 8 of the bound British Parliamentary Papers published in 1971 by the Irish University Press.

Two journals are cited here with sufficient frequency that they are abbreviated among the secondary references that appear below. They are *The Journal of the Barbados Museum and Historical Society* (*JBMHS*) and the *Nieuwe West-Indische Gids* or *New West Indian Guide* (*NWIG*).

Abrahams, R.D. 1974. *Deep the Water, Shallow the Shore*. Publications of the American Folklore Society. Memoir series, vol. 60. Austin: University of Texas Press.

Acosta, Y., and J. Casimir. 1985. "Social origins of the counter-plantation system in St Lucia". In *Rural Development in the Caribbean*, edited by P.I. Gomes. New York: St Martin's Press.

Adams, J.E. 1971. "Historical geography of whaling in Bequia island, West Indies". *Caribbean Studies* 11, no. 3 (October): 55–74.

———. 1973. "Shore whaling in St Vincent, West Indies". *Caribbean Quarterly* 19: 42–50.

_____. 1994. "Last of the Caribbean whalemen". *Natural History* 103, no. 11 (November): 64–72.

Adamson, A.H. 1972. *Sugar without Slaves: The Political Economy of British Guiana, 1838–1904*. New Haven: Yale University Press.

Barker, D., and D.F.M. McGregor, eds. 1995. *Environment and Development in the Caribbean: Geographical Perspectives*. Kingston, Jamaica: The Press University of the West Indies.

Barrow, C. 1992. *Family Land and Development in St Lucia*. Cave Hill, Barbados: Institute of Social and Economic Research.

Barry, R.G., and R.J. Chorley, 1992. *Atmosphere, weather, and climate*. London: Routledge, 6th ed.

Bayley, I. 1949. "The bush-teas of Barbados". *JBMHS*, 16: 103–12.

Beachey, R.W. [1957] 1978. *The British West Indies Sugar Industry in the Late 19th Century*. Reprint, Westport, CT: Greenwood Press.

Beck, H. 1976. "The bubble trade". *Natural History* 85 (December): 38–47.

Beck, J.C. 1977. "West Indian sea magic". *Folklore* 88: 194–202.

Beckles, H.M. 1990. *A History of Barbados: From Amerindian Settlement to Nation-state*. Cambridge: Cambridge University Press.

Bell, H.J. 1893. *Obeah: Witchcraft in the West Indies*. London: Sampson Low, Marston & Co., 2d ed.

Berleant-Schiller, R., and L.M. Pulsipher. 1986. "Subsistence cultivation in the Caribbean". *NWIG*. 60: 1–40.

Besson, J. 1987. "A paradox in Caribbean attitudes to land". In *Land and Development in the Caribbean*, edited by J. Besson and J. Momsen, 13–45. London: Macmillan Caribbean.

Besson, J., and J. Momsen. eds. 1987. *Land and Development in the Caribbean*. London: Macmillan.

Blackburn, F. 1984. *Sugar-cane*. London: Longman.

Blaikie, P., and H. Brookfield. 1987. *Land Degradation and Society*. London: Methuen.

Bolland, O.N. 1984. Reply to W. A. Green's "The perils of comparative history". *Comparative Studies in Society and History* 26: 120–25.

Boyce, R.W. 1910. *Health Progress and Administration in the West Indies*. London: John Murray.

Brierley, J.S. 1987. "Land fragmentation and land-use patterns in Grenada". In *Land and Development in the Caribbean*, edited by J. Besson and J. Momsen, 194–209. London: Macmillan Caribbean.

_____. 1991. "Kitchen gardens in the Caribbean, past and present: their role in small-farm development". *Caribbean Geography* 3: 15–28.

Brizan, G. 1984. *Grenada, Island of Conflict: From Amerindians to People's Revolution, 1498–1979*. London: Zed Books.

Campbell, Carl C. 1992. *Colony and Nation: A Short History of Education in Trinidad & Tobago, 1834–1986*. Jamaica: Ian Randle Publishers.

Carmichael, G. 1961. *The History of the West Indian Islands of Trinidad and Tobago, 1498–1900*. London: Alvin Redman.

Carrington, G. 1898. *Our West Indian Colonies*. London: The Anti-Bounty League.

Collins, R.H. 1990. *Theodore Roosevelt's Caribbean: The Panama Canal, the Monroe Doctrine, and the Latin American Context.* Baton Rouge: Louisiana State University Press.

Correspondence Relating to the Hurricane on 10th–12th September 1898, and the Relief of Distress Caused Thereby. 1899. London. HMSO.

Correspondence Relating to the Sugar Industry in the West Indies. 1897. London: HMSO.

Cox, Edward L. 1996. Rethinking the ancestral memory: King JaJa of Opobo's exile on Barbados and St Vincent, 1888–1891. Elsa Goveia Memorial Lecture. Cave Hill, Barbados: University of the West Indies (October).

Craton, M. 1982. *Testing the Chains: Resistance to Slavery in the British West Indies.* Ithaca: Cornell University Press.

_____. 1992. "The transition from slavery to free wage labour in the Caribbean, 1780–1890: a survey with particular reference to recent scholarship". *Slavery and Abolition* 13, no. 2 (August): 37–67.

_____. 1994. "Reshuffling the pack: the transition from slavery to other forms of labor in the British Caribbean, ca. 1790–1890". *NWIG* 68: 23–75.

Crichlow, M.A. 1994. "An alternative approach to family land tenure in the anglophone Caribbean: the case of St Lucia". *NWIG* 68 (nos. 1 & 2): 77–99.

Cronon, W. 1983. *Changes in the Land: Indians, Colonists, and the Ecology of New England.* New York: Hill and Wang.

Crook, D.P. 1984. *Benjamin Kidd: Portrait of a Social Darwinist.* Cambridge: Cambridge University Press.

Crowder, M. 1966. *A Short History of Nigeria.* New York: Praeger.

Cumpston, I.M., ed. 1973. *The Growth of the British Commonwealth, 1880–1932.* London: Edward Arnold.

Curtin, P.D. 1989. *Death by Migration: Europe's Encounter with the Tropical World in the Nineteenth Century.* Cambridge: Cambridge University Press.

_____. 1990. *The Rise and Fall of the Plantation Complex: Essays in Atlantic History.* Cambridge: Cambridge University Press.

Curtin, P.D., ed. 1971. *Imperialism.* New York: Walker and Company.

Deerr, N. 1949–1950. *The History of Sugar.* 2 volumes. London: Chapman and Hall.

DeGraff, J.V. 1991. "Determining the significance of landslide activity: examples from the Eastern Caribbean". *Caribbean Geography* 3: 29–42.

Dillon, W.P., N.T. Edgar, K.M. Scanlon, and K.D. Klitgord. 1987. "Geology of the Caribbean". *Oceanus* 30, no. 4: 42–52.

Dirks, R. 1987. *The Black Saturnalia: Conflict and its Ritual Expression on British West Indian Slave Plantations.* Gainesville: University of Florida Press.

Duerden, J.E. 1901. "The marine resources of the British West Indies". *West Indian Bulletin*, Imperial Department of Agriculture for the West Indies, volume 2, 121–63.

Dunn, R.S. 1972. *Sugar and Slaves: The Rise of the Planter Class in the English West Indies, 1624–1713.* Chapel Hill: University of North Carolina Press.

Edwards, J.R. 1970. *British History, 1815–1839.* New York: Humanities Press.

"Eruption of la Soufrière, 1902". 1983. *Sojourn* (St Vincent) 1, no. 1 (July–August): 2–4, 6, 12–13.

Fenger, F.A. 1917. *Alone in the Caribbean*. New York: George H. Doran Company.

Fredrich, B.E. 1978. "Dooryard medicinal plants of St Lucia". *Yearbook of the Association of Pacific Coast Geographers* 40: 65–78.

Froude, J.A. 1888. *The English in the West Indies, or the Bow of Ulysses*. London: Longmans.

Galloway, J.H. 1989. *The Sugar Cane Industry: An Historical Geography from its Origins to 1914*. Cambridge: Cambridge University Press.

_____. 1996. Botany in the service of empire: the Barbados cane-breeding program and the revival of the Caribbean sugar industry, 1880s–1930s. *Annals, Association of American Geographers* 86, no. 4: 682–706.

Garesche, W.A. 1902. *The Complete Story of the Martinique and St Vincent Horrors*. New York: L.G. Stahl.

Garrod, W.H.E. 1952. "Our water supply". *JBMHS* 19: 107–11.

Gaspar, D.B. 1985. *Bondmen and Rebels: A Study of Master-Slave Relations in Antigua*. Baltimore: Johns Hopkins University Press.

Gilpin, R. 1981. *War and Change in World Politics*. Cambridge: Cambridge University Press.

Gould, S.J. 1981. *The Mismeasure of Man*. New York: Norton.

Green, W.A. 1976. *British Slave Emancipation: The Sugar Colonies and the Great Experiment, 1830–1865*. Oxford: Clarendon Press.

_____. 1984. "The perils of comparative history: Belize and the British sugar colonies after slavery". *Comparative Studies in Society and History* 26, no. 1 (January): 112–19.

Greene, J.P. 1993. *The Intellectual Construction of America: Exceptionalism and Identity from 1492 to 1800*. Chapel Hill: University of North Carolina Press.

Grenada: Country Environmental Profile. 1991. Barbados. The Caribbean Conservation Association.

The Grenada Handbook, Directory and Almanac. 1910. London: Wyman & Sons.

Grove, R. 1991. "St Vincent, the birthplace of modern conservation: the eighteenth century context of the Kings Hill forest legislation". International Conference on the History of Environmental Institutions, St Vincent, 2–5 April.

Grove, R.H. 1992. "Origins of Western environmentalism". *Scientific American* 267 (July): 42–47.

_____. 1995. *Green Imperialism: Colonial Expansion, Tropical Island Edens and the Origins of Environmentalism*. Cambridge: Cambridge University Press.

Hamel-Smith, H. 1901. *Some Notes on Cocoa-planting in the West Indies*. London.

Handler, J.S. 1971. "The history of arrowroot and the origin of peasantries in the British West Indies". *Journal of Caribbean History* 2: 46–93.

Hearn, L. [1890] 1923. *Two Years in the French West Indies*. Reprint, New York: Harper & Brothers.

Heuman, G. 1994. *'The Killing Time': The Morant Bay Rebellion in Jamaica*. Knoxville: University of Tennessee Press.

Higman, B.W. 1986. "Ecological determinism in Caribbean history". Elsa Goveia Memorial Lecture at the University of the West Indies, Cave Hill, Barbados. (This lecture is published in *Inside Slavery: Process and Legacy in the Caribbean Experi-*

ence, edited by Hilary Beckles [Kingston, Jamaica: Canoe Press University of the West Indies, 1996].)

_____. 1988. *Jamaica Surveyed: Plantation Maps and Plans of the Eighteenth and Nineteenth Centuries*. Kingston: Institute of Jamaica Publications.

Hobsbawn, E.J. 1989. *The Age of Empire, 1875–1914*. New York: Vintage Books.

Holt, T.C. 1992. *The Problem of Freedom: Race, Labor, and Politics in Jamaica and Britain, 1832–1938*. Baltimore: John Hopkins University Press.

Howard, R. 1954. "A history of the botanic garden of St Vincent, British West Indies". *Geographical Review* 44, no. 3 (July): 381–93.

Howard R., and J. Howard, eds. 1983. *Alexander Anderson's Geography and History of St Vincent*. Cambridge, MA.

Hurricane 'Janet' at Barbados. 1956. *JBMHS* 23: 153–64.

The hurricane of August 1831. 1966. *JBMHS* 31: 180–88.

Hutson, F.C. 1973. "The Bridgetown dry dock". *JBMHS* 34 (March): 104–7.

_____. 1974. "Sugar manufacture *c.* 1900". *JBMHS* 34: 209–16.

Hyam, R. 1976. *Britain's Imperial Century, 1815–1914: A Study of Empire and Expansion*. New York: Barnes & Noble.

Jordon, P. 1985. *Schistosomiasis: The St Lucia Project*. Cambridge: Cambridge University Press.

Kidd, B. 1898. *The Control of the Tropics*. New York: Macmillan.

Kingsley, C. 1871. *At Last: A Christmas in the West Indies*. London: Macmillan.

Kubicek, R.V. 1969. *The Administration of Imperialism: Joseph Chamberlain at the Colonial Office*. Durham, NC: Duke University Press.

Levy, C. 1980. *Emancipation, Sugar, and Federalism: Barbados and the West Indies, 1833–1876*. Gainsville: University Presses of Florida.

Lewis, G.K. 1983. *Main Currents in Caribbean Thought: The Historical Evolution of Caribbean Society in its Ideological Aspects, 1492–1900*. Baltimore: Johns Hopkins University Press.

Livingstone, D.N. 1991. "Climate's moral economy. Science, race, and place in post-Darwinian British and American geography". Paper presented at a conference on "Geography and Empire", Queen's University, Kingston, Ontario.

_____. 1991. "The moral discourse of climate: historical considerations on race, place, and virtue". *Journal of Historical Geography* 17: 413–34.

London Trades Council. 1888. *Conference of Delegates from the Organized Trades of the United Kingdom in Favour of Free Trade and Condemnatory of Foreign State Bounties*. London: Co-operative Printing Society.

Louis, M. 1982. *'An Equal Right to the Soil': The Rise of a Peasantry in St Lucia*. PhD diss., Johns Hopkins University.

Lowenthal, D. 1957. "The population of Barbados". *Social and Economic Studies* 6: 445–501.

_____. 1960. "The range and variation of Caribbean societies". *Annals of the New York Academy of Sciences* 83: 786–95.

_____. 1961. "Caribbean views of Caribbean land". *Canadian Geographer* 5: 1–9.

Lucas, C.P. 1890. *A Historical Geography of the British Colonies*. Oxford: Clarendon Press.

Marsh, P.T. 1994. *Joseph Chamberlain: Entrepreneur in Politics*. New Haven: Yale University Press.

Marshall, W.K. 1991. "Provision ground and plantation labour in four Windward Islands: competition for resources during slavery". *Slavery and Abolition* 12: 48–67.

Martínez-Fernández, L. 1994. *Torn between Empires: Economy, Society, and Patterns of Political Thought in the Hispanic Caribbean, 1840–1878*. Athens: University of Georgia Press.

Merchant, C. 1989. *Ecological Revolution: Nature, Gender, and Science in New England*. Chapel Hill: University of North Carolina Press.

Milstead, H.P. 1940. "Cacao industry of Grenada". *Economic Geography* 16: 195–203.

Mintz, S.W. 1964. "Foreword" to *Sugar and Society in the Caribbean: An Economic History of Cuban Agriculture* by R. Guerra y Sánchez, xi–xliv. New Haven: Yale University Press.

_____. 1974. "The Caribbean region". *Daedalus* 103 (Spring): 45–71.

_____. 1974. *Caribbean Transformations*. Chicago: Aldine.

_____. 1985. *Sweetness and Power: The Place of Sugar in Modern History*. New York: Viking.

Momsen, J. 1987. "Land settlement as an imposed solution". In *Land and Development in the Caribbean*, edited by J. Besson and J. Momsen, 46–69. London: Macmillan Caribbean.

Moreno Fraginals, M. 1985. "Plantations in the Caribbean: Cuba, Puerto Rico, and the Dominican Republic in the late nineteenth century". In *Between Slavery and Free Labor: The Spanish-speaking Caribbean in the Nineteenth Century*, edited by M. Moreno Fraginals, F. Moya Pons, and S.L. Engerman, 3–21. Baltimore: Johns Hopkins University Press, 3–21.

Morison, S.E. 1942. *Admiral of the Ocean Sea: A Life of Christopher Columbus*. Boston: Little, Brown & Co.

Morris, D. 1887. "Botanical federation in the West Indies". *Nature* 35 (13 January): 248–50.

_____. 1898. *Report on the Economic Resources of the West Indies*. London: HMSO.

Murray, J.A., ed. 1991. *The Islands and the Sea: Five Centuries of Nature Writing from the Caribbean*. New York: Oxford University Press.

O'Loughlin, Carleen. 1968. *Economic and Political Change in the Leeward and Windward Islands*. New Haven: Yale University Press.

Olivier, S. 1906. *The Economics of Coloured Labour*. London: Alexander & Shepheard.

_____. [1929] 1971. *White Capital and Coloured Labour*. Reprint, New York: Russell & Russell.

Paterson, N.J., comp. 1902. *Grenada . . . Census of 1901*. St George: Government Printing Office.

Price, E.T. 1962. "Notes on the geography of Barbados". *JBMHS* 29: 119–54.

Pyle, D.C. 1981. *Clean Sweet Wind: Sailing Craft of the Lesser Antilles*. Preston, MD: Easy Reach Press.

Rathjen, W.F., and J.R. Sullivan. 1970. "West Indies whaling". *Sea Frontiers* 16, no. 3 (May–June): 130–37.

Report of the Royal Commission Appointed in December, 1882, to Inquire into the Public

Revenues . . . 1884. Part II: Grenada, St Vincent, Tobago, and St Lucia. London: Eyre and Spottiswoode.

Report of the West India Royal Commission. 1897. London: HMSO.

Richards, G. 1987. "Collective violence in plantation societies: the case of the St Kitts labour protests of 1896 and 1935". Mimeo, Institute of Commonwealth Studies, University of London.

Richardson, B.C. 1984. "Slavery to freedom in the British Caribbean: ecological considerations". *Caribbean Geography* 1: 164–75.

_____. 1985. *Panama Money in Barbados, 1900–1920.* Knoxville: University of Tennessee Press.

_____. 1989. "Catastrophes and change on St Vincent". *National Geographic Research* 5, no. 1 (Winter): 111–25.

_____. 1989. "Human mobility in the Windward Caribbean, 1884–1902". *Plantation Society* 2, no. 3 (May): 301–19.

_____. 1992. "Depression riots and the calling of the 1897 West India royal commission". *NWIG* 66, nos. 3 & 4: 169–91.

_____. 1993. "A 'respectable' riot: Guy Fawkes night in St George's Grenada, 1885". *Journal of Caribbean History* 27, no. 1: 21–35.

_____. 1996. "Detrimental determinists: applied environmentalism as bureaucratic self-interest in the fin-de-siècle British Caribbean". *Annals of the Association of American Geographers* 86, no. 2 (June): 213–34.

Rodney, W. 1981. *A History of the Guyanese Working People, 1881–1905.* Baltimore: Johns Hopkins University Press.

Root, J.W. 1899. *The British West Indies and the Sugar Industry.* Liverpool: J.W. Root.

Ryan, M.T. 1981. "Assimilating new worlds in the sixteenth and seventeenth centuries". *Comparative Studies in Society and History* 23: 519–38.

St Lucia: Country Environmental Profile. 1991. Barbados: The Caribbean Conservation Association.

St Vincent and the Grenadines: Country Environmental Profile. 1991. Barbados: The Caribbean Conservation Association.

Salmon, C.S. 1883. *Capital and Labour in the West Indies.* London: Civil Service Printing and Publishing Co.

_____. 1884. *Depression in the West Indies: Free Trade the Only Remedy.* London: Cassell & Co.

_____. 1888. *The Caribbean Confederation: A Plan for the Union of the Fifteen British West Indian Colonies.* London: Cassell & Co.

Sambon, L.W. 1898. "Acclimatization of Europeans in tropical lands". *Geographical Journal* 12: 589–606.

Sauer, C.O. 1966. *The Early Spanish Main.* Berkeley: University of California Press.

Schwartz, R. 1989. *Lawless Liberators: Political Banditry and Cuban Independence.* Durham, NC: Duke University Press.

Schwartz, S.B. 1992. "The hurricane of San Ciriaco: Disaster, politics, and society in Puerto Rico, 1899–1901". *Hispanic American Historical Review,* 72, no. 3: 303–34.

Shepherd, C.Y. 1947. "Peasant agriculture in the Leeward and Windward islands". *Tropical Agriculture* 24: 61–71.

Sigurdsson, H. 1982. "In the volcano". *Natural History* 91, no. 3 (March): 60–66, 68.

Singh, K. 1988. *Bloodstained Tombs: The Muharram Massacre, 1884*. London: Macmillan.

Snelling, R.C., and T.J. Barron 1972. The Colonial Office and its permanent officials, 1801–1914. In *Studies in the Growth of Nineteenth-century Government*, edited by G. Sutherland, 139–66. London: Routledge & Kegan Paul.

Solow, B.L., and S.L. Engerman, 1987. *British Capitalism and Caribbean Slavery: The Legacy of Eric Williams*. Cambridge: Cambridge University Press.

South Place Institute. 1900. *British America*. London: Kegan Paul, Trench, Trübner & Co.

Stark, J.H. 1893. *Stark's History and Guide to Barbados and the Caribbee Islands*. Boston: Photo-Electrotype Co.

Starkey, O.P. 1939. *The Economic Geography of Barbados: A Study of the Relationships between Environmental Variations and Economic Development*. New York: Columbia University Press.

Stevenson, G.C. 1959. "Sugar cane varieties in Barbados: a historical review". *JBMHS* 26: 67–93.

Sutton Moxly, J.H. 1886. *An Account of a West Indian Sanatorium and a Guide to Barbados*. London: Sampson Low, Marston, Searle, and Rivington.

Thomas, J.J. [1889] 1969. *Froudacity*. Reprint, London: New Beacon Books.

Tomich, D. 1990. *Slavery in the Circuit of Sugar: Martinique and the World Economy, 1830–1848*. Baltimore: Johns Hopkins University Press.

Trotman, D.V. 1986. *Crime in Trinidad: Conflict and Control in a Plantation Society, 1838–1900*. Knoxville: University of Tennessee Press.

Trouillot, M.R. 1988. *Peasants and Capital: Dominica in the World Economy*. Baltimore: Johns Hopkins University Press.

_____. 1989. "Discourse of rule and the acknowledgment of the peasantry in Dominica, WI, 1838–1928". *American Ethnologist* 16, no. 4 (November): 704–18.

Udal, J.S. 1915. "Obeah in the West Indies". *Folklore* 26: 255–95.

Vernon, K.C., and D.M. Carroll. 1965. *Soil and Land-use Surveys, no. 18: Barbados*. Trinidad: Imperial College of Tropical Agriculture.

Verrill, A.H. 1917. *The Book of the West Indies*. New York: E.P. Dutton.

Walker, H. de R. 1901. *The West Indies and the Empire: Study and Travel in the Winter of 1900-01*. London: T. Fisher Unwin.

Watts, D. 1987. *The West Indies: Patterns of Development, Culture and Environmental Change since 1492*. Cambridge: Cambridge University Press.

The West Indies: General Information for Intending Settlers. 1904. London: HMSO.

Whitbeck, R.H. 1933. "The Lesser Antilles: past and present". *Annals of the Association of American Geographers* 23: 21-26.

Who Was Who, 1897–1915. 1966. London: Adam & Charles Black.

Will, H.A. 1970. "Colonial policy and economic development in the British West Indies, 1895–1903". *Economic History Review* 23: 129–47.

_____. 1970. *Constitutional Change in the British West Indies, 1880–1903: With Special Reference to Jamaica, British Guiana, and Trinidad*. Oxford: Clarendon Press.

Williams. E. 1970. *From Columbus to Castro: The History of the Caribbean, 1492–1969.* London: André Deutsch.

Williams, R. 1913. *How I Became a Governor.* London: John Murray.

Wolf, E.R. 1982. *Europe and the People without History.* Berkeley: University of California Press.

Wood, D. 1968. *Trinidad in Transition: The Years after Slavery.* London: Oxford University Press.

Wood, G.A.R., and R.A. Lass. 1985. *Cocoa.* New York: Longman, 4th ed.

Wright, G. 1929. "Economic conditions in St Vincent, BWI". *Economic Geography* 5, no. 3 (July): 236–59.

Index